PRAISE FOR
Learning to Eat Soup with a Knife

"It's past time to make *Learning to Eat Soup with a Knife*
required reading at the White House."
–Trudy Rubin, *Philadelphia Inquirer*

"The last time Defense Secretary Donald Rumsfeld visited Baghdad, back in
December, the top U.S. military commander there gave him an unusual gift.
Gen. George Casey passed him a copy of *Learning to Eat Soup with a Knife*.
. . . In the book, Col. Nagl, who served last year in Iraq, contrasts the U.S.
Army's failure with the British experience in Malaya in the 1950s. The differ-
ence: the British, who eventually prevailed, quickly saw the folly of using mas-
sive force to annihilate a shadowy communist enemy. . . . Col. Nagl's
book is one of a half dozen Vietnam histories . . . that are changing
the military's views on how to fight guerrilla wars."
–Greg Jaffe, *The Wall Street Journal*

"John Nagl's brilliant book . . . is probably the best book on counterinsurgency
written by an American in modern times."
–Newt Gingrich, *Fox News*

"I read this book upon returning from my tour in Iraq after commanding a
company on the ground for a year. I was amazed at how insightful and 'true'
the conclusions were and wished that I had read it before I deployed."
–Nick Ayers, *Armor*

"It has only been comparatively recently that U.S. commanders have begun
to address the problem [of the demands of counter-insurgency] . . . Perhaps
the most influential thinking came from a book originally published in 2002
and called intriguingly *Learning to Eat Soup with a Knife*. The quote is again
from Lawrence whose whole sentence was: 'To make war upon rebellion is
messy and slow, like eating soup with a knife.'"
–Paul Reynolds, BBC

"[A] highly regarded counterinsurgency manual."
–Michael Schrage, *Washington Post*

"*Learning to Eat Soup with a Knife* revives the great tradition of writers like Bernard Brodie who focused scholarship on the most pressing security issues of the day. By assessing the British and American experience with counterinsurgency using modern conceptual tools like the idea of 'learning organizations,' Dr. Nagl illustrates the immense complexity of this type of conflict but also suggests ways to master it. This combination of rigorous, original scholarship and sound strategic advice is both rare and invaluable."
–Dr. Steven Metz, U.S. Army War College

"The success of DPhil papers by Oxford students is usually gauged by the amount of dust they gather on library shelves. But there is one that is so influential that General George Casey, the U.S. commander in Iraq, is said to carry it with him everywhere. Most of his staff have been ordered to read it and he pressed a copy into the hands of Donald Rumsfeld when he visited Baghdad in December. *Learning to Eat Soup with a Knife* (a title taken from T. E. Lawrence—himself no slouch in guerrilla warfare) is a study of how the British army succeeded in snuffing out the Malayan insurgency between 1948 and 1960—and why the Americans failed in Vietnam. . . . It is helping to transform the American military in the face of its greatest test since Vietnam."
–Tom Baldwin, *Times* (UK)

"The capacity to adapt is always a key contributor to military success. Nagl combines historical analysis with a comprehensive examination of organizational theory to rationalize why . . . 'military organizations often demonstrate remarkable resistance to doctrinal change,' and fail to be as adaptive as required."
–Nigel R. F. Aylwin-Foster, *Military Review*

"Excellent . . . Nagl has an unusual Anglo-American perspective, which may have helped him to get inside the British military mind and at the same time have a developed view of his own institution. . . . He is careful to avoid the idea that the Vietnam and Malaya campaigns were similar and is more concerned that both insurgencies faced the respective armies with comparable learning challenges."
–John Mackinlay, King's College, London

"Those interested in understanding the difficulties faced by Coalition forces in Iraq and Afghanistan, or who want to grasp the intricacies of the most likely form of conflict for the near future, will gain applicable lessons. [*Learning to Eat Soup with a Knife*] offers insights about how to mold America's armed forces into modern learning organizations. As the Pentagon ponders its future . . . one can only hope that Nagl's invaluable lesson in learning and adapting is being exploited."
–Frank G. Hoffman, *Proceedings of the United State Naval Institute*

Learning to Eat Soup with a Knife

"To make war upon rebellion is messy and slow,
like eating soup with a knife."
—T.E. Lawrence, *Seven Pillars of Wisdom*

Learning to Eat Soup with a Knife

Counterinsurgency Lessons from Malaya and Vietnam

JOHN A. NAGL

With a new Preface by
the Author

Foreword by
General Peter J. Schoomaker

THE UNIVERSITY OF CHICAGO PRESS · CHICAGO & LONDON

The University of Chicago Press, Chicago, 60637

First published in 2002.

University of Chicago Press paperback edition 2005

Printed in the United States of America

15 14 13 12 11 10 09 08 07   8 9

ISBN 0-226-56770-2

Library of Congress Cataloging-in-Publication Data

Nagl, John A., 1966–
    [Counterinsurgency lessons from Malaya and Vietnam]
    Learning to eat soup with a knife : counterinsurgency lessons
from Malaya and Vietnam / John A. Nagl ; with a new preface by
the author ; foreword by General Peter J. Schoomaker.—
Paperback ed.
        p. cm.
    Originally published: Counterinsurgency lessons from Malaya and
Vietnam. Westport, Conn. : Praeger, 2002.
    Includes bibliographical references (p.) and index.
    ISBN 0-226-56770-2 (pbk. : alk. paper)
    1. Malaya—History—Malayan Emergency, 1948–1960.
2. Counterinsurgency—Malaysia—Malaya. 3. Great Britain.
Army—History—Malayan Emergency, 1948–1960. 4. Vietnamese
Conflict, 1961–1975—Underground movements. 5. Counter-
insurgency—Vietnam. 6. United States. Army—History
—Vietnamese Conflict, 1961–1975. I. Title.
    DS597.N27 2005
    959.5'04—dc22
                                                2005008015

⊗ The Paper used in this publication meets the minimum
requirements of the American National Standard for Information
Sciences—Permanence of Paper for Printed Library Materials,
ANSI Z39.48-1992

Contents

Part III. Vietnam

Part IV. Lessons from Malaya and Vietnam

Illustrations

Foreword

Lieutenant Colonel John Nagl's study of counterinsurgency examines the learning processes of the British Army during the Malayan Emergency of 1948–1960 and of the United States Army during the Vietnam War. In both cases, the armies of these two great nations were challenged to transform to meet the demands of a different kind of war than the one they had planned for. The British Army was more successful in transforming itself largely because it was a more effective "learning organization" than the U.S. Army, which to a disturbing extent attempted to continue business as usual even when the old techniques no longer applied to the kind of enemy it faced. The organizational culture of the U.S. Army, predisposed to fight a conventional enemy that fought using conventional tactics, overpowered innovative ideas from within the Army and from outside it. As a result, the U.S. Army was not as effective at learning as it should have been, and its failures in Vietnam had grave implications for both the Army and the nation.

Today the U.S. Army is again facing new challenges. When the historians review the events of our day, will the record for our Army at the start of the twenty-first century show an adaptive and learning organization? I think so, and we are committed to making it so. We are leveraging the momentum of the global war on terror to transform our Army's organization and culture. Our Army leaders and Soldiers are responding magnificently to significant organizational changes by demonstrating initiative, resilience, and innovation at all levels.

As soon as we capture lessons from military operations, our Army is immediately integrating these lessons into our training so that each follow-on unit learns from the experience of those in contact with the enemy. Our non-commissioned officers and officers with recent combat experience are now teaching in our Army schools, ensuring that our education programs and doctrine stay relevant to the current operational environment.

Even while modern technology is evolving with incredible speed and dramatically improving our capabilities, our most important resource remains our people. Self-aware, thinking Soldiers and leaders build learning, adaptive teams and organizations. For the twenty-first century, we must have an Army characterized by a culture of innovation and imagination.

Nagl's study is especially relevant today, and one that military leaders and interested citizens at all levels should read. It suggests how to encourage the spirit of innovation—a spirit that helped the British Army succeed in Malaya and that is currently transforming America's Army in Afghanistan, in Iraq, and around the globe.

General Peter J. Schoomaker
United States Army

This foreword is the opinion of the author and does not constitute an endorsement by the Department of the Army or the United States.

Preface to the Paperback Edition

Spilling Soup on Myself

Authors generally learn something about their subject matter, and then write about it. I took the opposite approach. Eight years after beginning my research into counterinsurgency and a year almost to the day after the publication of the first edition of this book, I deployed to Iraq to practice counterinsurgency as the Operations Officer of the First Battalion of the 34th Armored Regiment, the "Centurions." From September 24, 2003, through September 10, 2004, I was privileged to serve as Centurion 3 in Khalidiyah, a town of some 30,000 between Fallujah and Ramadi in the Sunni Triangle.

The experience was searing. The Task Force was built around a tank battalion that had been designed, organized, trained, and equipped for conventional combat operations. The enemy we confronted was implacable, ruthless, and all too often invisible. Our yearlong confrontation in Al Anbar Province was bloody and difficult for the insurgents, for our soldiers, and for the population of the region. It was without a doubt the most intense learning period of my life.

The experience of fighting insurgents in Iraq made me think again about the views expressed in this book—assessments of the British army in Malaya and, especially, of the American army in Vietnam. Rereading my work now, I am surprised by how much I was able to understand of counterinsurgency before practicing it myself and simultaneously appalled at some of my presumptions and errors. In the few pages of this preface I hope to point out omissions and missteps from that first edition, written before my own physical immersion in counterinsurgency, while highlighting some of the things I feel I got right the first time. It is my sincere hope that the book may be of use to those attempting to make our armed forces more effective in what promises to be a long struggle against enemies who fight freedom with the ancient art of insurgency.

LEARNING TO EAT SOUP WITH A KNIFE

T. E. Lawrence's aphorism that "Making war upon insurgents is messy and slow, like eating soup with a knife" is difficult to fully appreciate until you have done it. Intellectually grasping the concept that fighting insurgents is messy and slow is a different thing from knowing how to defeat them; knowing how to win, in turn, is a different thing from implementing the measures required to do it.

This is perhaps the most basic flaw in the book that follows. There is something of a blithe sense that defeating the Communist insurgents in Malaya was easy once Sir Gerald Templer and Harold Briggs showed the British army what to do, and that the American army could similarly have won in Vietnam if only it had adopted earlier the changes promulgated by Creighton Abrams and Bob Komer. The truth is rather more complex. Changing an army is an extraordinarily challenging undertaking. Britain was able to adapt to defeat the insurgency in Malaya for many reasons, but those reasons certainly included the British army's comparatively small size and its organizational culture that had been honed in a number of small wars fought over generations.[1] Changing the American army is a task of an entirely different scale, a challenge that the organization struggled with during the Vietnam War.

The army's adaptations in Vietnam were ultimately too little too late to defeat the insurgency there. By contrast, the army has adapted much more rapidly to the challenge of insurgency in Iraq. My own personal experience is illustrative of the larger challenge and response. Task Force 1-34 Armor was preparing for high-intensity combined arms warfare in July of 2003 when it was notified that it would deploy to Iraq; by September, two of its three tank companies were conducting combat operations in the Sunni Triangle mounted on Humvees and dismounting to fight as dragoons, with just one company fighting from M1A1s. In the intervening sixty days, the battalion had been issued new weapons systems and vehicles ranging from machine guns to up-armored Humvees. It reorganized its combat vehicle crews and maintenance teams, designed and implemented counterinsurgency training, and deployed halfway around the world to fight a kind of war that, if not new, was new to the soldiers of Task Force 1-34 Armor.

Difficult as these transformations were, the combat soldiers of the Task Force in some ways had an easier time adapting than the staff. The essence of the line soldiers' mission remained closing with and destroying the enemy. Their additional tasks of supporting the local government and winning the trust of the local people were subordinate to and in some ways a natural outgrowth of their ability to provide security. The battalion staff had to change its entire approach to combat, shifting its focus from battle-tracking enemy tank platoons and infantry squads who fought in plain sight to identifying and locating an insurgent enemy who hid in plain sight. This much more difficult change demanded an entirely different way of thinking about combat—a different level of professional knowledge about a different kind of war. The enemy we faced could only be defeated if we knew both his name and his address—and, often, the addresses of his extended family as well.[2]

Understanding tribal loyalties, political motivations, and family relationships was essential to defeating the enemy we faced, a task more akin to breaking up a Mafia crime ring than dismantling a conventional enemy battalion or brigade. "Link diagrams" depicting who talked with whom became a daily chore for a small intelligence staff more used to analyzing the ranges of enemy artillery systems.

The book that follows pays ritual obeisance to the importance of intelligence in counterinsurgency operations, and to the canard that "To defeat an insurgency you have to know who the insurgents are—and to find that out, you have to win and keep the support of the people." All true, truer than I knew at the time I wrote it. But the task of winning and keeping the support of the population is far more complex than I had understood. In the following pages, I note that the British did a better job of gaining the trust of the Malay population, but I don't properly emphasize that when the insurgency began they had been in the country for well over a century, developing long-term relationships and cultural awareness that bore fruit in actionable intelligence.

The United States is working diligently in Iraq, as it did in Vietnam, to improve the lives of the people. Dollars are bullets in this fight; the Commander's Emergency Response Program (CERP), which provides field commanders funds to perform essential projects, wins hearts and minds twice over—once by repairing infrastructure, and again by employing local citizens who are otherwise ready recruits for the insurgents. CERP is helping with the painstaking process of building relationships with the Iraqi people, resulting in some intelligence from those we help—but not enough, not yet.

One of the most frustrating aspects of the war on the ground in Iraq is responding to the scene of an attack, whether on U.S. or Iraqi security forces, with the sure knowledge that at least some of the bystanders have critical information on those responsible, but being unable to obtain that information from them. The people know the insurgents; they are often tied to them through blood or marriage or long association. The combination of these bonds and the likelihood that they will be killed in the night if they are seen talking to security forces in the day all too often intimidates those who genuinely want peace in Iraq, but see no way to achieve it at a bearable personal cost. Winning the Iraqi people's willingness to turn in their terrorist neighbors will mark the tipping point in defeating the insurgency.[3] Those who contend that "American forces have lost the support of the Iraqi population and probably cannot regain it"[4] are incorrect; in fact, the majority of the Iraqi population prefers the American vision of a democratic and free Iraq to the Salafist version of Iraq as Islamic theocracy. The key challenge is empowering the intimidated majority to enable Iraqi and American security forces to eliminate the criminal insurgents.

THE IRREPLACEABLE ROLE OF LOCAL FORCES

When I wrote this book, I underestimated the challenge of adapting an army for the purposes of defeating an insurgency while simultaneously maintaining the army's ability to fight a conventional war. I also understated the importance of local forces in defeating an insurgency and the difficulty of raising, training, and equipping them. Creating reliable, dedicated local forces during the course of an insurgency that targets not just the local soldiers and police but also their families truly is a task as difficult as "eating soup with a knife."

Local forces have inherent advantages over outsiders in a counterinsurgency campaign. They can gain intelligence through the public support that naturally adheres to a nation's own armed forces. They don't need to allocate translators to combat patrols. They understand the tribal loyalties and family relationships that play such an important role in the politics and economies of many developing nations. They have an innate understanding of local patterns of behavior that is simply unattainable by foreigners. All these advantages make local forces enormously effective counterinsurgents. It is perhaps only a slight exaggeration to suggest that, on their own, foreign forces cannot defeat an insurgency; the best they can hope for is to create the conditions that will enable local forces to win it for them.

In their turn, however, foreign forces have much to offer local forces battling an insurgency. Western armies bring communications packages, training advantages, artillery and close air support, medical evacuation, and Quick Reaction Forces that together contribute dramatically to the confidence, morale, and effectiveness of the local forces, especially when trainers are embedded with the locals.

The fact that the insurgents often attack local forces suggests that they realize how essential those forces are. Task Force 1-34 Armor worked diligently to mentor the local police force and two battalions of the Iraqi National Guard during its year in Khalidiyah. Recruiting, organizing, training, equipping, and employing these forces often appeared to be an uphill fight, as the Iraqi leadership both wanted and resented American leadership and logistical and financial support. Building trust through joint operations and shared risks ultimately resulted in some intelligence sharing, but the task of creating reliable forces that could independently guarantee local security was incomplete when the Task Force passed responsibility for these units to its follow-on force, the Currahees of Task Force 1-506 Infantry. The effort to raise, train, and equip these forces is likely to take much time and energy, but it could not be more important.[5] The British forces in Malaya had earlier and better success with this process than did the Americans in Vietnam, with the possible exception of the Marines' Combined Action Platoon program in I Corps. Some of the lessons of the British and Marine experiences may be of use today as the United States increasingly turns its attention to the task of creating Iraqi security forces that can defend Iraq against both internal and external threats. Their success is the key to unlocking victory in Iraq—victory for, and by, the Iraqis.

INNOVATION UNDER FIRE

This book suggests that tactical leaders in the field can spur innovation that, when accepted by higher commanders, dramatically reshapes an army in combat. The experience of the U.S. Army in Iraq certainly supports that contention. Tank battalions, which just weeks previously had been required to execute missions no more politically complicated than "Attack" and "Defend," learned while in combat how to conduct Area Denial operations and Special Forces–style raids even as their battalion leadership conducted political negotiations with local leaders and trained and equipped Iraqi police and National Guard forces.[6] Task Force 1-34 Armor learned to integrate Civil Affairs, Psychological Operations, and Counterintelligence Teams into its daily counterinsurgency operations. Linking up in theater and inventing doctrine on the run, these Counterinsurgency Teams were essential to the success of the battalion in winning the hearts and minds of the good guys—and of uncovering, capturing, and killing the bad ones.[7]

The United States Army has taken remarkable strides to adapt to the demands of counterinsurgency in Iraq in a process it calls the "Modular Army." Stepping away from the 15,000-soldier division as the center of gravity of the army, this program creates more nimble 4000-soldier Units of Action able to operate independently over a wide area. The army is also taking steps to increase the numbers of soldiers with much-needed special skills including the counterintelligence and civil affairs soldiers that Task Force 1-34 Armor put to such good use in Khalidiyah. Programs to recruit additional Arabic speakers are underway in both the Active Army and in the National Guard, adding another essential weapon to the counterinsurgency capability of the nation. Much more remains to be done as the army creates a force capable of the cultural and linguistic sophistication necessary to defeat a very capable enemy.

WINNING THE LONG WAR: THE INTEGRATION OF NATIONAL POWER

The army is adapting to the demands of counterinsurgency in Iraq at many levels, from the tactical and operational through the training base in the United States. However, Iraq is but one front in a broader war against

Salafist extremists dedicated to eliminating Western influence from the Islamic world; winning the struggle may take decades. There is a growing realization that the most likely conflicts of the next fifty years will be irregular warfare in an "Arc of Instability" that encompasses much of the greater Middle East and parts of Africa and Central and South Asia.[8] To cope more effectively with the messy reality that in the twenty-first century many of our enemies will be insurgents, America's armed forces must continue to change.

The 2005 Quadrennial Defense Review specifically evaluates the ability of the Department of Defense to prevail in irregular warfare.[9] However, the fight to create a secure, democratic Iraq that does not provide a safe haven for terror is not primarily a military task. Counterinsurgency requires the integration of all elements of national power—diplomacy, information operations, intelligence, financial, and military—to achieve the predominantly political objectives of establishing a stable national government that can secure itself against internal and external threats. Britain was able to employ all of these elements of power remarkably well in Malaya; the process of integration took the United States longer in Vietnam.

Final victory in today's fight depends upon the integration of the nations in the Arc of Instability into the globalized world's economic and political system.[10] The army is working hard to adapt to the challenge of the global insurgency. The other departments of the federal government, and governments throughout the entire world, are steeling themselves for a protracted struggle. They also must adapt themselves to prevail in this fight, creating an operational capability to influence the actions of other nations and of subnational groups in the Arc of Instability.

Much of the burden of that struggle will continue to be borne by the young men and women of the American armed services and by their local force comrades in arms. It was truly an honor and an inspiration to serve in Iraq with some of the finest soldiers our country has ever produced. Their spirit of selfless service and determination to fight so that others can live in freedom should humble all of us. It is to them that I dedicate this edition.

NOTES

1. The task was also made much easier by the ethnic composition of the insurgency and by Malaya's geography; external support is almost always a prerequisite for a successful insurgency.

2. A task made rather more difficult by the fact that there are no street addresses in rural Iraq. For a discussion of this point, and an excellent analysis of the challenges the Task Force faced during its first three months in Khalidiyah, see Peter Maass, "Professor Nagl's War," *New York Times Sunday Magazine,* 11 January 2004.

3. Several units, including Task Force 1-34 Armor, created "Tips Lines" to allow anonymous contact between the population and security forces. These will become more effective as more people gain access to telephones, but are hampered by the absence of addresses noted earlier.

4. James Dobbins, "Iraq: Winning the Unwinnable War," *Foreign Affairs*, January/February 2005.

5. Eric Schmitt, "Effort to Train New Iraqi Security Forces Is Facing Delays," *New York Times*, 20 September 2004.

6. One of the best innovators was Captain Nick Ayers and his Bravo Company, Task Force 1-16 Infantry. For an analysis of the challenges Ayers faced in Ramadi and how he overcame them, see Greg Jaffe, "Trial by Fire: On Ground in Iraq, Capt. Ayers Writes His Own Playbook," *Wall Street Journal*, 22 September 2004.

7. See Greg Jaffe, "Soldier Uses Wits to Hunt Insurgents," *Wall Street Journal*, 10 September 2004, for the story of Sergeant John McCary, a counterintelligence specialist assigned to the task force whose knowledge of Arabic language and Iraqi culture—and dogged determination—made him perhaps the task force's most valuable player.

8. The idea of the "Arc of Instability" is taken from Thomas P. M. Barnett, *The Pentagon's New Map: War and Peace in the Twenty-First Century* (New York: G. P. Putnam's Sons, 2004).

9. See Bradley Graham, "Pentagon Prepares to Rethink Focus on Conventional Warfare; New Emphasis on Insurgencies and Terrorism Is Planned," *Washington Post*, 26 January 2005.

10. See David Ignatius, "Achieving Real Victory Could Take Decades," *Washington Post*, 26 December 2004, for CENTCOM Combatant Commander General John Abizaid's views on what he calls "The Long War."

Acknowledgments

Making war upon insurgents is messy and slow. To the extent that the writing of this book was not, first thanks are owed to Professor Robert O'Neill, veteran of the Vietnam War and of my M.Phil. and D.Phil. theses. He suggested the topic and saw it through to the end. Just as important was the support of the United States Military Academy's Department of Social Sciences; I owe a great deal to its former Chair and the current Dean of West Point, Brigadier General Daniel J. Kaufman, another Vietnam veteran and scholar. Sincere thanks to all of my colleagues during three wonderful years of teaching at West Point.

The American and British armies were very helpful and open in the course of my inquiry. A large number of veterans of the Malayan Emergency and the Vietnam War were kind enough to share their thoughts and memories; their names are listed in the Bibliography. The custodians of several archives in Britain and in the United States were extremely helpful; I should cite Brigadier (Retired) Gavin Bulloch and Lieutenant Colonel (Retired) Tim Harris of the Tactical Doctrine Retrieval Cell, Dr. Conrad Wood of the Imperial War Museum, and Dr. Peter Boyden of the National Army Museum; and in the United States, Dr. Richard Sommers of the Military History Institute and Dr. Richard Hunt and Dr. Jim Wright of the Center for Military History. I owe special thanks to Miles Templer, who opened his father's papers to me and thus enriched my understanding of the Malayan Emergency.

Professor Williamson Murray is both a veteran of the Vietnam War and one of the most important thinkers on military adaptation; knowing him has been a personal and professional boon. Colonel Richard Downie is another soldier-scholar whose work has been influential in my own intellectual development; I appreciate his generosity. Dr. Jim Miller gave me a home and an education in the Office of the Secretary of Defense. Dr. Jim Smith of the U.S. Air Force Academy's Institute for National Security Studies has been both a friend and a source of research funds, I appreciate all of his contributions. Brigadier (Retired) Michael Addison, Dr. Sam Gregg, and Dr. Nick Redman read drafts and provided many helpful comments, as did Chris Traugott, fifteen-year friend and provider of a permanent patrol base in Washington. Thanks to Dr. Heather Staines and everyone at Greenwood Press who worked so hard to make this book a reality.

Special thanks to my mother and mother-in-law, both of whom found books and provided emotional support and diversions from writing. Like mother, like daughter: Susi has battled insurgents in her pot plants and over the kitchen table as well as on the computer keyboard. Jack Frederick joined the project late but made the final editing process both more challenging and more fun.

With so much assistance, I can claim credit for little that follows except the errors of fact and interpretation that remain despite the best efforts of all of those listed here.

Introduction

Two months to the day after the attacks of 11 September 2001, U.S. Army Special Forces soldiers played a critical role in the defeat of Taliban forces at Mazar-i-Sharif. The victors displayed a remarkable ability to improvise, calling in precision-guided munitions while riding horses into battle. This was not a war the American military had prepared to fight; none of the Special Forces soldiers were trained in horse cavalry tactics. But the circumstances of the war in Afghanistan demanded that the Army adapt its traditional way of fighting and the Special Forces were able to learn on the fly, leading to the collapse of the Taliban regime in a remarkably innovative campaign.[1]

Secretary of Defense Donald Rumsfeld uses the horse cavalry charge at Mazar-i-Sharif to make a telling point about the military in the twenty-first century. He writes, "The lesson from the Afghan campaign is not that the U.S. Army should start stockpiling saddles. Rather, it is that preparing for the future will require new ways of thinking, and the development of forces and abilities that can adapt quickly to new challenges and unexpected circumstances."[2] This book explains how to build military organizations that can adapt more quickly and effectively to future changes in warfare.

Otto von Bismarck suggested that fools learn by experience whereas wise men learn from other peoples' experience.[3] This book examines how two armies learned when they were confronted with situations for which they were not prepared by training, organization, and doctrine: the British army in the Malayan Emergency and the American army in the Vietnam War. These cases are of particular interest today because both armies confronted opponents who chose to fight them asymmetrically, avoiding their strengths while exploiting their weaknesses. Despite the difficulty of the task, the British army adapted itself to meet the demands of defeating a Communist rural insurgency, whereas the United States Army was less successful in learning how to conduct a counterinsurgency campaign. The comparison offers some interesting lessons in how armies can adapt to changed conditions.[4]

The Malayan Emergency and the Vietnam War have been the subject of comparative study before, notably in Richard Clutterbuck's *The Long, Long War: Counterinsurgency in Malaya and Vietnam*[5] and more recently in Sam Sarkesian's *Unconventional Conflicts in a New Security Era: Lessons from Malaya and Vietnam.*[6] This study differs from these earlier works in that it analyzes the performance of the British and American armies, acting as executive agents for a number of government agencies, in learning how to deal with a situation for which they were originally unprepared. It follows the learning process by using the technique of *process tracing*, defined by the political scientist Alexander George as "attempts to assess the possibility of a causal relationship between independent and dependent variables by identifying intervening steps, or cause-and-effect links, between them."[7]

The cases of Malaya and Vietnam were not selected primarily because the two wars are similar in geographical location, colonial history, or time span, although these surface similarities do serve to make more apparent both the differences in the philosophy of counterinsurgency practiced by the British and American armies and the differing abilities of the two armies to learn and change during the course of a conflict.[8] This book does not attempt to provide the definitive answer as to why the United States "lost" the war in Vietnam, nor why the British "won" in Malaya—although the conclusions it will draw about the organizational culture and learning ability of the two armies certainly demonstrate some of the reasons for the differing results of the two conflicts.

The primary argument of the book is that the better performance of the British army in learning and implementing a successful counterinsurgency doctrine in Malaya (as compared to the American army's failure to learn and implement successful counterinsurgency doctrine in Vietnam) is best explained by the differing organizational cultures of the two armies; in short, that the British army was a learning institution and the American army was not. This difference in organizational culture between the two armies is the primary cause for their markedly different performances in learning and applying the lessons of counterinsurgency. The United States Army resisted any true attempt to learn how to fight an insurgency during the course of the Vietnam War, preferring to treat the war as a conventional conflict in the tradition of the Korean War and World War II. The British army, because of its traditional role as a colonial police force and the organizational culture that its history and the national culture created, was better able to learn quickly and apply the lessons of counterinsurgency during the course of the Malayan Emergency.

The organizational learning approach has not previously been applied to explain cases of military adaptation during the course of a conflict. Efforts to understand adaptive behavior in organizations have their roots in theories of bureaucratic politics, the fledgling field of organizational science, and recent attempts to apply theories of psychology and cognition to international relations. Because of the lack of consensus on the essential attributes of learning organizations and the absence of previous explanations of military adaptation during conflicts using this approach, the author has been forced to develop his own criteria by which to conduct what George describes as a "structured, focused comparison"[9] of British army counterinsurgency learning in Malaya and United States army learning in Vietnam. Literature on learning and cognitive psychology, the histories of successful and unsuccessful military organizations, and the author's own experiences of military organizations were all drawn upon in structuring and focusing the comparison. Particularly helpful was Richard Downie's *Learning from Conflict: The U.S. Military in Vietnam, El Salvador, and the Drug War.* Downie examines United States Army counterinsurgency learning after Vietnam, using a theoretical framework upon which this study is built.[10]

The sheer volume of writing on the Malayan Emergency and (especially) on the Vietnam War can be too much of a good thing. Research for this book began with the use of secondary sources to sketch narratives of the two conflicts and published compilations of primary documentation.[11] This preliminary work allowed a focused research effort on the critical points at which learning happened—or was blocked—during the two conflicts. Documentary evidence, some never before seen, and interviews with both high-level decision makers and their more junior "eyes and ears" provided many answers. Oral histories, the midpoint between documents and interviews, were surprisingly useful in this regard.

The single most important archival source on British army learning during the Malayan Emergency are the papers of Gerald Templer: thirty boxes archived at the National Army Museum in Chelsea to which the author was only the third researcher granted access.[12] Of these, the most important are the thirty-nine letters exchanged between Templer and Colonial Secretary Oliver Lyttelton between 20 February 1952 and 25 May 1954; it would be difficult to overstate their significance. The papers of General Robert Lockhart, also catalogued at the National Army Museum, are open but underutilized in explanations of British army performance in Malaya.

Many of the critical decision makers in both conflicts studied have reached an age and a position in life at which they enjoy recalling their role and are no longer hesitant about placing blame for mistakes made on other participants or, in rare cases, on their own heads. Many were willing to talk more openly and of different topics with a serving army officer than they would have been with a purely academic researcher. Of the British army participants in the Malayan Emergency, General Sir Frank Kitson, who served at the operational level, and Major General David Lloyd Owen, Templer's Military Assistant and the provider of an invaluable perspective on high-level decision making, were particularly important.

The Colonial Policeman R. J. W. Craig MC was significant not just for revealing his insights into the importance of police forces in defeating the insurgency but also for opening the door to the Imperial War Museum's Department of Sound Records, where the archivist Dr. Conrad X. Wood has painstakingly compiled nearly one hundred interviews with participants in the Malayan Emergency, ranging from private soldiers through to the postwar Malaysian secretary of defence, Sir Robert Thompson. This resource has not been cited in any other work on the subject known to this author; Dr. Wood shares the author's hope that this project will emphasize its value and availability to future researchers.

Archival resources on the Vietnam War are vast. An invaluable road map to those that proved most relevant to this study was provided by Andrew Krepinevich's *The Army and Vietnam*.[13] It led to the U.S. army Center for Military History, which houses the twenty boxes of the Westmoreland History notes, a diarylike account of the most important United States Army decisions on Vietnam by the most significant American commander there. They were most valuable, as were the Signature Files of both General Westmoreland and of his deputy and successor, General Creighton Abrams. The U.S. Army Military History Institute is the repository of other important archives and of oral history interviews of the army's key decision makers conducted by U.S. Army War College students; like those held at the Imperial War Museum, these are open but underused.

Interviews on Vietnam ranged from the lowest officer ranks through the highest, including the Secretary of Defense. Again, the author's status as a serving army officer and the fact that the research was conducted under U.S. Army sponsorship and auspices both opened many doors and made those inside more willing to talk more openly about their experiences. Of these, the interview with Mr. McNamara was extremely useful despite his insistence that it remain background only. A brief meeting with General and Mrs. Westmoreland also provided important background knowledge, and Westmoreland's operations deputy during the critical year of 1966, Major General John Tillson III, was of great substantive help, as was the deputy MACV commander during the transition from Westmoreland to Abrams, General Andrew J. Goodpaster. Many of these participants will soon be lost to researchers; the author is extremely grateful for the chance to learn from them and for their assistance in providing context for the written record.

Through the selective use of archival sources, interviews, and oral histories, this book attempts to explain the differing performance of the British army in Malaya and the United States Army in Vietnam in "learning" how to defeat two very different Communist insurgencies during the cold war. The two conflicts were very different in scale, geography, and level of external support provided to the insurgents; they were similar in requiring an adaptive response from the Western armies involved. One army adapted successfully; the other did not, with profound effect on the international relations of the postwar era.

Chapter 1 builds on current research into innovation in military organizations, organizational culture, and organizational learning theories to construct a model of a military learning organization and tests with which to evaluate the ability of military organizations to "learn." The second chapter discusses the long history of guerrilla warfare, the changing nature of revolutionary warfare from Napoleon through Mao, and the definition of a successful counterinsurgency strategy, which is necessary to evaluate the performance of the British and American armies in developing their own counterinsurgency doctrines. The third chapter examines the organizational culture of the British and American armies before 1945 and their differing proclivities to reinforce learning behavior.

The book then examines the specific cases of the British in Malaya and the Americans in Vietnam to determine how, why, and how successfully the two armies adapted to the demands of revolutionary warfare. Finally, it draws some conclusions concerning the ability of military organizations to learn from their own experience and from that of other armies, as well as the ability of Western militaries to deal with insurgencies. It concludes with a discussion of ways to ensure that military organizations follow Bismarck's advice to learn, not just from their own experiences, but from those of other militaries as well, in the hope that more armies can prepare to fight the next war rather than the last one.

NOTES

1. Evan Thomas and John Barry, "A Fight over the Next Front," *Newsweek* (October 22, 2001), 43.

2. Donald A. Rumsfeld, "Transforming the Military," *Foreign Affairs* 81: 3 (May/June 2002), 22.

3. Quoted in Kenneth N. Waltz, *Man, the State, and War* (New York: Columbia University Press, 1959), 220.

4. The political scientist Alexander George suggested studying "cases of both success and failure in order to identify the conditions and variables that [seem] to account for this difference in the outcome." Alexander L. George, "Case Studies and Theory Development: The Method of Structured, Focused Comparison," in Paul Gordon Lauren, ed., *Diplomacy: New Approaches in History, Theory, and Policy* (New York: Macmillan, 1979), 44.

5. Richard Clutterbuck, *The Long, Long War: Counterinsurgency in Malaya and Vietnam* (Westport, CT: Praeger, 1966).

6. Sam Sarkesian, *Unconventional Conflicts in a New Security Era: Lessons from Malaya and Vietnam* (Westport, CT: Greenwood Press, 1993).

7. George, "Case Studies and Theory Development," in Lauren, *Diplomacy*, 40.

8. Robert Thompson discusses the comparison in his own book, *Defeating Communist Insurgency: Experiences from Malaya and Vietnam* (London: Chatto & Windus, 1972). "We have, then, a Malaya in comparison smaller, more prosperous and better administered: all great advantages in counter-insurgency. But perhaps the greatest advantage of all was that Malaya was completely isolated from outside Communist support." He goes on to note several advantages that the Vietnamese enjoyed, including "almost unlimited support from the American government" (19–20). Thompson, who worked on behalf of the American effort in Vietnam as head of the British Advisory Mission, did not always find the support of the American government to be an advantage.

9. George, "Case Studies and Theory Development," in Lauren, *Diplomacy*, 62.

10. Richard Downie, *Learning from Conflict: The U.S. Military in Vietnam, El Salvador, and the Drug War* (Westport, CT: Praeger, 1998). The author is grateful for Downie's research assistance, especially during a meeting at the Pentagon on 19 September 1996.

11. Primarily A.J. Stockwell, ed., *British Documents on the End of Empire: Malaya*, 3 volumes (London: HMSO, 1995), and *The Pentagon Papers: The Defense Department History of United States Decisionmaking on Vietnam*, Senator Gravel Edition, 4 volumes (Boston: Beacon Press, 1971).

12. The author is grateful to Miles Templer for permission to use his father's papers.

13. Andrew Krepinevich, *The Army and Vietnam* (Baltimore: Johns Hopkins University Press, 1986). Lieutenant Colonel (Retired) Krepinevich provided more assistance during a 17 September 1996 interview in Washington, D.C.

List of Abbreviations

AID	Agency for International Development
ARVN	Army of the Republic of Vietnam
BMD	British Military Doctrine
BRIAM	British Advisory Mission
CAP	U.S. Marine Corps Combined Action Platoon
CEPS	Combined Emergency Planning Staff
CG	Civil Guard
CIA	Central Intelligence Agency
CIDG	Civilian Irregular Defense Group
CINPAC	Commander-in-Chief Pacific
CMH	U.S. Army Center for Military History
CO	Colonial Office
COIN	Counterinsurgency
COMUS-MACV	Commander, U.S. Military Assistance Command Vietnam
CORDS	Civil Operations and Revolutionary Development Support
CPO	Chief Police Officer
CSA	Chief of Staff of the Army
CT	Communist Terrorist
DRV	Democratic Republic of (North) Vietnam
DSR	Department for Sound Records, Imperial War Museum

DWEC	District War Executive Committee
FARELF	Far East Land Force
FM	Field Marshal
FWEC	Federal War Executive Committee
GVN	Government of (South) Vietnam
IISS	International Institute for Strategic Studies
ISA	International Security Affairs
IWM	Imperial War Museum
JCS	Joint Chiefs of Staff
LIC	Low Intensity Conflict
MAAG	Military Assistance Advisory Group
MACV	Military Assistance Command, Vietnam
MAF	Marine Amphibious Force
MCA	Malayan Chinese Association
MCP	Malayan Communist Party
MHI	U.S. Army Military History Institute
MOOTW	Military Operations Other Than War
MPAJA	Malayan People's Anti-Japanese Army
MPAJU	Malayan People's Anti-Japanese Union
MRLA	Malayan Races Liberation Army
NATO	North Atlantic Treaty Organization
NITM	Notes and Information on Training Matters
OCPD	Officer in Charge of the Police District
OOTW	Operations Other Than War
PFF	Police Field Force
PRO	Public Records Office
PROVN	Program for the Pacification and Long-Term Development of South Vietnam
RAMC	Royal Army Medical Corps
RAND	Research and Development Corporation
RD	Revolutionary Development
RF/PF	Regional Forces and Popular Forces
RSA	Royal School of Artillery
RVNAF	Republic of Vietnam Armed Forces
SAS	Special Air Service
SB	Special Branch
SDC	Self-Defense Corps

SEP	Surrendered Enemy Personnel
SOE	Special Operations Executive
SOOHP	U.S. Army Military History Institute Senior Officer Oral History Project
SOV	Special Operations Volunteer
SWEC	State War Executive Committee
TDRC	British Army Tactical Doctrine Retrieval Cell
TRIM	Training Relations and Instruction Mission
UMNO	United Malays National Organization
USA	U.S. Army
USIA	U.S. Information Agency
VA	Voice Aircraft
WO	War Office

I

SETTING THE STAGE

How Armies Learn

INTERNAL AND EXTERNAL MODELS OF MILITARY INNOVATION

There is substantial disagreement over what spurs military innovation. An early debate in the American academy centered on whether it was possible for military organizations to adapt to changes in their environment without substantial pressure from outside. Barry Posen argued that fundamental change in military organizations occurs as a result of the efforts of external civilian reformers, often with the assistance of individual military officers he called "mavericks." These reformers respond to the emergence of national security threats that current military doctrine is unable to meet. Other writers also focus on pressures outside the military that they feel are the key to doctrinal change.[1] A common feature of their arguments is the belief that military organizations are essentially conservative and reflexively opposed to change; thus, in order to simplify their possible responses to the uncertain environment of future war, they focus on offensive military doctrine, regardless of whether it is appropriate to the nature of the warfare of the time or to the strategic situation of their nation. In this view, civilian leaders intervene to force changes in doctrine only during times of imminent crisis. This has been called the "Cult of the Offensive" explanation.[2]

In 1991, Stephen P. Rosen argued that neither defeat in wartime nor civilian intervention to assist military "mavericks" is a necessary prerequisite for military innovation. Instead, senior military officers who create new military tasks and missions for their service, inspire a generation of young officers to take up this new career path, and are assisted by senior government civilians can create major changes in military doctrine.[3] This could be described as an internal model of military innovation.

In 1993, Ricky Lynn Waddell compared the usefulness of the theories of Stephen Rosen and Barry Posen to explain developments in U.S. Army Low-Intensity Conflict Doctrine from 1961 to 1993.[4] He found that civilian reformers and members of the army combined to cause changes in military doctrine, but that maverick officers were not necessary for doctrine to change in response to changes in the international system and the requirements of new forms of warfare. Waddell thus combined the internal and external schools of military innovation in an integrative model of doctrinal change. He is joined in this approach by Kimberly Martin Zisk, who believes that military organizations innovate in response to foreign doctrinal shifts that they view as a threat, even in the absence of civilian intervention,[5] and by Deborah Avant, author of *Political Institutions and Military Change*.[6] Avant's book, which compares the performance of the British army in the Boer War and the Malayan Emergency with that of the American army in Vietnam, concludes that the parliamentary British system of government has created a more adaptable army than has the presidential American system.

An integrative perspective is also adopted by Williamson Murray and Allan R. Millett in *Military Innovation in the Interwar Period*, although their explanation of causality differs from Avant's.[7] Murray and Barry Watts conclude, "Without the emergence of bureaucratic acceptance by senior *military* leaders, including adequate funding for new enterprises and viable career paths to attract bright officers, it is difficult, if not impossible, for new ways of fighting to take root within existing military institutions."[8]

Organizational and Strategic Culture

Although these studies provide valuable perspectives on the factors that spur innovation in military organizations, they do not adequately evaluate how different military forces create, assimilate, and disseminate doctrinal change during the course of conflicts, nor why some military forces are more successful at the process than are others. One possible explanation originates in the realm of organizational theory.

Organizational theory suggests that organizations are created in order to accomplish certain missions. Over time certain missions become more important than other missions to the leadership of the organization. According to an early proponent of organizational theory, the essence of an organization is the view of the dominant group in that organization on the best roles and missions for that organization.[9] The essence is "the notion held by members of an organization as to what the main capabilities and primary mission of the organization should be."[10] Morton Halperin lists a number of ways by which organizations demonstrate the importance of their essence. Organizations favor policies that will increase the importance of the organization, fight for the capabilities that they view as essential to their essence, seek to protect those capabilities viewed as essential, and demonstrate comparative indifference to functions not viewed as essential.[11] Leaders of organizations have substantial influence over their own destinies: "Career officials of an organization believe that they are in a better position than others to determine what capabilities they should have and how they should best fulfill their mission. They attach very high priority to controlling their own resources so that these can be used to support the essence of the organization."[12]

In order to contribute to the concept of the organization as successful, organizations reward those members who contribute to the essence of the organization. Thus, as Halperin observes, "military officers compete for roles in what is seen as the essence of the services' activity rather than other functions where promotion is less likely . . . Army officers compete for roles in combat organizations rather than advisory missions."[13] Maintaining morale in organizations can become even more important than accomplishing the missions of that organization: "Short-run accomplishment of goals and even increases in budgets take second place to the long-run health of the organization." Halperin notes the example of the army's one year tour of duty for officers in Vietnam, which many observers think contributed to the poor performance of the army in that conflict. The army was dedicated to the policy because it gave the greatest possible number of officers the opportunity to experience combat, widely viewed as necessary for promotion.[14]

As thinking about the sources of military innovation evolved, some analysts turned to the idea of strategic culture to explain differing responses from different organizations to similar situations. In the words of James Wilson, "Every organization has a culture, that is, a persistent, patterned way of thinking about the central tasks of and human relationships within an organization."[15] This school of thought believes that, whereas military organizations are alike in many ways, different militaries have different organizational cultures.[16] The British and American armies played very different roles in the international system and in the lives of their nations in the years before they joined in an alliance to defeat Nazi Germany; it is not surprising that their organizational cultures are very different. These differences were magnified in the postwar era, as the American army focused itself on preparing to fight the forces of the Warsaw Pact in Europe. Although the British army also had substantial responsibilities to the North Atlantic Treaty Organization (NATO), it simultaneously engaged in a series of what have been described as "Brushfire Wars" during the devolution of empire. These modified the British army's own concept of its role in the international system.

In the 1990s Lieutenant General Theodore G. Stroup demonstrated how pervasive the concept of strategic culture has become: "The Army's culture is its personality. It reflects the Army's values, philosophy, norms, and unwritten rules. Our culture has a powerful effect because our common underlying assumptions guide behavior and the way the Army processes information as an organization."[17] The essence of the American army, in the eyes of its career officers, is ground combat by organized regular divisional units. Although the American army tolerates the existence of subcultures that do not directly contribute to the essence of the organization, these peripheral organizations do not receive the support accorded to the army core constituencies of armor, infantry, and artillery.[18] It is these combat arms that exert most influence on the way the army approaches conflicts.

The varying strategic and organizational cultures of different organizations play a critical role in the organizations' abilities to adapt their structure and functions to the demands placed on them. As Elizabeth Kier notes: "Culture has independent explanatory power. . . . The organizational culture is the intervening variable between civilian decisions and military doctrine."[19] The U.S. Army's organizational culture, for example, led it only haltingly and grudgingly to implement President John F. Kennedy's instructions to focus on counterinsurgency in the early 1960s. Organizational culture also plays a critical role in determining how effectively organizations can learn from their own experiences.

ORGANIZATIONAL LEARNING THEORIES

An evolving body of organizational learning literature examines how organizations "learn" from their experiences.[20] It suggests a cyclical process through which doctrine and standard operating procedures evolve in all organizations.[21] The institutional learning process begins with the recognition of shortcomings in organizational knowledge or performance. It moves through the critical phase of searching for and achieving consensus on the right solution for the shortcomings to the adoption and dissemination of the modified doctrine. The process then repeats itself endlessly.[22] This study will follow Richard Downie in defining learning as "a process by which an organization uses new knowledge or understanding gained from experience or study to adjust institutional norms, doctrine and procedures in ways designed to minimize previous gaps in performance and maximize future successes."[23]

Essential to any examination of organizational learning, but especially to learning in military organizations, is the concept of institutional memory. The institutional memory of an organization is the conventional wisdom of an organization about how to perform its tasks and missions. Although organizations are admittedly collections of individuals, individual learning is not sufficient for the organization to change its practices; a more complicated process involving the institutional memory is required. As Bo Hedberg puts it, "Members come and go, and leadership changes, but organizations' memories preserve certain behaviors, mental maps, norms, and values over time."[24]

An army codifies its institutional memory in doctrine. According to the most recent edition of Field Manual 3-0, *Operations*, the capstone of the American army's thinking about war, doctrine is the "concise expression of how Army forces contribute to unified action in campaigns, major operations, battles, and engagements. . . . Army doctrine provides a common language and a common understanding of how Army forces conduct operations."[25]

Although the British army definition of doctrine echoes the American as a result of NATO standardization agreements, published doctrine is a relatively recent phenomenon in the British Army.[26] In fact, General Sir Nigel Bagnall was the first Chief of the General Staff to insist that it be written in the British army; his successor, Sir John Chapple, found it necessary in 1989 to reply to "some who say that laying down doctrine like this is not the British way" by stating: "The modern battlefield is not a place where we could hope to succeed by muddling through. Doctrine is not in itself a prescription for success as a set of rules. . . . What it does provide is the basis for thought, further selective study and reading which is the personal responsibility of all of us."[27] A British doctrine writer concurs: "The first safe assumption is that war will occur where it is little expected and that warfare will assume at least a partly unforeseen form." As a result, in wartime the services "must be able to react positively to the unexpected, adjusting their methods of operation rapidly to the circumstances actually prevailing."[28]

Doctrinal changes are not the only way in which military organizations demonstrate learning, although the published nature of formalized doctrine makes it convincing evidence of change. Learning is also demonstrated in the curricula of military schools and training institutions, in the structure of military organizations, in the creation of new organizations to deal with new or changed situations, and in myriad other institutional responses to change. As a result of the long process required to revise or rewrite published doctrine and ensure its approval through all of the levels of military bureaucracy through which it must pass prior to publication, doctrinal change is in many ways a trailing indicator of institutional learning. Responsive, flexible military institutions often publish "Lessons Learned" notes, incorporating information gained locally during the course of a conflict, and pull forces out of a conflict for periodic retraining in new techniques or new weaponry. Such cases should be accepted as indicators of the flexibility of the organization and its willingness to learn; however, the changes are generally incorporated into published doctrine at the first opportunity.

Figure 1-1
The Institutional Learning Cycle: The Process of Doctrinal Change

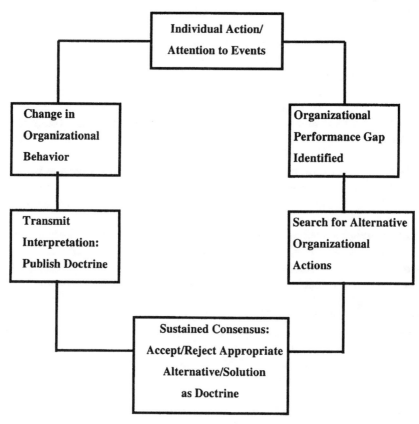

Doctrine is thus an efficient way to track the development of learning in military organizations; changes in doctrine are prima facie evidence of military learning. Figure 1-1 depicts Richard Downie's application of the complete learning cycle to military institutions, with the learning process demonstrated through published and disseminated changes in doctrine.[29]

Resistance to Learning

Military organizations often demonstrate remarkable resistance to doctrinal change as a result of their organizational cultures. Organizational learning, when it does occur, tends to happen only in the wake of a particularly unpleasant or unproductive event. The British army finally scrapped the "Purchase System" as a means of selecting its officers as a result of the spectacularly poor performance of many of its officers during the Crimean War, though there was a substantial time lag—the system was not reformed until Edward Cardwell, the secretary of state for war, introduced the Regulation of Forces Act of 1871.[30] Even spectacular failures do not necessarily promote adaptation, however; Richard Downie found that the American army's counterinsurgency doctrine did not change substantially in the fifteen years after its failure in Vietnam.

An early and particularly interesting examination of the importance of organizational culture as a factor creating resistance to adaptation in military organizations is Edward L. Katzenbach's "The Horse Cavalry in the Twentieth Century: A Study in Policy Response."[31] Katzenbach examines the institutional forces that allowed the horse cavalry to survive in the face of four profound changes in military technology: the invention of automatic weapons, the introduction of internal combustion engines to the battlefield in the air and on the ground, the creation of airborne forces, and the development of nuclear weapons. To explain the remarkable adherence of cavalrymen in both Europe and the United States to their mounts despite these developments (the Belgian General Staff suggested the reintroduction of the horse into its military forces in 1956 for mobility on the nuclear battlefield!), Katzenbach dissected the organizational culture of the cavalry. He discovered that emotional faith in battle-tested systems, the hierarchy of the military culture, the lack of peacetime pressure to make changes whose actual importance to the state becomes clear only in war, and the lack of desire of civilian leadership to spend money on military change in peacetime all conspired to keep horses in the cavalry.[32] Since the military bureaucracy could not overcome the organizational culture to create needed change, Katzenbach supported the external theory of military innovation: "The greatest instigation of new weapons development has in the past come from civilian interest plus industrial pressure. The civilian governors get the weapons systems *they* want."[33]

Successful adaptations of military doctrine in the course of a war are interesting cases of organizational adaptation under extreme pressure. One such case is the development of infiltration tactics by the German Army in 1917, after three hard years of trench warfare[34]; another is the adaptation of the American army to *bocage* fighting in the hedgerows of Normandy.[35] This book will examine the British army's process of learning successful counterinsurgency doctrine in 1951 after three unsuccessful years fighting Communist insurgents in Malaya; the conclusion of the Malayan Emergency in 1960 marked one of the few Western successes in counterinsurgency. The American army, in contrast, did not learn how to defeat an insurgency during the course of its war, and it also failed to learn from a British Advisory Mission invited to Vietnam for the sole purpose of imparting lessons learned from the Malayan conflict.

Figure 1-2
Question Set #1: Was the Army a "Learning Institution"?

1.) Does the army promote suggestions from the field?

2.) Are subordinates encouraged to question superiors and policies?

3.) Does the organization regularly question its basic assumptions?

4.) Are high-ranking officers routinely in close contact with those on the ground and open to their suggestions?

5.) Are Standard Operating Procedures (SOPs) generated locally and informally or imposed from the center?

EVALUATING ARMIES AS LEARNING INSTITUTIONS

Although there is no universally accepted question set that can be used to determine whether a specific institution performs as a "learning organization," the characteristics of such institutions are generally well accepted. A recent book by the former U.S. Army chief of staff, Gordon R. Sullivan, and one of his strategic planners, Colonel Michael V. Harper, applies this consensus in a study of the early post–cold war performance of the U.S. Army.[36] Chapter 11 of *Hope Is Not a Method*, specifically dedicated to "Growing the Learning Organization," argues, "The [U.S.] Army began its journey to becoming a learning organization in the 1970's."[37] Sullivan and Harper posit a six-step organizational learning process, with the steps very similar to those presented by Richard Downie in his organizational learning cycle: targeting opportunity, collecting data, creating knowledge, distributing knowledge, performing short-term applications, and performing long-term applications.[38]

This study draws on these six steps in building Question Set #1 (Figure 1-2), but also on what Sullivan and Harper describe as "the three key elements" in meeting "the learning challenge": "the right culture, the knowledge itself, and access to the knowledge."[39] The questions aim at determining not just whether an army is interested in the collection of data—promoting suggestions from those engaged in combat—but, far more important, whether the institution is willing and able to apply the information to create change in procedures, organization, training, and thinking about conflict. In the words of a student of U.S. Army learning during conflicts, "An army learns lessons *after* it incorporates the conclusions derived from experience into institutional form."[40] It is therefore essential that the army leadership be willing to accept, or at least consider, even what at first appear to be heretical ideas. The 1902 *Combat Training* manual of the British army explains an institutional culture that would earn full marks from Question Set #1:

Success in war cannot be expected unless all ranks have been trained in peace to use their wits. Generals and commanding officers are, therefore, not only to encourage their subordinates in so doing by affording them constant opportunities of acting on their own responsibility but, they will also check all practices which interfere with the free exercise of the judgment, and will break down, by every means in their power, the paralyzing habit of an unreasoning and mechanical adherence to the letter of orders and to routine, when acting under service conditions.[41]

The answers to the "structured, focused" questions in Question Set #1 will demonstrate that the British army was in fact a "learning institution" during the period of this study as a result of its organizational culture. The army developed a successful counterinsurgency doctrine in Malaya largely as a result of its performance as a "learning institution." The answers to the same questions will show that the American army was not a learning institution during its involvement in Vietnam but was in fact organizationally disposed against learning how to fight and win counterinsurgency warfare. It was as a result of this failure to become a "learning institution" that the American army did not learn how to fight a counterinsurgency war in Vietnam, and that the British Advisory Mission to Vietnam was ineffective in passing on counterinsurgency lessons from the recent British success in Malaya to the American army in Vietnam.

The next chapter will discuss the long history of guerrilla warfare, the changing nature of revolutionary warfare from Napoleon through Mao, and the definition of a successful counterinsurgency strategy, all of which are necessary to evaluate the performance of the British and American armies in developing their own counterinsurgency doctrines.

NOTES

1. They include Steven Van Evera, "Why Cooperation Failed in 1914," in Kenneth Oye, ed., *Cooperation Under Anarchy* (Princeton, NJ: Princeton University Press, 1986); Jack Snyder, *The Ideology of the Offensive* (Ithaca, NY: Cornell University Press, 1984); and Van Evera, "The Cult of the Offensive and the Origins of the First World War," *International Security* 9/1 (Summer 1984), 58–107.

2. Christopher M. Gacek, *The Logic of Force: The Dilemma of Limited War in American Foreign Policy* (New York: Columbia University Press, 1994), 6. Gacek argues that the tension between concepts of limited war and "Total Victory" has driven postwar American decisions regarding the use of force in international relations; see p. 20.

3. Stephen P. Rosen, *Winning the Next War: Innovation and the Modern Military* (Ithaca, NY: Cornell University Press, 1991).

4. Ricky Lynn Waddell, *The Army and Peacetime Low Intensity Conflict, 1961–1993: The Process of Peripheral and Fundamental Military Change* (Unpublished Ph.D. Thesis, Columbia University, 1993).

5. Kimberly Martin Zisk, *Engaging the Enemy: Organization Theory and Soviet Military Innovation, 1955–1991* (Princeton, NJ: Princeton University Press, 1993).

6. Deborah Avant, *Political Institutions and Military Change* (Ithaca, NY: Cornell University Press, 1994).

7. Williamson Murray and Allan R. Millett, eds., *Military Innovation in the Interwar Period* (Cambridge: Cambridge University Press, 1996). This study further develops the work done by Millett and Murray in their three volumes on *Military Effectiveness* (London: Allen & Unwin, 1988), focusing on the learning process during the interwar years.

8. Watts and Murray, "Innovation in Peacetime," in Murray and Millett, *Military Innovation*, 409.

9. Morton Halperin, *Bureaucratic Politics and Foreign Policy* (Washington, DC: Brookings, 1974), 26–28. This discussion of the concept of organizational culture relies heavily on Halperin, who was one of the first and most perceptive analysts of the organizational culture of the American army. The organizational culture of the British army has not been extensively studied; Patrick Mileham's *Ethos: British Army Officership, 1962–1992* (Camberley: Strategic and Combat Studies Institute Occasional Paper #19) is a recent exception that also helps to explain the cause of the neglect: "Aversion to abstract theory is a known and well documented British national characteristic" (4).

10. Morton Halperin and Arnold Kanter, "The Bureaucratic Perspective," in Robert J. Art and Robert Jervis, eds., *International Politics: Anarchy, Force, Political Economy, and Decision Making*, 2d ed. (Boston: Addison-Wesley, 1985), 444.

11. Halperin, *Bureaucratic Politics and Foreign Policy*, 39–40.

12. Ibid., 51.

13. Ibid., 55.

14. Ibid., 56.

15. James Q. Wilson, *Bureaucracy* (New York: Basic Books, 1989), 91.

16. The evolution of strategic culture explanations for military policies is reviewed by Alastair Iain Johnston, "Thinking About Strategic Culture," *International Security* 19/4 (Spring 1995), 32–64.

17. Theodore G. Stroup, Jr., "Leadership and Organizational Culture: Actions Speak Louder than Words," *Military Review* LXXVI, No. 1 (January/February 1996), 45.

18. Halperin, *Bureaucratic Politics and Foreign Policy*, 34–35.

19. Elizabeth Kier, "Culture and Military Doctrine: France Between the Wars," *International Security* 19/4 (Spring 1995), 66.

20. The best review of organizational learning theory as applied to international relations is Jack S. Levy, "Learning and Foreign Policy: Sweeping a Conceptual Minefield," *International Organization* 48, 2 (Spring 1994), 279–312. See also Barbara Levitt and James G. March, "Organizational Learning," in Michael D. Cohen and Lee S. Sproul, eds., *Organizational Learning* (London: Sage, 1996), 516–540.

21. Richard Downie, *Learning from Conflict: The U.S. Military in Vietnam, El Salvador, and that Drug War* (Westport, CT: Praeger, 1998), 9. Downie examines the learning ability of the American army by tracing the development of American counterinsurgency doctrine after Vietnam and in El Salvador, and by evaluating counterdrug doctrine in the Andean Ridge. This study applies Downie's theoretical

base to cases of military innovation during the course of conflicts and to a cross-cultural comparison to determine the relative importance of the learning institution in accounting for military success and failure.

22. James C. March and Johan P. Olsen, "Organizational Learning and the Ambiguity of the Past," in March and Olsen, eds., *Ambiguity and Choice in Organizations* (Oslo, Sweden: Universitet forlaget, 1976).

23. Downie, *Learning from Conflict*, 22.

24. Bo Hedberg, "How Organizations Learn and Unlearn," in Paul C. Nystrom and William H. Starbuck, eds., *Handbook of Organizational Design* (Oxford: Oxford University Press, 1981), 6.

25. Headquarters, Department of the Army, Field Manual 3–0, *Operations* (Washington, DC: GPO, 2001), 1–45 and 1–46.

26. When asked why it was that the British army began to publish doctrine so late in its history, General Sir Frank Kitson harumphed, "No one would read it if they did write it down." Interview in Devon, 12 December 1995.

27. Army Code 71451, *Design for Military Operations: The British Military Doctrine* (1989), vii.

28. Ibid., 21.

29. The concept is familiar in organizational learning literature; for example, "The Experiential Learning Cycle" consists of "Experience, Reflection, Generalization, and Experimentation" in a feedback loop process in Gervase R. Bushe and A.B. Shani, *Parallel Learning Structures: Increasing Innovation in Bureaucracies* (Wokingham, England: Addison-Wesley, 1991), 141. This cycle owes its intellectual heritage to Colonel John Boyd, developer of the "Boyd Cycle" or "OODA Loop" in which fighter pilots are taught to observe, orient, decide, and act faster than their opponents can. See "Colonel John Boyd Dies, Revolutionized Air Combat Tactics," *International Herald Tribune* (14 March 1997), 2.

30. Cecil Woodham-Smith, *The Reason Why* (London: Constable, 1955), 22–25. Another good analysis is Correlli Barnett, *Britain and Her Army* (London: Penguin, 1970), 283–291.

31. Edward L. Katzenbach, "The Horse Cavalry in the Twentieth Century: A Study in Policy Response," *Public Policy* (1958), 120–149.

32. Ibid., 121.

33. Ibid., 148.

34. Timothy T. Lupfer, *The Dynamics of Doctrine: The Changes in German Tactical Doctrine During the First World War* (Fort Leavenworth, KS: Combat Studies Institute, 1981).

35. Michael D. Doubler, *Closing with the Enemy* (Lawrence: University of Kansas Press, 1994).

36. Gordon R. Sullivan and Michael V. Harper, *Hope Is Not a Method: What Business Leaders Can Learn from America's Army* (New York: Random House/Times Business, 1996). The author is grateful to Sir Douglas Haig of Templeton College for an invitation to attend a seminar based on this book led by Colonel Harper at Templeton on 12 November 1996 and to Colonel Harper for his help in defining "learning institutions."

37. Ibid., 190. The quotation implies that the U.S. Army was not a learning organization during the Vietnam War, a conclusion with which this study agrees.

38. Ibid., 206–207.

39. Ibid., 206. These questions are also influenced by those asked by Allan R. Millett, Williamson Murray, and Kenneth H. Watman in "The Effectiveness of Military Organizations," the first chapter of Allan R. Millet and Williamson Murray, eds., *Military Effectiveness*. Volume I, *The First World War* (London: Allen and Unwin, 1988), 1–30.

40. Dennis J. Vetock, *Lessons Learned: A History of U.S. Army Lesson Learning* (Carlisle Barracks, PA: U.S. Army Military History Institute, 1988), 128. This is a good historical survey of U.S. Army use of its combat experiences to learn lessons in wartime, although it downplays the importance of organizational culture. This author disagrees with Vetock's conclusion that "the most effective procedures for managing the [U.S.] Army's usable combat experience involved the centralization of responsibility, control and operation" (127); this conclusion is true only for the major conflicts that have represented the organizational essence of the U.S. Army throughout its history.

41. Great Britain War Office, *Combined Training (Provisional)* (London: Harrison and Sons, 1902), 4. Quoted in Michael J. Meese, "Institutionalizing Maneuver Warfare: The Process of Organizational Change," in Richard D. Hooker, Jr., ed., *Maneuver Warfare: An Anthology* (Novato, CA: Presidio, 1993), 204. The author is grateful to then-Major Meese for his assistance at West Point on 6 September 1996.

2

The Hard Lesson of Insurgency

Low-intensity conflict has been more common throughout the history of warfare than has conflict between nations represented by armies on a "conventional" field of battle. Until relatively recently, however, those who took up arms against the state were referred to as bandits or criminals rather than as combatants in irregular warfare; it was only the rise of nationalism, and the corresponding growth of acceptance of individual liberty and responsibility, that provided a sort of legitimacy to violence directed against the state.[1]

The essential features of guerrilla warfare are avoiding the enemy's strength—his main fighting forces—while striking at outposts and logistical support from unexpected directions. This principle is now often described as "asymmetric," but it is as old as the word *guerrilla* itself. The term is derived from the Spanish term for "small war" and springs from the Spanish rebellion of 1808 against an occupying French army. The combined efforts of Wellington's 60,000 men, a small Spanish army, and the Spanish *guerrilleros* tied up more than 250,000 French troops and supported Henry IV's remark that "Spain is a country where small armies are beaten and large ones starve."[2] Henry's appreciation for the unpleasant fate that befell foreign armies invading Spain echoes the Roman experience there in the second century B.C.; Napoleon was not the first to be checked by Spanish guerrillas!

Henry focused on the country of Spain, but the combination of difficult, broken terrain and a proud people who refuse to bow before a foreign invader is one of the constants of guerrilla warfare. A more contemporary observer describes the essential nature of terrain in increasing the ability of guerrillas to defeat a conventional army, noting that such terrain includes

swamps, mountains and forests where mobility is limited to movements on foot and in light vehicles. The fact that the partisan operates in such terrain will be to his advantage for in an environment of this nature the regular forces lose the use of their vehicles and artillery as well as the ability to mass superior numbers. In essence, the terrain reduces the better equipped, better trained, and better armed regular force to a level where the partisan is equal.[3]

The essential features of guerrilla warfare—the tactics of applying weakness against strength and the clever use of terrain to conceal guerrilla forces from the enemy's main body—have barely changed since the days of the Romans and Persians. What has changed, and made guerrilla warfare an altogether more potent form of conflict for the accomplishment of political goals, is the addition of revolutionary politics to the mix. The man who first wrote penetratingly on these changes fought at the same time as the campaigns that gave guerrilla warfare its name: Carl von Clausewitz.

CLAUSEWITZ AND PEOPLE'S WARS

Carl von Clausewitz's *On War* is important for our purposes both because it places guerrilla warfare in the context of conventional warfare and because it has exerted considerable influence on Western armies attempting to defeat insurgency—often through the medium of Clausewitz's contemporary, Henri Jomini.[4]

Clausewitz fought against Napoleon and later wrote about the Corsican's remarkable success in revolutionizing war. In comparison to the set-piece battles of the eighteenth century, in which European armies fought by mutual consent and a single battle often decided a war, Napoleon's use of the French nation to support his campaigns constituted nothing less than a revolution in military affairs. In pre-Napoleonic European warfare, the role of the army, acting as the striking hand of the national sovereign, had so overshadowed the role of the people of a nation in supporting war that warfare had been called "the sport of kings" for centuries. Armies acted as the instruments of state power for national leaders who often personally led them into battle. Warfare involved governments and armies, arousing surprisingly little interest in the majority of the population, who often did not notice a change in rulers that resulted from battles won or lost.

Napoleon's decisive contribution was his discovery that armies and kings needed no longer fight in isolation from the people of their states. Building upon changes that had emerged during the French Revolution, Napoleon harnessed the power of the French people to make warfare a "remarkable trinity" composed of the people, the army, and the government. Clausewitz described what Napoleon grasped almost instinctively: war is "a paradox-ical trinity—composed of primordial violence, hatred, and enmity, which are to be regarded as a blind natural force; of the play of chance and probability within which the creative spirit is free to roam; and of its ele-ment of subordination, as an instrument of policy, which makes it subject to reason alone. The first of these three aspects mainly concerns the people; the second the commander and his army; the third the government."[5]

Another element has been added to warfare; the sport of kings has be-come the business of the people. Although the common people had always played an important role in warfare by providing the men, taxes, and food-stuffs with which the army was supplied, the rise in nationalism meant that people and armies were much more intimately linked. The people increased in relative importance, forming the raw material for a mass army; the new spirit of enraged nationalism often kept them fighting even when the na-tional government or army had been conquered or ceased to exist. Clau-sewitz's "remarkable trinity" of the people, the army, and the government is an effective way to depict the evolution of the concept of "people's war" and will also be very useful in understanding why some armies are better than others at comprehending how to combat revolutionary war.

Absolute Victory: Jomini, Clausewitz, and the Propagation of an Idea

Clausewitz's interpretation of Napoleon's revolution in military affairs is neither the only nor the most influential interpretation. The ideas of Clausewitz's contemporary, Antoine-Henri Jomini, are important both in their own right and in their shaping of the influence of Clausewitz on his-tory. Jomini was a Swiss banker who, like Clausewitz, was swept up in the events unleashed by the French Revolution. A bookish soldier, he took a position on Marshal Ney's staff and began to publish works on military history in 1803. The key principles of all of his years of writing (he lived another sixty-five years) were clearly laid out in Jomini's first book:

- Strategy is the key to warfare.
- All strategy is controlled by invariable scientific principles.
- These principles prescribe *offensive action* to *mass forces* against weaker enemy forces at some *decisive point* if strategy is to lead to victory.[6]

Jomini served in the Ulm, Jena, Eylau, Spanish, and Russian campaigns, earning some renown as a soldier but much more as the dominant military historian and theorist of his day. His most famous book, *A Summary of the Art of War*, was published in 1837; it maintained his emphasis on scientific principles of warfare and on massive battles of annihilation. Like

Clausewitz, Jomini hungered for but never enjoyed the command of troops in battle. Jomini deserted Napoleon in 1813 to serve on the Russian General Staff; again, he never gained independent command. This lifelong position on the perimeter of power led Jomini to proclaim in his writing that the military commander should have absolute control of decisions in campaigns; his models were Frederick the Great and Napoleon. The principle they followed was the same one he advocated: mass your own armies to threaten a decisive point; then defeat a fraction of the enemy army with all of your own.

Jomini is important because of his prescription of the annihilation of the opponent's force as the best route to victory, a sentiment often and mistakenly attributed to Clausewitz. The Prussian was actually much too subtle to say that anything was always the best route to victory—except the accomplishment of the political objectives for which the war was being fought. That Jomini's most famous prescription is misattributed to Clausewitz, who disliked Jomini personally and thought his ideas rubbish, is more than ironic; as John Shy says in *Makers of Modern Strategy*, "If there can be such a thing as a joke in military history, surely this is it."[7] The question of how this ironic joke came about has much to do with the historical impact of Clausewitz versus Jomini and can be explained very simply. Soldiers—and most statesmen—are uncomfortable with ambiguity, with Clausewitzian "it depends" answers. They like checklists of simple principles that always apply, ideas such as "Annihilate the enemy's force in the field and you will win the war." Jomini had given his audience what it wanted; Michael Howard notes, "This was the kind of thing that appealed to practical soldiers."[8]

It was Moltke more than any other who popularized Jominian ideas and called them Clausewitzian, for instance, "Victory through the application of armed force is the decisive factor in war. . . . It is not the occupation of a slice of territory or the capture of a fortress but the destruction of the enemy forces which will decide the outcome of the war. This destruction thus constitutes the principal object of operations."[9] Moltke supported such statements with quotations from Clausewitz, but certainly by the end of his life Clausewitz had developed a much more nuanced view of warfare than always prescribing the destruction of the enemy forces. That was a Jominian idea, misattributed to Clausewitz by Moltke, who muddied the waters for future generations of strategists still unborn.

This misattribution is important not just because it confuses military historians, but also because the Jominian concept of victory through annihilation of the enemy forces influenced other thinkers about strategy as well as generations of practitioners. The belief that annihilating the enemy army was the certain route to victory was corrupted before World War I into the concept that offense was both practically and morally superior to defense in all cases, a concept Clausewitz would have abhorred but in the defense of which he was repeatedly quoted. When ideas that were decidedly non-Clausewitzian resulted in the bloody stalemate of World War I, he was again quoted out of context to justify the continuation of the slaughter for no possible political gain. This occurred despite the fact that, as Bernard Brodie points out, German Army chief of staff Schlieffen himself was "sufficiently a student of Clausewitz" to have absorbed the concept of the primacy of the political over the military, "for he is on record as having urged in writing that if the Plan should fail, as of course it did in 1914, Germany should at once seek a negotiated peace."[10] No matter. After the war, Clausewitz took the blame for the conduct of a war of annihilation of which he would most certainly have disapproved.

The importance of Jomini for a student of counterinsurgency learning is evident: Jomini emphasizes the destruction of the enemy army in the field, despite Clausewitz's understanding that the true power of armies in the wake of Napoleon rests in the people and their government.[11] Nonetheless, armies ever since have clung to what they continue to describe as "Clausewitzian" (actually Jominian) principles of destroying the enemy army as the key to victory.

Clausewitz was primarily concerned with understanding conventional war fought by national armies, albeit armies inspired by the then-revolutionary ideas and currents unleashed by the ideals of liberty, equality, fraternity, and love of *patrie*. However, the feelings, aspirations, and energies of the people that Napoleon harnessed for the benefit of the state in conventional warfare would play a dramatic role in modifying the nature of unconventional warfare as well. Clausewitz describes "the people in arms" as "smoldering embers," which

consume the basic foundations of the enemy forces. Since it needs time to be effective, a state of tension will develop while the two elements interact. This tension will either gradually relax, if the insurgency is suppressed in some places and slowly burns itself out in others, or else it will build up to a crisis: a general conflagration closes in on the enemy, driving him out of the country before he is faced with total destruction.[12]

His theoretical description would come to life more than a century later, half a world away from Prussia. The man who fanned the embers of the most populous nation in the world was the son of a Chinese peasant. His name was Mao Tse-Tung.

FROM CLAUSEWITZ TO MAO: THE REVOLUTION CONTINUES

"However much we may seek it elsewhere, the basic text for ideas about revolutionary war is in the writings of Mao Tse-Tung."[13]
—John Shy and Thomas W. Collier

Mao Tse-Tung was born in Hunan province in central China in 1893. His father was a "middle peasant," a man who earned enough money to ensure that his family had enough to eat. Mao had a hard childhood; his father was strict but provided him with the comparative luxury of a high school education. Mao responded by reading everything he could and was a keen observer of the inability of the Chinese government to meet the needs of the peasants with whom he grew up. His service as a private soldier in a corrupt and inefficient army further increased his political awareness; Mao was "the Chinese version of an angry young man" when he began working in the library of the University of Peking in 1917.[14] He soon had contact with the precepts of communism and helped organize the Chinese Communist Party in Shanghai in 1921.

Mao described the China in which he grew up as "semi-colonial and feudal."[15] It was a country in which 400 million peasants "ate bitterness" throughout their difficult lives and that had been exploited by Western nations for over a century. Griffith notes that "a potential revolutionary situation exists in any country where the government consistently fails in its obligation to ensure at least a minimally decent standard of life for the great majority of its citizens."[16] It would be hard to imagine a better case in support of Griffith's argument than Mao's China of the 1920s, though the very use of the word *government* is somewhat misleading; in fact, there were several rival governments in China, and the standard of living was probably improving—though not fast enough to suit Mao.

The Chinese Communist Party took advantage of the corruption and inefficiency of the government to recruit the proletariat for membership in trade unions. Mao was sent to his home province of Hunan to recruit in 1926; he was surprised by the groundswell of peasant support for the National Revolutionary Army in 1926. Mao fled to the Chingkang Mountains of southern Hunan province after leading four auxiliary regiments in the abortive Autumn Harvest Uprising of September 1927. Chu Teh, another survivor of the coup, joined Mao in 1928; after a series of defeats in attacks on Nationalist-held cities in 1930, they jointly decided that in China the revolution had to be based on the peasant rather than the urban proletariat. Douglas Blaufarb notes, "The problem confronted by Mao in China in 1927 was that of writing Hamlet with a midget prince of Denmark."[17] China was simply not industrialized enough for the urban workers to form a viable base for revolution. Griffith calls this shift in emphasis from urban workers to rural peasants "the single most vital decision in the history of the Chinese Communist Party."[18]

Chiang Kai-Shek, heartened by the Communist defeat at Changsha that had led to Mao's decision to focus on the peasants, announced a "Bandit Suppression Campaign" in October 1930. It failed miserably, as did three similar campaigns in following years. The Nationalist troops displayed the conduct that would prove to be their downfall: Chiang's "divisions flailed over the land like locusts, further alienating peasants, the ill-treated, illiterate soldiers frequently deserting to the Communists."[19] Only when Chiang Kai-Shek accepted the advice of his German adviser, General von Falkenhausen, who drew on the British lessons of the Boer War and advanced slowly and methodically through the Communist base areas with a force of some 500,000 supported by artillery and aircraft, did the Communists begin to feel the pressure of the counterinsurgency campaign.

The Communists broke through the Nationalist lines to begin the "Long March" of some 6,000 miles to a new base in Shensi province in October 1934. Over twelve months later, some 30,000 survivors of the 130,000 who began the march arrived in Shensi; Mao's wife died on the march. Costly as it was, the Long March demonstrated the will of the people to support the revolutionaries.[20] It also taught Mao a great deal about revolutionary warfare; it was while he was rebuilding Communist strength in Yenan after escaping yet another attack by Chiang Kai-Shek in 1936 that Mao wrote *Guerrilla Warfare*.

The continuing encroachment of Japan into China gave Mao's Communists the political issue they needed to mobilize the people behind their cause. Chiang's refusal to ally his forces with Mao's in a national front against the invader allowed Mao to "appropriate nationalism from the Nationalists and [make] it a powerful Communist weapon."[21] Chiang agreed to the creation of a united front only after literally being kidnapped by his own forces shortly before the Japanese invasion in 1937. The Japanese invasion was a blessing in disguise for Mao and the Communists: it "broke the hold of parochialism on the Chinese peasant. Before the Japanese invasion the Chinese peasant was indifferent to 'Chinese' politics, being wholly absorbed in local affairs. The war totally destroyed the rural society order and sensitized the Chinese peasantry to a new spectrum of possible associations, identities, and purposes. Foremost among the new political concepts were those of 'China' and 'Chinese nationality.'"[22]

Mao turned the principles of guerrilla warfare he had used against the Nationalists to the struggle against the Japanese, simultaneously husbanding his own forces for the battle against Chiang's forces once the Japanese had been evicted. Both sides kept their eye on the real prize: the eventual total control of China. Mao's ideas on how to accomplish that task with his poorly armed, unprofessional band of Communist peasants would lead to the greatest revolution in military thought since the ideas of Clausewitz.

Mao's contribution to the theory of warfare is an even closer interlinking of the people, the army, and the government than that discovered by Napoleon and analyzed by Clausewitz. In fact, the people in and of themselves were the greatest weapon the Communists possessed, both in their struggle against the Japanese invaders and in the temporarily postponed fight against the Nationalists. In Mao's own words, "The richest source of power to wage war lies in the masses of the people."[23]

This doctrine was largely one of necessity: it was essential that the army, without an established government to provide logistical support, retain the goodwill of the people in order to ensure its own survival. Hence Mao's insistence on "a unity of spirit" between troops and local inhabitants, which is evident in a code known as "The Three Rules and the Eight Remarks" which guided the activities of the Communist Eighth Route Army:[24]

Rules
1. All actions are subject to command.
2. Do not steal from the people.
3. Be neither selfish nor unjust.

Remarks
1. Replace the door when you leave the house.
2. Roll up the bedding on which you have slept.
3. Be courteous.
4. Be honest in your transactions.
5. Return what you borrow.
6. Replace what you break.
7. Do not bathe in the presence of women.
8. Do not without authority search those you arrest.

The implementation of such precepts allowed the army of the people to be truly an army of the people; it was strict adherence to these regulations that emphasized to the common people that the Communists were on their side and that the Nationalist armies were not much better than the Japanese. Full implementation would create an organized Chinese populace, aroused against the Japanese invaders (and later, the Chinese Nationalists): "The Japanese aggressor, like a mad bull crashing into a ring of flames, will be surrounded by hundreds of millions of our people standing upright, the mere sound of their voices will strike terror into him, and he will be burned to death."[25]

This is a new conceptualization of the idea of "people's war," with even more emphasis on the decisive role of an aroused populace fighting against a conventional army weakened by corruption and inefficiency and crippled by the hatred of the local populace. The army and the government were now of the populace, living within it and emerging to strike at the enemy before fading back into the cover provided by the population.

It is nearly impossible to overstate the emphasis that Mao placed on ensuring the support of the people for the revolutionary war that he saw ahead. He returns to the point throughout his writing: "This question of the political mobilization of the army and the people is indeed of the greatest importance. We have dwelt on it at the risk of repetition precisely because victory is impossible without it. There are, of course, many other conditions indispensable to victory, but political mobilization is the most fundamental."[26]

Revolutionary war is protracted. Mao foresaw three phases through which the war of national liberation would pass: one of organization, consolidation, and preservation; one of progressive expansion; and the final decisive phase culminating in the destruction of the enemy. During the first phase, military operations would be limited and sporadic; the revolution would focus on training cadres, organizing the peasantry, and gathering its strength. The second phase exploits the gathering strength of the revolution to attack isolated enemy outposts and patrols with two motives: undermining the faith of the populace in the government while increasing the prestige of the revolutionaries and taking arms, ammunition, and equipment from government forces to serve as the "storehouse of the revolution." In the decisive third phase, the guerrilla fighters transform themselves into conventional military forces that confront and defeat the government in open battle. All phases can and should occur simultaneously; recruitment and training of cadres, consolidation of public support, and guerrilla operations will all be conducted in support of the decisive battles of phase III.

The patience and willingness to suffer over a long period in order to achieve ardently desired revolutionary goals have led one observer of the phenomenon to note, "Insurgents start with nothing but a cause and grow to strength, while the counter-insurgents start with everything but a cause and gradually decline in strength and grow to weakness."[27]

This is exactly what happened in the aftermath of the Japanese defeat in World War II. Chiang Kai-Shek's Nationalist forces, despite overwhelming material advantages and the logistical support of the United States, were defeated by those of Mao, buoyed by the support of the vast majority of the Chinese people. Admittedly, the Chinese Communist victory of 1949 reflected a conventional operation, but the guerrilla war against the Nationalists of 1930–1936, and that against the Japanese of 1937–1945, had set the stage. The impact of Mao's victory on the nations of the West would be hard to overstate: in the words of one observer, "The fall of the Chinese nationalist regime in 1949 to the Communists led by Mao, more than any other event, created a new Western consciousness of how protracted armed conflict, using guerrilla tactics and guided by a heterodox version of Marxism-Leninism, might achieve decisive revolutionary victory."[28] The revolution in military affairs that Mao unleashed would soon be adopted by disciples of the Chinese revolution taking advantage of the changes in the international system that occurred in the wake of World War II. These included the end of imperialism, the rise of modern media, the increase in portability and effectiveness of weaponry, and the rise of political awareness in the peoples of former colonies of the West.

INSURGENCY: A SPECIAL KIND OF REVOLUTIONARY WAR

> "The reader will agree with us when we say that once barriers are torn
> down they are not so easily set up again."
>
> —Carl von Clausewitz[29]

John Shy and Thomas Collier begin their essay "Revolutionary War" in *Makers of Modern Strategy* (1986) by noting that the 1941 edition of the book did not have a chapter on the subject. The reason for the increased importance of revolutionary warfare in the fifty years since the first edition is "the sudden decline in power and prestige of the traditional nation-state system. . . . The crumbling of European empires under colonial and even domestic assault, and the rapid appearance amidst the imperial ruins of new successor states, often weak, are the main reasons why we see this new dimension of military theory where none was apparent in 1941."[30]

Although the rise of nationalism and relative decline of imperial powers are certainly the primary reasons for the increased importance of revolutionary warfare after World War II, they are only part of the answer. Nationalism and the supranational philosophy of communism were important motivations for peoples seeking to form governments responsive to their own needs; these are the ends of a revolutionary strategy. The means changed as well. The proliferation of portable and extremely effective killing machines in the wake of World War II dramatically increased the amount of firepower available to groups wishing to overthrow governments and continues to be a substantial problem today.[31] Just as important is the increase in the ability of the media to get close to even the most distant conflicts and to transmit pictures and sounds to both the local population and the population of any foreign power intervening in a revolutionary conflict. T.E. Lawrence noted, "The printing press is the greatest weapon in the armory of the modern commander."[32] All of these factors, along with a growing disinclination in the national publics of major powers to accept casualties[33] or any evidence of oppression by their forces, have made the phenomenon of revolutionary warfare both more prevalent and far more important than it was when the Spanish guerrillas inflicted such punishment on French forces in the Peninsular campaign.

These changes in the ends of insurgency, that is, communist or nationalist (or both) domination of the government of a nation, and in the means, including more effective weaponry and the use of the media as an important weapon of the insurgent, changed the nature of revolutionary warfare as well. Clausewitz believed that people's war could serve only as a strategic defensive; changes in the ends and means of insurgency allowed revolutionary warfare to become not just an adjunct to conventional conflict but a strategically offensive form of warfare in its own right. The weapons of modern war in the hands of a politically aware and motivated populace appeared to create a new kind of war; even if the tactics had not changed since Alexander the Great, the means and ends had. As Robert Taber notes in the wonderfully titled *The War of the Flea*, "The specifically modern aspect of guerrilla warfare is in its use as a tool of political revolution— the single sure method by which an unarmed population can overcome mechanized armies, or failing to overcome them, can stalemate them and make them irrelevant."[34]

One of the advantages fleas enjoy in their attacks on much larger creatures is their autonomy. Similarly, nations composed of a large number of small, autonomous villages are hard to conquer, as each individual village will fight on individually after the defeat of the national army and will have to be individually subdued. Mao took advantage of this knowledge, gained from hard-won experience, to organize his Communists into a number of independent cells that could not be defeated en masse. The original revolutionaries proselytize to create small groups of believers in outlying villages, often through the threat of force: "power flows from the barrel of a gun." These groups in turn both create local armed forces to operate as guerrillas against the occupying power and further expand the reach of the organization. Over time, district committees are formed to control the various village cells, while larger military formations are created from the best of the local guerrilla forces.

Far from Communist insurgency's being a new kind of war, it is in fact merely an adaptation of Clausewitz's "remarkable trinity." Changes in weaponry (including the media) and especially in the increased role of the people as the logistical support; recruiting base; providers of intelligence, cover, and concealment; and armory of the army meant that enemy forces could no longer be defeated by mere defeat of the enemy army, as had previously been the case. Now defeating the army required that the people be defeated as well—or at least persuaded not to fight on behalf of, nor even support, the insurgents. In the words of a perceptive United States Army officer:

When there are no economic and political foundations for the guerrilla movement, there will be no guerrilla movement. The bulk of any guerrilla movement joins out of belief in what it is doing; the hard core of leaders keeps going because of political beliefs. If the bulk of the band find they can live as decent human beings, do not have to rob to live, and can have land and homes, they will be poor guerrillas from then on. If the great mass of the population knows it will be protected by a strong, just government, it has no reason to cooperate with the guerrillas, and the system of intelligence and supply that sustains all guerrilla movements breaks down. Without popular support the mopping up of the hard-core die-hards is fairly easy.[35]

COUNTERINSURGENCY: TWO APPROACHES

Revolutions are, by their very nature, hard to understand for those who live through them. Because revolutions in any field represent a dramatic shift in understanding of the way society is organized and in the precepts that have previously governed social behavior, it is not surprising that they result in questions about the best way to counter them. Napoleon's grasp of revolutionary warfare necessitated a coalition of Prussia, Russia, and Britain to defeat him; Mao's revolutionary warfare would also present major conceptual challenges to the nations of the West. The challenge posed by Mao would be even more difficult to confront because conventional military forces have always had difficulties in engaging guerrillas.

The difficult nature of guerrilla warfare led to two different approaches to countering insurgencies, exemplified by differing approaches to the problem of subduing the Welsh in the Norman era. The Norman King William II (Rufus) waged a ruthless campaign against the Welsh under Gruffydd in 1097 in which William "intended to abolish and utterly destroy all of the people until there should be alive not so much as a dog. He had purposed also to cut down all of the woods and groves so that there might not be shelter nor defence for the men of Gwynedd henceforth."[36]

Another approach is presented in Gerald of Wales's *Description of Wales*, written in 1194. He offers instructions in more appropriate techniques for subduing the Welsh: "The prince who would wish to subdue this nation and govern it peaceably, must use this method. . . . Let him divide their strength and by bribes and promises endeavor to stir up one against the other. . . . In the autumn let not only the marshes, but also the interior part of the country be strongly fortified with castles, provisions and confidential families."[37]

These two different approaches—annihilating versus turning the loyalty of the people—are the foundation of the two approaches to counterinsurgency (COIN) to which armies have turned throughout history. The newest edition of the British army's Counterinsurgency Manual explains the advantages and disadvantages of each approach, demonstrating that the British have come a long way from the counterinsurgency principles of William Rufus:

A straightforward attritional approach is one option. Such strategies have been adopted and some have worked. Absolute repression was used by the Germans in response to guerrilla attacks during the Second World War. Saddam Hussein's use of chemical weapons against the Kurds and his campaign against the Marsh Arabs in Southern Iraq are contemporary examples of the use of attrition. . . . None of the attritional "solutions" described above is appropriate in a liberal democracy and it is considered that a "gloves off" approach to any insurgency problem has a strictly limited role to play in modern COIN operations.

Furthermore, the record of success for attrition in COIN operations is generally a poor one. Undue focus on military action clouds the key political realities, which can result in a military-dominated campaign plan that misses the real focus of an insurgency. An inability to match the insurgent's concept with an appropriate government one—likened by [Sir Robert] Thompson to trying to play chess whilst the enemy is actually playing poker—is conceptually flawed and will not achieve success. Having deployed conventionally trained troops and large amounts of firepower, the attritionalist commander generally feels compelled to use them. The head of the US Mission to South Vietnam, General Harkins, claimed in September 1962 that what was required to defeat the Viet Cong within 3 years were "Three Ms"—men, money, and material. The result of this approach (normally to the delight of an insurgent) is an escalating and indiscriminate use of military firepower. The wider consequences of this approach, seen both in South Vietnam and elsewhere, will often be an upward spiral of civilian alienation.[38]

The two approaches to counterinsurgency in many ways resemble the two approaches often taken to conventional warfare, known as the direct and the indirect approach. A participant in the counterinsurgency effort in Vietnam explains:

In essence, military strategy generally boils down to a choice between direct and indirect methods. Direct methods imply the physical destruction of the enemy's means to make war as a preliminary to the imposition of one's physical will on the enemy, and are exemplified by the Franco-Prussian War and by the Western Front of the First World War. Indirect methods seek to attain the political objective of the war by avoidance of a frontal clash between opposing forces.[39]

The direct approach to defeating guerrillas and insurgents is well represented by Harry Summer's phrase "A war is a war is a war." The indirect approach can be clearly explained through reference to Mao's own concept that the revolutionaries are like fish that swim in the water of the people; defeating insurgents is then a matter of "separating the fish from the water."

The Direct Approach: A War Is a War Is a War

The central thesis of the direct approach to fighting a revolutionary war is that unconventional war is much like conventional war in the European setting; in the words of the American Army Colonel Harry Summers, "A war is a war is a war."[40] In order to defeat the enemy, it is only necessary to defeat his armed forces. This approach is based on a Jominian interpretation of the wars of Napoleon. Armies that resort to this method to defeat insurgents are not fighting the last war, but rather, fighting the last revolution in warfare: the Napoleonic nation in arms rather than Mao's armed nation. This is a standard military misinterpretation based on substantial experience in conventional warfare according to the European model.

Western armies often attempt to apply the same concept to the defeat of a people's army: the counterinsurgent army focuses on the defeat of the guerrilla fighters. The essence of Mao's theory of revolutionary warfare is that the warriors are part of the people, living among them during the day and striking at night; this makes difficult the determination of which are legitimate targets of a counterinsurgency campaign. One answer is the killing of all natives down to and including domestic animals as advocated by William Rufus.

The Indirect Approach: Separate the Fish from the Water

The other approach to defeating an insurgency is a function of a better understanding of Mao and a change in the perception of the nature of revolutionary warfare. While continuing to attack the armed elements of the insurgency, the indirect approach recognizes that it is essential also to attack the support of the people for the insurgents. The approach is well described in the following passage from Frank Kitson's *Low Intensity Operations*, which plays on Mao's description of a revolutionary army as relying on the people for support "like fish swimming in the water of the population:"

In attempting to counter subversion it is necessary to take account of three separate elements. The first two constitute the target proper, that is to say the Party or Front and its cells and committees on the one hand, and the armed groups who are supporting them and being supported by them on the other. They may be said to constitute the head and the body of a fish. The third element is the population and this represents the water in which the fish swims. Fish vary from place to place in accordance with the water in which they are designed to live, and the same can be said of subversive organizations. If a fish has got to be destroyed it can be attacked directly by rod or net, providing it is in the sort of position which gives these methods a chance of success. But if rod and net cannot succeed by themselves it may be necessary to do something to the water which will force the fish into a position where it can be caught. Conceivably it might be necessary to kill the fish by polluting the water, but this is unlikely to be a desirable course of action.[41]

The indirect approach of defeating an insurgency by focusing on dividing the people from the insurgents, removing the support that they require to challenge the government effectively, is rather different from the direct approach and in the long term is usually more effective. Once the local and regular armed units are cut off from their sources of supply, personnel, and, most importantly, intelligence, they wither on the vine or are easily coerced to surrender or destroyed by the security forces with the aid of the local populace. Winning that support is the critical battle in a counterin-

Figure 2-1
Five Principles of Counterinsurgency

1. "The government must have a clear political aim: to establish and maintain a free, independent and united country which is politically and economically stable and viable."

2. "The government must function in accordance with law."

3. "The government must have an overall plan."

4. "The government must give priority to defeating the political subversion, not the guerrillas."

5. "In the guerrilla phase of an insurgency, a government must secure its base areas first."

surgency campaign—as Robert Thompson emphasizes in his Five Principles of Counterinsurgency (Figure 2-1).[42]

EVALUATING COUNTERINSURGENCY DOCTRINE AND PRACTICE

Figure 2-2 details the questions by which the learning performance of the British army in Malaya and the American army in Vietnam will be compared. They are derived from an analysis of the objectives and techniques of insurgency as posited in this chapter and are heavily informed by Robert Thompson's Five Principles of Counterinsurgency, themselves drawn from a study of the theory and practice of insurgency.

The first point of comparison, *victory*, may seem to be an unfair one, as the achievement of national objectives depends to a great extent on factors outside the control of the army conducting a counterinsurgency campaign, including geography, strength of the local government and of the insurgents, and degree of popular support for the campaign in the nation supporting the beleaguered government. Nonetheless, the ultimate determinant of the success or failure of counterinsurgency theory and practice is the attainment of national objectives; neglecting the explicit consideration of this characteristic would only relegate it to the realm of unstated but inescapable facts. It is better to confront it directly.

Although the achievement of national goals may not be determined entirely by the army's counterinsurgency doctrine and practice, the army as a powerful bureaucratic actor inevitably affects the definition of national *objectives* for the conflict. Whether these are capable of realization will to a large degree determine whether victory in the campaign is attained—and the army contributes materially to the determination of which tasks it can and cannot do, and how, and why.

As Thompson's Five Principles make clear, the achievement of these goals depends to a great extent on the creation of an effective local government that earns the support of the people; note that Thompson does not even mention the counterinsurgent army or armies. An army that subordinates

Figure 2-2
Question Set #2: Did the Army Develop a Successful Counterinsurgency Doctrine?

1.) **Victory**: Did the doctrine adopted achieve national goals in the conflict?

2.) **Objective**: Did the army contribute to the setting of realistic national goals in the conflict?

3.) **Unity of Command**: Did the military accept subordination to political objectives?

4.) **Minimum Force**: Did the military use the minimum amount of force necessary to accomplish the mission?

5.) **Mass**: Did the military structure itself in an appropriate manner to deal with the threat at hand?

all military action to the achievement of these political goals facilitates *unity of command* over all the organizations attempting to defeat the insurgency—and makes accomplishment of the objective more likely.

Similarly, Thompson's principles highlight the fact that the counterinsurgency forces must use force in support of the government's effort to establish legitimacy at the expense of the insurgents. Military operations that do not exercise *minimum force* instead diminish the support of the people for the government, which they feel should protect them—not destroy them. In a metaphor proposed by Brigadier Michael Addison, "economy of force" is the principle of war that states that a sledgehammer should not be used to crack a nut because the sledgehammer might be better employed elsewhere. The doctrine of "minimum force" forbids the use of a sledgehammer to protect the nut inside the shell.[43]

Finally, military forces that structure themselves for conventional warfare will not succeed in protecting and hence earning the support of the populace. It is essential that they use the principle of *mass* to protect the critical battleground over which the campaign is being fought: the people.

These five questions are not the only ones that might be used as a basis of focused comparison for the cases of British army counterinsurgency doctrine in Malaya and American army counterinsurgency doctrine in Vietnam; they do have the merit of being based on both the history and the theory of insurgency and guerrilla warfare. They also provide a critical perspective for comparison of learning during the conduct of the two campaigns. First, however, it is essential to examine briefly the organizational cultures of the two armies that confronted a new kind of war in Malaya and Vietnam.

NOTES

1. John Ellis, *A Short History of Guerrilla Warfare* (London: Ian Allen, 1975), 7. Though now somewhat dated, this remains a good short survey of the topic.

The best single source is Robert B. Asprey's *War in the Shadows: The Guerrilla in History* (New York: William Morris, 1994).

2. Thomas E. Griess, ed., *The Wars of Napoleon* (West Point: Avery Publishing Group, 1985), 100–101.

3. A.H. Sollom, "Nowhere Yet Everywhere," in Franklin Mark Osanka, ed., *Modern Guerrilla Warfare: Fighting Communist Guerrilla Movements, 1941–1961* (New York: The Free Press of Glencoe, 1962). The author, a United States Marine Corps lieutenant colonel, originally published this article in the *Marine Corps Gazette* of June 1958.

4. One good source is Peter Paret's "Clausewitz and the Nineteenth Century," in Michael Howard, ed., *The Theory and Practice of War* (London: Indiana University Press, 1965), 21–41. Perhaps the best book on Clausewitz and his ideas is Michael Howard's *Clausewitz* (Oxford: Oxford University Press, 1983).

5. Carl von Clausewitz, translated by Michael Howard and Peter Paret, *On War* (Princeton, NJ: Princeton University Press, 1984), 89.

6. John Shy, "Jomini," in Peter Paret, ed., *Makers of Modern Strategy from Machiavelli to the Nuclear Age* (Princeton, NJ: Princeton University Press, 1986), 146. Emphasis in original.

7. Ibid., 177.

8. Michael Howard, "The Influence of Clausewitz," in Clausewitz, *On War*, 30.

9. Ibid.

10. Bernard Brodie, "The Continuing Relevance of *On War*," in Clausewitz, *On War*, 56.

11. This is the supreme irony of Harry Summer's modestly titled book, *On Strategy: A Critical Analysis of the Vietnam War* (Novato, CA: Presidio, 1982) which uses what Summers calls "Clausewitzian" principles of war to explain that the reason the U.S. Army lost the war in Vietnam is that it was not allowed to annihilate the opponent's force in the field—a clearly Jominian argument. In fact, by focusing on the Jominian concept of destroying the enemy army at all costs, the U.S. Army ignored the one absolute principle of Clausewitz: that war must always be subordinate to the political goals for which it is fought.

12. Clausewitz, *On War*, 479–480.

13. John Shy and Thomas W. Collier, "Revolutionary War," in Paret, *Makers of Modern Strategy*, 838–839.

14. Asprey, *War in the Shadows*, 246.

15. Mao Tse-Tung, translated by Samuel Griffith, *On Guerrilla Warfare* (London: Cassell, 1965), 14.

16. Ibid., 8.

17. Douglas Blaufarb, *The Counterinsurgency Era: U.S. Doctrine and Performance* (New York: The Free Press, 1977), 3.

18. Mao, *On Guerrilla Warfare*, 16.

19. Asprey, *War in the Shadows*, 249.

20. Dick Wilson, *The Long March 1935: The Epic of Chinese Communism's Survival* (New York: Penguin, 1982).

21. J.A. Harrison, *China Since 1800* (New York: Harcourt Brace & World, 1967), 168, in Asprey, *War in the Shadows*, 252.

22. Chalmers Johnson, *Peasant Nationalism and Communist Power* (Stanford,

CA: Stanford University Press, 1962), 5, in Blaufarb, *The Counterinsurgency Era,* 7.

23. Mao Tse-Tung, *Selected Military Writings of Mao Tse-Tung* (Peking: Foreign Language Press, 1966), 260.

24. Mao, *On Guerrilla Warfare,* 66–67.

25. Mao, *Selected Military Writings of Mao Tse-Tung,* 260.

26. Ibid., 261.

27. Frank Kitson, *Low Intensity Operations: Subversion, Insurgency and Peacekeeping* (London: Faber & Faber, 1971), 29.

28. John Shy and Thomas W. Collier, "Revolutionary War," in Paret, *Makers of Modern Strategy,* 845. The story of American advice and assistance to Chiang Kai-Shek and the resistance of the Nationalist government to suggestions for political and military reforms is well told in Barbara Tuchman, *Sand Against the Wind: Stillwell and the American Experience in China, 1911–1945* (London: Futura, 1985).

29. Clausewitz, *On War,* Book VIII, quoted in Howard, *The Theory and Practice of War,* 35.

30. Shy and Collier, "Revolutionary War," in Paret, *Makers of Modern Strategy,* 816.

31. A fascinating if horrifying examination of this issue is John Ellis, *The Social History of the Machine Gun* (Baltimore: Johns Hopkins University Press, 1987).

32. Asprey, *War in the Shadows,* 262.

33. For an examination of the modern phenomenon of casualty aversion, see Don M. Snider, John A. Nagl, and Tony Pfaff, *Army Professionalism, the Military Ethic, and Officership in the 21st Century* (Carlisle, PA: U.S. Army War College Strategic Studies Institute, 1999).

34. Robert Taber, *The War of the Flea: A Study of Guerrilla Warfare, Theory and Practice* (New York: Citadel Press, 1965), 131–132.

35. Frederick Wilkins, "Guerrilla Warfare," in Franklin Mark Osanka, ed., *Modern Guerrilla Warfare: Fighting Communist Guerrilla Movements, 1941–1961* (New York: The Free Press of Glencoe, 1962), 14. The author, a retired lieutenant colonel of the United States Army, first published this article in the *U.S. Naval Institute Proceedings* of March 1954.

36. A. Jones, trans., *The History of Gruffydd ap Cynan* (Manchester: Manchester University Press, 1910), 141, in Ellis, *A Short History of Guerrilla Warfare,* 33. This is both the standard military response to insurgency and the typical response from the population that suffers from a scorched-earth counterinsurgency policy.

37. Gerald of Wales, translated by T. Wright, *The Historical Works of Geraldius Cambriensis* (H.G. Bohn, London, 1863), 511–512 and 517–518, in Ellis, *A Short History of Guerrilla Warfare,* 35.

38. British Army Code No 71596 (Part 2), Army Field Manual, Volume V, *Operations Other Than War,* Section B, *Counter Insurgency Operations,* Part 2, *The Conduct of Counter Insurgency Operations,* 2–1 through 2–2.

39. Robert J. O'Neill, *Vietnam Task: The 5th Battalion, Royal Australian Regiment* (Marrickville, Australia: Southwood Press, 1968), 185.

40. Harry Summers, "A War is a War is a War is a War," in Loren B. Thompson, ed., *Low Intensity Conflict: The Pattern of Warfare in the Modern World* (Lexington, MA: Lexington Books, 1989).

41. Frank Kitson, *Low Intensity Operations: Subversion, Insurgency and Peace-keeping* (London: Faber & Faber, 1971), 49.

42. Robert F. Thompson, *Defeating Communist Insurgency: Experiences from Malaya and Vietnam* (London: Chatto & Windus, 1972), 50–60.

43. Brigadier (Retd) Michael Addison, private correspondence with the author, 11 February 1997.

3

The British and American Armies: Separated by a Common Language

The first chapter examined the concept of organizational culture, the idea that every organization has "a persistent, patterned way of thinking about the central tasks of and human relationships within an organization."[1] The organizational culture of an army is a reflection of the nation from which it springs; in the words of General Sir John Hackett, "The pattern of a parent society is faithfully reflected in the military institutions to which it gives birth."[2] There are an almost incalculable number of factors that combine to create a national military culture; Hanson W. Baldwin notes that what he describes as a military philosophy "grows from the minds and hearts, social mores and customs, traditions and environment of a people. It is the product of national and racial attributes, geography, the nature of a potential enemy threat, standards of living and national traditions, influenced and modified by great military philosophers, like Clausewitz and Mahan, and by great national leaders like Napoleon."[3]

This is a particularly historical approach to the questions of what drives military policy, informed by the belief that "a nation's behavior toward the rest of the world cannot be adequately explained as a function of the universal factors of power and interest"[4]—at least, not exclusively. Instead, this study assumes that "a remembered past has always more or less constricted both action in the present and thinking about the future."[5]

THE ORGANIZATIONAL CULTURE OF THE BRITISH ARMY

Although this section is organized chronologically, it is designed to illustrate several themes that form the basis of the organizational culture of the British army. The most important of these is the limited Continental commitment of the British army. Protected by the English Channel, the North Sea, and the Atlantic Ocean, the British nation reserved primacy in the national heart for the Royal Navy. This is noted in such works as B.H. Liddell-Hart's *The British Way in Warfare*, which argued that "the distinctively British practice of war" was based on the two principles of mobility and surprise, best achieved through the use of sea power.[6] A more recent observer has argued that the British strategic culture is currently based on a certain degree of commitment to the security of Europe, the legacy of great power status, and a political culture that values evolutionary change, continuity, and tradition.[7] The army's role has traditionally been service as an expeditionary force when European affairs absolutely demanded British involvement. In order to act effectively in Europe and secure her national interests, Britain resorted to the creation of expeditionary forces when required. "Instead of the continuous development of a national army, as on the Continent, there is a succession of sudden expansions to meet particular emergencies, followed by a relapse into peacetime stagnation and sudden neglect. . . . The British army has always enjoyed in its continental wars an advantage denied to Europeans; it can legitimately run away."[8] Or in the words of Richard Holmes, the role of the British army has traditionally been "to be landed by the Royal Navy and be taken off the continent in moments of growing adversity."[9]

A later development is the requirement to police the far-flung reaches of the British empire. This mission was informed by the recognition that the army's role was the pacification of people who would someday become imperial subjects and was therefore marked by the use of limited force; the small size of the British imperial armies further served to limit the application of force. The imperial army developed its own attitudes toward the recognition of civil-military cooperation in the administration of local political problems. Warfare on the Continent was to be avoided if at all possible; this was Britain's solution to a problem noted by Eliot Cohen: "It is the characteristic military dilemma of a world power that it finds itself forced to prepare for two entirely different kinds of wars, large-scale conflicts on the continent of Europe, on the one hand, and lesser battles on its periphery or on other continents, on the other."[10]

Another theme is the slightly antiintellectual tilt of the British army. There is a cartoon in the Sandhurst library of a knight in armor speaking to a young cadet carrying a stack of books under his arms. The knight says, "In my day we didn't read many books, but we hit hard."[11] Even more than most armies, the British have maintained the emphasis on hitting hard rather than on reading and theorizing about the nature of its business.

A final theme is the variety of experiences endured by the very different regiments that the British army comprises, what Richard Holmes has called "a collection of regiments in loose voluntary association." Cohen argues that the regimental system, which he calls "quasi-tribal," "sustained the fighting spirit of soldiers stationed for years in the remote and alien locations where British power was needed" by creating a sort of surrogate family. These regiments fought what were in many ways several different wars in World War I and World War II, against several different enemies; the campaigns in Burma had little in common with those in Western Europe except that they happened at the same time. Without a shared common experience, relevant local experience counted for everything. British soldiers and officers learned on the job, and often their job had nothing to do with what they had been trained to do. The fact that domestic theory about soldiering had little to do with colonial practice led to a general mistrust of theory.

These themes, which differ markedly from those that inform the culture of the American army, will recur throughout the short history of the British army's role in the national history that follows. They contributed over time to a uniquely British approach to warfare.

Unpleasantness in the Colonies

The most important cause of the defeat of the Redcoats by the insurgent American colonials is noted by Larry Cable:

> The British, being blissfully unaware that governmental authority rested on the twin bases of perceived legitimacy and credible capacity to coerce, lost the opportunity to prevent or abort insurgency by failing to engage in pre-emptive reforms or other actions which would have reinforced their legitimacy while under-cutting that of the dissidents. By being equally unaware that coercion was defined by the recipient and instead relying upon the undeniable, but ultimately irrelevant, fact of the traditional military supremacy over the rudimentary armed forces of the insurgents, the British fatally undercut their capacity to win.[12]

Confounded by the insurgency in America, the British had more success in leading a coalition to defeat Napoleon on the mainland of Europe in a more conventional campaign, as well as in India. However, there is some evidence to indicate that the British army in the Peninsular Campaigns adopted some elements of the Spanish partisan strategy against Napoleon, even if not necessarily of their own volition. Lieutenant Simmons of the Ninety-fifth Regiment of Foot wrote in 1809, "My jacket is brown instead of green. Never has seen such a motley group of fellows . . . I am a perfect guerrilla, having broken my sword, lost my sash and am as ragged as a sweep."[13]

Once the Napoleonic threat had been defeated, the soldier was again restored to his proper position in British society. The limited role of the British army in keeping the peace reasserted itself. "Relieved of an internal police function, the British Army did not hold to the assumption that its primary task was to force British standards of behavior on unfriendly states. Instead, it was able to implement a variety of political objectives. Whether in Continental Europe, in colonial expeditions, or in policing sea lanes, the British military was charged with the task of limited objectives."[14] These limited objectives often consisted of assisting a colonial government to maintain control over a large native population with a comparatively small number of administrators and soldiers. The British system of colonial administration was usually a thin veneer of British officers, military or civil, commanding a much larger native population.

Policing the Empire

With peace restored in Europe—at least so far as the British were concerned—and at home, the focus of the British army turned elsewhere. "In the nineteenth century the history of the British army is the history of British colonial policy and British involvement overseas."[15] This history is often one of the use of superior firepower and discipline to slaughter overmatched African or Asian opponents.

The campaigns of the three Victorian heroes, Roberts, Wolseley and Kitchener, represented essentially all the British people knew of modern war. It was in fact a highly specialized form, which contrasted sharply with war as fought between great industrial powers. There was emphasis on the man rather than on the system, on smallness instead of greatness of scale, on great variety of task and terrain instead of a single eventuality, on overwhelming superiority of instead of equality of armaments, and on minute casualties and easy victories instead of heavy losses and prolonged fighting.[16]

Out of these wars emerged one of the classics of military thought on defeating insurgents: Major General Sir Ernest Swinton's *The Defence of Duffer's Drift*.[17] Describing a successful action against Boer insurgents through the use of unconventional tactics, this little book remains both a worthwhile tactical primer and a great narrative of the tactical problems that junior leaders must overcome to defeat insurgents. Swinton's book provides a good example of an important theme in British military history and culture: the odd intellectual officer in a profoundly unintellectual environment who thinks, reads, and writes about his own experiences and their implications for the future of warfare. In an army that was only loosely controlled and directed from Whitehall, such individuals had a deep impact on the development of British military thought.[18]

This is particularly true of British doctrine for colonial warfare; Gavin Bulloch notes, "Despite the extensive experience gained by the British Army in counter-insurgency during the Twentieth century, relatively little has been recorded as official doctrine in any military publications. A large amount has been written about counter-insurgency unofficially and partly through this, military doctrine has evolved and developed. Official doctrine, when published, has always lagged behind events."[19]

One of the first of these unofficial doctrinal manuals was Major Charles Callwell's *Small Wars—Their Principles and Practice*, first published in 1896.[20] It became an important reference, used to teach at the Staff College into the 1920s, and only superseded by Sir Charles Gwynn's *Imperial Policing* in 1934. Callwell's book is important not just because it is the first attempt to distill a doctrine for fighting "small wars" from the many such British campaigns, but also because it drew upon the experiences of Spain in Cuba and the United States in the Philippines.[21] The British army was to have a continuing need for such manuals, whether formally accepted or not. Trouble in India, though it had subsided after a stern response to the Great Mutiny of 1857–1858, appeared again in the northeastern province of Bengal before World War I.[22]

The Great War

Against the background of these small and relatively cheap wars, the stalemate resulting from the success of the British Expeditionary Force in France and Belgium and the resulting need for a mass army to intervene on the Continent were unpleasant surprises for the British public and the British army. Accustomed to relatively easy victories and armed with only a limited appreciation of the nature of warfare against industrialized European opponents, the British army did not fare well in the quality of its officership.

[The army's] other-rank personnel were improving [in the First World War], with a rising standard of living, but its officer corps was still the preserve of young men of good social standing who had the outlook of amateurs, which is what they mostly were. They were ill-paid, with "half a day's pay for half a day's work," and so had to be of independent means. This meant that most were hard to teach, and many were unteachable. They were not well trained and were expected to be neither industrious nor particularly intelligent. From men such as these came the commanders of the First World War. As a foreign observer put it, among the officers of the British army bravery had often to compensate for lack of ability.[23]

The price among both the officer corps and the rank and file of the Commonwealth armies that bore the brunt of the casualties of the World War I led to one of the revolutions of modern military thought.

Interwar and Empire

The reaction in Britain to the slaughter of the Western Front was the evolution of doctrine for the use of a British attempt to minimize casualties while achieving a decisive breakthrough: the tank. Although the tank was initially developed by Winston Churchill's Admiralty, the postwar mechanization of the British army lagged behind that of the Germans—more proof of the dictum that defeat can be a strong incentive for change.[24] In Britain, under governments convinced that war in Europe was no longer a likely contingency, the army returned to its prewar tasks of colonial policing.

It did so still without the benefit of written doctrine or much guidance from London. In the words of John Shy and Thomas Collier, "Separate organizations divided the colonial military experience from problems of European warfare, and helped to keep the thinkers of the national war colleges unconcerned with strategies for dealing with revolutions."[25] As a result, "the rich legacy of operational experience in the colonies was kept largely separated from the theory and practice of the home armies before World War I."[26]

Not all of the colonial experience was far from British shores. Lord Salisbury, British prime minister at the turn of the century, described "the internal history of Ireland," then linked with Britain in the United Kingdom for a full century, as "a continuous tempest of agitation, broken by occasional flashes of insurrection."[27] Richard Popplewell argues that

the lessons of Ireland . . . seem clear with hindsight. Good police intelligence was at the heart of counterinsurgency. This alone could nip trouble in the bud, and this alone could provide the army with the information necessary for effective operations against the insurgents. Of equal importance was the "hearts and minds" campaign, which was all but non-existent on the government side right up to the last year of the conflict, though highly effective on the part of the IRA.[28]

World War II

Against this background, World War II again led to a vast expansion of the British army and to a wide variety of experiences in a number of theaters. British officers again led colonial troops in difficult fighting, including a force of British officers in command of a group of resistance fighters against the occupying Japanese army in Malaya.

There was a gradual acceptance of the idea that the war did indeed have to be fought on the main front on the continent—the reluctance a legacy of the horrific casualties of World War I—after a series of attempts to implement B.H. Liddell Hart's ideas about warfare on the periphery—and on the cheap. The weight of the United States Army began to tell in the Alliance and with it the beginnings of British acceptance of junior partner status, though tempered by a firm conviction that the experience of administering a colonial empire and centuries of experience in European affairs lent British political judgment a great deal of clout.

Perhaps most important of all for the campaign in Malaya, the experiences of the British army in Burma under Slim leavened a substantial portion of the army with the experience of fighting a very different kind of warfare from that fought in Europe.[29] The very costly raids of Orde Wingate's Chindits merit Slim's assessment "If anything was learnt of air supply or jungle fighting it was a costly schooling."[30] Slim's evaluation of the Burma campaign, and his comparison of it with the American Pacific campaign, is of interest:

In Burma we fought on a lower scale of transport, supplies, equipment, supporting arms, and amenities than was accepted in any other British theatre. Yet, largely because of this lack of material resources, we learned to use those we had in fresh ways to achieve more than would have been possible had we clung to conventional methods. We had not only to devise new tactics but to delve deeply into the motive forces of human conduct and to change our traditional outlook on many things. The result was, I think it true to say, a kind of warfare more modern in essence than that fought by other British forces. Indeed, by any Allied force, with the exception of the Americans in the Pacific. There, their problem, the opposite of ours, was to use the immense resources that became increasingly available to them most effectively in the peculiar circumstances of an ocean war. They solved it brilliantly and evolved a new material technique. We, also in strange conditions, evolved our technique of war, not so much material as human.[31]

Postwar

The exhilarating experience of playing a decisive role in a national struggle for survival meant that the veterans of the European war carried greater weight in the British army than ever before: "In the five years that followed the end of the war the methods and concepts of 1939–1945 provided the foundation of official military thought, pragmatic and complacent as always, mistrustful of the theories of 'military bolshies' and long-haired armchair strategists."[32] The emphasis on conventional war could not completely overwhelm the many veterans of Slim's campaigns whose memories of small-unit jungle fighting, often leading Gurkhas or other non-British troops, contributed to the organizational ethos of an army that would soon face another sort of challenge in Malaya.

Robert O'Neill has argued that the British army developed a characteristic way of warfare in the years after 1945.[33] The key features of this way of warfare include an understanding of the nature of the peoples and politics of the areas of engagement, ability to work with them (as opposed to ignoring or alienating them) and to understand that a military solution stands or falls as the people affected decide to support or oppose it, historical experience, the availability of old colonial and third world hands, British infrastructure in the colonies, a recognized need to work within the constraints set by public opinion, the supremacy of political objectives and control, the ability to work effectively with allies, the economical use of manpower, the availability of a broad range of civil expertise to support the armed forces, and flexible and original operating techniques.

These attitudes, the product of many years of experience as an expeditionary army for the European continent and as a colonial police force, would be put to good use in the years following World War II. In addition to making a substantial contribution to the United Nations effort in Korea, the British army would soon find itself embroiled in what Michael Dewar described as "Brushfire Wars":

Buglers and men with banners inscribed "Disperse or I fire" in English and Urdu were of marginal use in these vicious little wars. Soon the men on the spot were learning the trade; in Malaya for example, the Far East Land Forces training centre quickly became one of the best tactical schools of the postwar Army. It evolved a coherent philosophy of counter-guerrilla warfare; devised effective battle drills for the jungle; and trained every officer and soldier arriving in Malaya before he began his jungle operations.[34]

The first of these "Brushfire Wars" to confront the British army erupted in Palestine on 31 October 1945. The Jewish rebellion against both the Palestinians, who shared the territory, and the British, who were attempting to keep peace between the two groups, resulted in the creation of the state of Israel on 15 May 1948, but only after bitter fighting. In keeping with the tradition of minimum force, Sir Alan Cunningham, British high commissioner in Jerusalem, instructed that offensive military action was to be limited to "direct attack on terrorists or immediate searches for terrorists in areas where outrages have occurred, and such preventative action based on sound intelligence of specific intended terrorist acts, as the High Commissioner may approve."[35] This policy changed as results proved discouraging; the British campaign against the terrorists suffered from a lack of support among the local population and the absence of clear political direction. The British government acknowledged the intractability of the situation, turning the problem over to the United Nations in February 1947, and the last British troops had departed by May 1948. Despite the failure of British policy in Palestine, the army had reinforced a number of lessons it had learned over many years of imperial policing, lessons it would soon put to use in other theaters of the postwar world.[36]

The Organizational Culture of the British Army in 1948

In his seminal book *British Counterinsurgency 1919–60*, Thomas R. Mockaitis has convincingly argued that the British army developed three principles regulating its counterinsurgency operations: minimum force, civil-military cooperation, and tactical flexibility demonstrated through a "highly decentralized, small-unit approach."[37] Whereas Mockaitis argues that these principles evolved over time, beginning with the suppression of revolts in Ireland in 1919–1920, Richard Poppelwell has pointed out that similar principles were the basis of British rule in India during the nineteenth century.[38] This chapter has argued that the British army has throughout its history been an instrument of limited war, designed to achieve limited goals at limited cost, with a wide variety of experiences to draw on and with a limited belief in the validity of military doctrine that meets the needs of all situations. These attributes have contributed significantly to the success of the British army in the postwar era.

THE ORGANIZATIONAL CULTURE OF THE UNITED STATES ARMY

"Good fortune is often more fatal than adversity."
—Frederick the Great[39]

In contrast to the British army, whose role for most of its history was secondary to that of the Royal Navy, the American army's role from its very origins was the eradication of threats to national survival. Beginning with the War of Independence from a distant imperial nation, the United States was forged in war and confronted a struggle for national existence. The defeat of the Native American tribes was marked by the brutality advocated by King William II against the Welsh; the American Civil War was another bloody struggle for national survival. The United States felt a sense of ownership of its national army, in combination with an ambivalence toward its military forces. The history of the American nation in war encouraged the notion that politics ceases when war begins: once war is initiated, the military assumes primacy over politics. The American military thus has an exceptional degree of control over military strategy and policy. As Carl Builder notes, "The roots of modern American military strategies lie buried in the country's three most powerful institutions: the army, navy, and air force. Though many people outside the military institutions, including academics and presidents, may propose military strategies and concepts, these can be implemented only if and when military institutions accept and pursue them."[40] When the United States finally did develop a national approach to the use of force in international politics, "the strategy of annihilation became characteristically the American way in war."[41] The American way of war is marked by a belief that the nation is at war or at peace; the binary nature of war leaves no space for political-military interface.[42]

Other features that characterize the American approach are an overweening reliance on technology, a faith in the uniqueness and the moral mission of the United States, and a remarkable aversion to the use of unconventional tactics. These have their roots in what Eliot Cohen has called the "two dominant characteristics" of American strategic culture: "The preference for massing a large number of men and machines and the predilection for direct and violent assault."[43]

Creating a Nation and an Army: The War of Independence

Although American forces did resort to unconventional warfare (against General Washington's express desire) in the Revolutionary War, the primary experience of the colonists with guerrilla warfare was on the receiving end. The Native American bands presented an uncoordinated yet not inconsequential challenge to the fledgling nation, as they had in fact done when the colonies were still under British rule; Washington learned his military skills during the French and Indian War. It was in these battles against inferior opponents that the United States first demonstrated what would become the characteristic American way of war.

American Wars of the Nineteenth Century

Despite the fact that the young American army would fight various Native American tribes for over a century, engaging in these "small wars" never became recognized as an essential aspect of the business of the army. The Indian Wars never reverberated in the collective consciousness of the American army: "The Indians were unconventional warriors whose methods more closely resembled those of guerrillas than of conventional European armies, but the American army's schools and thinkers were so much more attracted by the Napoleonic glories of European war than by grubby skirmishes that the army never created a coherent body of guiding principles for Indian war."[44]

Despite the army's lack of enthusiasm for the wars it was actually fighting—Ian Beckett notes that "the United States Army continued to measure its professionalism against current European practice despite almost a century when its primary role had been frontier policing"[45]—it initiated several important counterinsurgency techniques during the numerous Indian campaigns of the nineteenth century. Brigadier General Nelson A. Miles took advantage of the Indians' limited mobility and reliance on food stores during snowy Great Plains winters to coerce the tribes to move to reservations. The American army also used General George Crook's innovation of small counterguerrilla patrols to sap the security and morale of Geronimo's Apache warriors in New Mexico; here "coercion was applied not to the body, but to the mind and soul" to force the Apaches to accept unfavorable treaties limiting their territory to apparently useless reservations.[46]

Neither the War of 1812, in which an overconfident American army hoped to occupy first Quebec and then all of Canada, but then settled for a status quo peace, nor the Mexican-American War of 1849, in which U.S. military forces advanced to Mexico City, eventually applying sufficient pressure to force a negotiated peace, altered the army's focus on European-style warfare. Despite the successes in small wars, the army saw European armies—and European wars—as its true raison d'être. "The gathering currents of military professionalism, centering on conventional wars of the future, left almost wholly untouched the unconventional wars of the present."[47] The first major war fought entirely on American soil would, however, kindle the enthusiasm of the army and shape the American way of war for generations.

War Between the States

The American Civil War demonstrated the vast latent military potential of the United States. Falling as it did in the midst of the industrial revolution, the war was marked by the first use in combat of the railroad, the telegraph, and rifled repeating firearms. Most importantly, it created and solidified the image of war as conventional battles between opposing mass armies in the mind of the nation and its generals. Those battles were won by the application of men and firepower at the decisive point in time; Weigley calls the victory of the North "a triumph of sheer power."[48]

Notably, concern for civilian suffering was minimal; General Sherman truly believed that war was hell and aimed to shorten the war by extending the suffering as widely as possible. Demonstrating the same resource denial strategy used to good effect in the Indian Wars by General Miles, Sherman deliberately terrorized the civilian population of Georgia and the Carolinas to "make old and young, rich and poor, feel the hard hand of war, as well as their organized armies."[49]

The Civil War continued to define the distinctively American practice of war in the minds of army officers at least through to General William Westmoreland, Military Assistance Command—Vietnam (MACV) Commander from 1965 through 1968, who noted that Vietnam was

somewhat analogous to the Civil War. There were certain troops in static positions, around base areas and airfields, but other than that it was a war of movement. Instead of having a horse, as was the case in the Civil War, we had the helicopter. . . . You "homed" in on the enemy as in the Civil War and tried to bring the enemy to combat. Once you've done that, then you regroup, move, and continue to try and find the enemy and force him to combat.[50]

The American Civil War, the first great national war of annihilation, fixed itself in the eyes of professional soldiers as what war should be. The American nation's next war would create a global span of influence, requiring the first intervention of the United States Army in Asia and revealing a very different side to the American army.

Entry to Empire: The Spanish-American War

The victory over Spain in 1898 necessitated the garrisoning of the Philippine Islands, which soon rose in rebellion against the occupying army. The army's response was unusual enough to warrant careful examination. Brigadier General J. Franklin Bell used an early form of population control during the Batangas campaign against Filipino guerrillas; he instructed his subordinates that they

will immediately specify and establish plainly marked limits surrounding each town bounding a zone within which it may be practical with an average size garrison to exercise efficient supervision . . . [and] will also see that orders are given at once and distributed to all of the inhabitants within the jurisdiction of towns over which they exercise supervision informing them of the danger of remaining outside of those limits . . . with all their moveable food supplies including rice, palay, chickens, livestock, etc. . . . After January 1st, 1902, any able-bodied male found by patrols or scouting detachments outside of protected zones without passes will be arrested and confined or shot if he runs away.[51]

John M. Gates, whose *Schoolbooks and Krags* is the best treatment of the army's counterinsurgency campaign, notes that

after 1900 the American stress on the isolation of the guerrilla and the protection of townspeople from terrorism and intimidation was an important element in the success of pacification operations. The deployment of American troops in strategic garrisons; wide dispersion of American units; increased surveillance of municipalities to detect insurgent agents, terrorists, and supporters; and, when necessary, population reconcentration enabled Filipinos to show their support for the Americans without fear of harm. At the same time, continuous action by American patrols kept the guerrillas on the run. Off balance, short of supplies, and in continuous flight, the guerrillas were unable to threaten either the American columns or the towns.[52]

Military measures were only one component of a broader political-military campaign that included effective propaganda, payment of cash bounties for weapons surrendered by the insurgents, and building of schools and hospitals in a comprehensive public works program. Those rebels who maintained their antagonism were deported, imprisoned, or defeated in the U.S. Army's most successful instance of counterinsurgency theory and practice. However, the hard-won lessons of the campaign were quickly lost to the belief that such wars were not the army's true business and submerged by those of another large war fought with conventional tactics against a conventional army.

World War I

The American experience in World War I confirmed what was emerging as the American way of war: large wars against conventional enemies, who were to be defeated by an overwhelming mass of men and material, particularly artillery. The American concept of war was again heavily influenced by the European conception. The impact of the war on the emerging army concept can be plainly seen in the U.S. Army Field Service Regulations of 1923, which state, "The ultimate objective of all military operations is the destruction of the enemy's armed forces by battle. Decisive defeat in battle breaks the enemy's will to war and forces him to sue for peace."[53] The focus would remain the same up to the verge of the next great war: "The ultimate objective of all military operations is the destruction of the enemy's armed forces in battle. Decisive defeat breaks the enemy's will to war and forces him to sue for peace which is the national aim," stated the 1939 version of Field Manual 100–5.[54]

While the United States Army was developing and refining its absolutist strategy of annihilation, the United States Marine Corps defined itself in terms of the limited warfare missions assigned to it in China and in Latin America. The latter experiences generated the *Marine Corps Small Wars Manual*.[55] Ronald Schaffer notes that the Marines landed in the Philippines, Cuba, Puerto Rico, Honduras, Mexico, Guam, Samoa, China, Nicaragua, and the Dominican Republic between 1898 and 1938; the Marines were America's version of the British colonial army.[56] Out of their experiences emerged the *Small Wars Manual*, which was similar to Charles Callwell's *Small Wars—Their Principles and Practice* in more than name. A key principle was the use of minimal force: the marines should use "as little military display as possible with a view to gaining the lasting friendship of the inhabitants."[57]

The use of force was not the only way in which the "small wars" that the marines faced habitually differed from conventional war:

In conventional war, violence was a last resort, used after diplomacy had failed. In small wars, military and political action went on simultaneously, for combat and diplomacy could be different aspects of the same thing. At the beginning of a conventional war, political leaders handed over to military men the problem that diplomacy had not solved and told them to deal with it. But in small wars political authorities never let the strings out of their hands.[58]

The *Small Wars Manual* is full of such appreciations of the difficulties and dangers inherent in fighting against guerrillas and is emphatic in noting that excessive use of force might "create sympathy for the revolutionists ... destroy lives and property of innocent people, and ... have adverse effects on the discipline of our own troops."[59] Unfortunately for American counterinsurgency doctrine, the United States Marine Corps (USMC) was soon to find a new raison d'être in amphibious assaults, and the *Small Wars Manual* faded from the Marine Corps's institutional memory. Schaffer remarks that the officer who wrote the 1960 USMC training manual *Anti-Guerrilla Warfare* did not know that the *Small Wars Manual* existed.[60] Nevertheless, the institutional culture of the United States Marine Corps differed substantially from that of the army, and these differences would play an important role in the way the two services fought Communist insurgency in Vietnam.

World War II

World War II marked the true emergence of the United States as a great power as it pulled away from the isolationism that had so greatly contributed to allowing the outbreak of war. The army took from the overwhelming military victory it had won a picture of what future wars should look like: large battalions of armor and infantry supported by vast quantities of artillery and close air support to annihilate opposing forces, all backed up by unquestioning public support for the war effort. George F. Kennan, who would serve as one of the American architects of the postwar world, explains the viewpoint:

The precedents of our Civil War, of the war with Spain, and of our participation in the two world wars of this century, had created not only in the minds of our soldiers and sailors but in the minds of many of our people an unspoken assumption that the normal objective of warfare was the total destruction of the enemy's ability and will to resist and his unconditional capitulation. . . . This sort of victory placed you in a position to command total obedience on the part of the defeated adversary; it thus opened the way to the unhindered realization of your political objectives, whatever they might be.[61]

Without a clear understanding of the role of force and the threat of force in international politics, the United States decided to demobilize its vast war machine. The advancing cold war burst into flames in another war that solidified the American army's concept of Jominian conventional warfare. But the stage had been set: "By the late 1940s, Army doctrine was oriented toward a European-type battlefield—an orientation which varied only slightly during the next 30 years."[62]

The Korean War

The Korean War not only vastly increased the size of America's armed forces; it also created a large standing army for the first time in the nation's history and provided it with a ready-made enemy. Many of the troop reinforcements drafted during the first year of the war went to stiffen the defense of Western Europe against an expected Soviet attack. After an extremely mobile first year in which a Pacific war–style amphibious assault played a critical role, the Korean conflict stabilized into a defensive war familiar to officers from the postwar European theater. The strategy and tactics perfected in Korea were very similar to those the army intended to use to defend the Fulda Gap: "The Army had become accustomed to massive amounts of firepower which came at the expense of mobility. The Army had also perfected its techniques of employing firepower and the defense to inflict huge losses on an attacker. Thus the Army focused upon attrition at the expense of maneuver and its offensive spirit."[63]

This concept of warfare would not stand the United States Army in good stead in the next war it was to face. Writing as the Vietnam conflict was beginning, an anonymous army officer noted the emerging problem: "Korea, instead of concentrating military attention on the decaying colonialism and revolutionary eruptions in the Far East, was considered an abnormal conflict; an Asiatic war was against the wrong enemy, at the wrong place, and at the wrong time. The true target was Moscow, and the fatal battleground would be in Western Europe. . . . If we have the weapons to win a big war we can certainly win a small one, Eisenhower said."[64]

The Organizational Culture of the U.S. Army Before Vietnam

The experience of the United States Army throughout its history tended toward the absolute defeat of its enemies as a matter of national survival. The Indian Wars, the American Civil War, the Spanish-American War, and both world wars are united by an American conception of warfare as a crusade to be won quickly and completely. This idea gained strength in the Korean War and overshadowed army interest in the "small wars" doctrine that the United States Marine Corps developed before World War II. Instead,

whenever after the Revolution the American army had to conduct a counterguerrilla campaign—in the Second Seminole War of 1835–1841, the Filipino Insurrection of 1899–1903, and in Vietnam in 1965–1973—it found itself almost without an institutional memory of such experiences, had to relearn appropriate tactics at exorbitant costs, and yet tended after each episode to regard it as an aberration that need not be repeated.[65]

The focus on large wars, fought with the American advantages of high technology and almost unlimited firepower, but without appreciation for the political context in which they were fought, would not work in the favor of the United States Army when it faced a revolutionary insurgency in Vietnam. It would also stand in the way of American efforts to learn from the British counterinsurgency effort in Malaya.

COMPARISON AND CONCLUSIONS: BRITISH AND AMERICAN ARMY ORGANIZATIONAL CULTURE AND COUNTERINSURGENCY BEFORE MALAYA AND VIETNAM

The British and American armies developed very different attitudes toward their respective national roles and places in the international system as a result of their differing national cultures, geographies, and histories. The United States Army viewed its task as the absolute defeat of an enemy on the field of battle, supported by all of the resources of the nation. The British attitude was necessarily different: "Military powers less able to assume superior strength over their enemies, such as the British, tended to talk less about annihilation."[66] Instead, the British army developed a limited war perspective, based on its history of close cooperation with the civil power in the administration and pacification of a colonial empire. This split is very similar to that described by Janowitz between the competing "absolute" and "pragmatic" schools of thought in the American military tradition, with the British army more pragmatic—not least because it did not have the resources for absolute warfare, and because it enjoyed some confidence based on success with more limited means in the past.[67]

The differences between the organizational cultures of the two armies by the end of the Korean War can be seen in the relative emphasis each placed on unconventional warfare in its Staff College. In 1956, of the 1,219 hours of instruction given to midgrade officers at the United States Army's Command and General Staff College, *none* was dedicated to the study of revolutionary warfare, the impact of Mao, nor even limited war. A total of 190 hours was spent on conventional Infantry Division Operations, as "It is believed that the graduate will have the greatest need for this knowledge."[68] In contrast, the British army Staff College at Camberley devoted 45 of its 1,042 hours of instruction to "Small Wars and Policing Duties" and another 6 hours to the study of "Warfare in Developing Countries."[69]

The differences between the British and American armies in terms of attitudes toward unconventional war through the end of World War II are summarized in Figure 3-1. The aftermath of the war would present more challenges to the Western powers, whose defeat in their colonial possessions by the Japanese early in the war removed the Western aura of invincibility and provided substantial incentives to disaffected locals to agitate for independence, following the model of revolutionary insurgency provided by Mao Tse-Tung. Confronting these revolutionary movements would prove a challenge for both the British and American armies. The American army would remain true to its organizational and strategic culture in Vietnam in spite of dramatic evidence that it was facing a new kind of war there; the

Figure 3-1
A Comparison of the Organizational Cultures and Counterinsurgency
Doctrines of the British and American Armies before Malaya and Vietnam

Characteristic	British Army	American Army
Nature of Threat	Limited / Empire	National Existence
Role of Force	Minimum Force	Massive Firepower / Technology
Role of Army	Expeditionary / Colonial	National Army
COIN Tactics	Close Civil-Military Cooperation	Military Domination of Politics in Theater
	Identify & Solve Political Problems with Civil Power	Solve Political Problems with Military
	Decentralized, Small Unit	Conventional Big Unit
National Character	Patience (Bulldog)	Impatient
Role of Special Forces	Limited / Gradual Increase	Coopted into Main Army
Commitment to Nation	Colonial / Assistance for Independence	Paternal / "We Can Fix This Better"
Nature of War	Shades of Gray	Binary
Nature of Victory	Long Haul / 51%	100% Now or Out
Location of Leadership	Local Leadership	Central Management

organizational culture of the British army would play a substantial role in the way it chose to deal with the emergency in Malaya and in the way it adapted to changes in warfare that were not already a part of its organizational culture.

NOTES

1. James Q. Wilson, *Bureaucracy* (New York: Basic Books, 1989), 91.

2. Sir John Hackett, *The Profession of Arms* (New York: Macmillan, 1983), 184.

3. *The New York Times Magazine Section* (3 November 1957), 13, in Morris Janowitz, *The Professional Soldier: A Social and Political Portrait* (New York: The Free Press, 1971), 278.

4. John Shy, "The American Military Experience: History and Learning," *Journal of Interdisciplinary History* 1, 2 (Winter 1971), 205.

5. Ibid., 210.

6. B.H. Liddell Hart, *The British Way in Warfare: Adaptability and Mobility* (Middlesex: Penguin, 1942).

7. Alan Macmillan, "Strategic Culture and National Ways in Warfare: The British Case," *RUSI Journal* 140, 5 (October 1995), 34–36.

8. Corelli Barnett, *Britain and Her Army 1509–1970: A Military, Political, and Social Survey* (London: Penguin, 1970), xix.

9. Richard Holmes, "The British Experience," lecture presented to the Conference on the Origins of Contemporary Military Doctrine, RSA Larkhill, 28 March 1996.

10. Eliot Cohen, "Constraints on America's Conduct of Small Wars," *International Security* 9/2 (Fall 1984), 151.

11. Holmes, "The British Experience."

12. Larry Cable, "Reinventing the Round Wheel: Insurgency, Counter-Insurgency, and Peacekeeping Post Cold War," *Small Wars and Insurgencies* 4/2 (Fall 1993), 230–231. On p. 3 of *The Long, Long War: The Emergency in Malaya 1948–1960* (London: Cassell, 1966), Richard Clutterbuck juxtaposes General Templer's observation "The answer lies not in pouring more troops into the jungle, but in the hearts and minds of the people," with John Adams's statement "The Revolution was in the hearts and minds of the people." Clutterbuck remarks that this "goes to show that the British have been learning the same lessons about counter-insurgency for nearly 200 years."

13. National Army Museum, Chelsea, exhibit on the Peninsular Campaign. For a fictional account of a soldier of the same unit who fought as a guerrilla in this campaign, see C.S. Forester, *Rifleman Dodd* (Quantico, VA: U.S. Marine Corps University Press, 1996).

14. Moritz Janowitz, *The Professional Soldier: A Social and Political Portrait* (New York: The Free Press, 1971), 263.

15. Barnett, *Britain and Her Army*, 273.

16. Ibid., 324.

17. E.D. Swinton, *The Defence of Duffer's Drift* (Wayne, NJ: Avery, 1986). Swinton was later Chichele Professor of the History of War at All Souls College, Oxford.

18. Jay Luvaas, *The Education of an Army: British Military Thought, 1815–1940* (London: Cassell, 1964).

19. Gavin Bulloch, "The Development of Doctrine for Counter Insurgency: The British Experience," *British Army Review* III (December 1995), 21–24. The quotation is from p. 21. Brigadier Bulloch is the author of Army Code No. 71596, *Counter Insurgency Operations* (1995), and of several other doctrinal manuals. During interviews on 30 October 1995 and 19 December 1995 he explained a great deal about doctrine in the British army in general, and about counterinsurgency doctrine in particular.

20. Charles Callwell, *Small Wars: Their Principles and Practice* (London: HMSO, 1896).

21. Ian F. Beckett, "The Study of Counter-Insurgency: A British Perspective," *Small Wars and Insurgencies* 1/1 (April 1990), 47–53.

22. For the importance of the campaign in Bengal in the development of British counterinsurgency doctrine, see Richard Poppelwell, "Lacking Intelligence: Some

Reflections on Recent Approaches to British Counter-Insurgency, 1900–1960," *Intelligence and National Security*, Vol. 10, No. 2 (April 1995), 336–352, especially p. 339.

23. Hackett, *The Profession of Arms*, 158.

24. For the role of Major General J.F.C. Fuller and Captain B. H. Liddell Hart in the evolution of armored forces doctrine, see Luvaas, *The Education of an Army*, 335–424. See also J.P. Harris, *Men, Ideas, and Tanks: British Military Thought and Armoured Forces, 1903–1939* (New York: St. Martin's Press, 1995). For the early evolution of American armored doctrine, see Dale E. Wilson, *Treat 'Em Rough: The Birth of American Armor, 1917–20* (Novato, CA: Presidio, 1989).

25. John Shy and Thomas W. Collier, "Revolutionary War," in Peter Paret, ed., *Makers of Modern Strategy* (Princeton, N.J.: Princeton University Press, 1986), 830.

26. Ibid., 830. See also Williamson Murray, "The Collapse of Empire: British Strategy, 1919–1945," in Williamson Murray, MacGregor Knox, and Alvin Bernstein, eds., *The Making of Modern Strategy: Rulers, States, and War* (Cambridge: Cambridge University Press, 1994), 393–427.

27. Charles Townsend, *Britian's Civil Wars: Counterinsurgency in the Twentieth Century* (London: Faber & Faber, 1986), 45. For a good summary of the Troubles, see pp. 45–77. Townsend's critique of army counterinsurgency methods in the 1920s is particularly apt; he notes that because the British heavy-handedness fueled local support, "Patrols in daylight had practically no chance of encountering rebels—except by being ambushed" (63).

28. Popplewell, "Lacking Intelligence," 345.

29. Field Marshal Sir William Slim, *Defeat into Victory* (London: Cassell, 1956).

30. Ibid., 163. See also Christopher Sykes, *Orde Wingate* (London: Collins, 1959), for a biography of the unconventional soldier who led the Chindits into history, if not always to victory.

31. Slim, *Defeat into Victory*, 541.

32. Alun Gwynne Jones (Lord Chalfont), "The British Army Since 1945," in Howard, *The Theory and Practice of War*, 315.

33. Robert O'Neill, "The British Way in Warfare," lecture to the British Army Higher Command and Staff College at Camberley, 4 January 1996.

34. Jones, "The British Army Since 1945," in Howard, *The Theory and Practice of War*, 318.

35. PRO CO 537/1731, "Palestine, Use of Armed Forces, Note by Joint Secretaries," 19 December 1946, in Thomas R. Mockaitis, *British Counterinsurgency, 1919–1960* (New York: St. Martin's, 1990), 107.

36. Mockaitis, *British Counterinsurgency*, 100–11.

37. Ibid., 13–14.

38. Richard Poppelwell, "Lacking Intelligence," 336–352.

39. Jay Luvaas, *The Education of an Army*, 3.

40. Carl H. Builder, *The Masks of War: American Military Styles in Strategy and Analysis* (Baltimore: Johns Hopkins University Press, 1989), 3. Quoted in Colin S. Gray, "Strategy in the Nuclear Age: The United States, 1945–1991," in Murray, Knox, and Bernstein, eds., *The Making of Strategy*, 587. This chapter is a particularly good exposition of American strategic culture; see especially pp. 589–598.

41. Russell F. Weigley, *The American Way of War: A History of United States Military Strategy and Policy* (Bloomington: Indiana University Press, 1973), xxii.

42. Morris Janowitz, *The Professional Soldier: A Social and Political Portrait* (New York: The Free Press, 1971), describes the difference between the absolute and pragmatic schools of thought on the nature of warfare in society on p. 264: As a result of what Janowitz calls "the frontier and punitive expedition tradition," the American way of war prior to Vietnam tended toward the absolute. Christopher Gacek believes that the conflict between the two schools has been a primary determinant of postwar American attitudes toward the use of force in international politics; see *The Logic of Force: The Dilemma of Limited War in American Foreign Policy* (New York: Columbia University Press, 1994).

43. Eliot A. Cohen, "The Strategy of Innocence? The United States, 1920–1945," in Murray, Knox, and Bernstein, *The Making of Strategy*, 464.

44. Weigley, *Makers of Modern Strategy*, 436–437.

45. Beckett, "The Study of Counter-Insurgency: A British Perspective," in *Small Wars and Insurgencies*, 48. This focus on the big European war that the army wants to fight rather than the smaller limited wars it actually did fight will recur repeatedly.

46. Cable, "Reinventing the Round Wheel: Insurgency, Counter-Insurgency, and Peacekeeping Post Cold War," in *Small Wars and Insurgencies*, 232.

47. Robert F. Utley, *Frontier Regulars: The United States Army and the Indian, 1866–1891* (Bloomington: Indiana University Press, 1973), 12. For a perspective of the campaigns from the insurgent side, see Dee Brown, *Bury My Heart at Wounded Knee: An Indian History of the American West* (London: Pan Books, 1970).

48. Weigley, *American Way of War*, 2.

49. Ibid., 149.

50. Interview of Westmoreland 15 May 1982 by Andrew F. Krepinevich, in Krepinevich, *The Army and Vietnam* (Baltimore: Johns Hopkins University Press, 1990), 167.

51. Senate Document No. 331, 57th Congress, "Hearing Before the Committee on the Philippines in Relation to Affairs in the Philippine Islands" (Washington, DC: GPO, 1902), 1607, 1619, in K. Bruce Galloway and Robert Bowie Johnson, Jr., *West Point: America's Power Fraternity* (New York: Simon & Schuster), 359.

52. John Morgan Gates, *Schoolbooks and Krags: The United States Army in the Philippines, 1898–1902* (London: Greenwood Press, 1973), 271.

53. *Field Service Regulations, U.S. Army, 1923* (Washington, DC: GPO, 1924), 77.

54. FM 100–5, Field Service Regulations (Tentative), Operations, 1939, Paragraph 91, in Weigley, *The American Way of War*, 4.

55. *United States Marine Corps Small Wars Manual* (Washington, DC: GPO, 1940), reprinted by Sunflower University Press (Manhattan, KS), with an introduction by Ronald Schaffer.

56. Ibid., v.

57. Ibid., vii.

58. Ibid., ix.

59. Ibid., xi.

60. Schaffer, in ibid., xii.

61. George F. Kennan, *Memoirs: 1925–1950* (Boston: Knopf, 1977), 308.

62. Robert M. Doughty, *The Evolution of U.S. Army Tactical Doctrine 1946–*

1976 (Leavenworth Paper No. 1) (Fort Leavenworth, KS: Combat Studies Institute, 1979), 7.

63. Ibid., 12.

64. "Letter to the Editor," *ARMY* (March 1962), 35. The letter continues, "Few officers, if any, have achieved general officer rank who have devoted time and effort to the development and implementation of the field of special warfare," (36).

65. Weigley, *Makers of Modern Strategy*, 411.

66. Russell F. Weigley, *Eisenhower's Lieutenants: The Campaign of France and Germany, 1944–1945* (Bloomington: Indiana University Press, 1981), 4.

67. Janowitz, *The Professional Soldier*, 264.

68. Colonel W.W. Culp, "Resident Courses of Instruction," *Military Review* XXXVI, No. 2 (May 1956), 17–18.

69. "Camberley," in *Military Review* XXXVI, No. 2 (May 1956), 3.

II

MALAYA

4

British Army Counterinsurgency Learning During the Malayan Emergency, 1948–1951

The Malayan Emergency of 1948–1960 shows the British army as a learning institution that replaced traditional but ineffective counterinsurgency techniques with new methods that contributed to the defeat of a Communist insurgency. Fresh from their victory against the conventional armies of Japan and Germany, British army commanders at first focused their attention on battalion sweeps aimed at the insurgent forces. Innovative younger officers then developed more effective techniques to defeat the guerrillas at their own game by gaining the support of the local people; flexible senior officers emphasized the interrelationship of political and military goals and encouraged the creation, testing, and implementation of more effective counterinsurgency doctrine. The new tactics yielded results, reinforcing the learning process by providing the innovative junior leaders with tangible proof of the importance of their efforts. The British public's patience and acceptance of the traditional role of the British army in policing the empire—limited wars to achieve limited objectives—provided support for a long effort that ended when the freely elected government of Malaya declared the emergency over in 1960. The British army had successfully adapted to overcome the challenges of a Communist insurgent war and an obsolete doctrine. After briefly examining the history of Malaya leading up to the insurgency, this chapter will follow British efforts to defeat the insurgency through the organizational learning process.

STRATEGIC GEOGRAPHY

Malaya is a peninsula of some 50,000 square miles with a short land border with Thailand; in 1948 its territory was 80 percent uncultivated jungle.[1] The Malay inhabitants of the peninsula originally emigrated from Melanesia; they occupied coastal plains and pushed the aborigine natives into the jungles.[2] When the British first established themselves in Malaya at the close of the eighteenth century, they imported Chinese immigrants to work the tin mines and rubber plantations. The main population centers of modern Malaya—including Kuala Lumpur, Ipoh, and Taiping—began as Chinese mining camps. By 1901, the Chinese formed 65 percent of the total population of the state of Selangor and 46 percent of the population of Perak. They refused to be ruled by the Malays; W.C. Blythe, the president of municipal commissioners in Singapore, noted in 1948 that "the Chinese will accept government by the British in Malaya but regard government by the Malays with contempt." The ethnic conflict first spurred British rule of Malaya in the nineteenth century and even in 1948 was a major cause of the emergency.[3]

By the late 1940s the population of 5.3 million included 49 percent Malay persons, 38 percent Chinese, 11 percent Indian, and slightly more than 1 percent aboriginal persons. There were some 12,000 Europeans, mostly rubber plantation owners and tin mine managers; the Federation army and police force, composed mostly of Malays, was led by British officers.[4]

ORIGINS OF THE INSURGENCY

The story of the Malayan Communist Party (MCP) is almost entirely a Chinese one.[5] The Malayan Communist Party was formed in 1930 from the remnants of the Chinese "South Seas" Communist Party, which had been established in Singapore in 1924. Although it was able to organize one effective strike in 1928 and hosted a conference in 1930 attended by a certain Ho Chi Minh then living in exile in Hong Kong, its achievements had been minimal. The Special Branch of the Singapore Police Force monitored this meeting and arrested a number of the Communist organizers, including Ho Chi Minh, who was imprisoned in Hong Kong until 1932.[6] According to papers captured at the meeting, the Malayan Communist Party had a membership of some 15,000 with another 10,000 active sympathizers.[7]

Although the Malayan Communist Party took a number of years to recover from the arrests, which decimated the Comintern's Far Eastern Bureau, during this time the MCP became much more closely attuned to the genuine local grievances that it was later to exploit. These were a result of the worldwide great depression and nascent anti-Japanese feelings in the Chinese population. The Malayan Communist Party was strong enough to organize a large strike at the Batu Arang coal mine in Selangor province in 1935, which resulted in wholesale deportation of the organizers to Chiang Kai-Shek's China, where they were not kindly received.[8]

Once Japan attacked China in 1937, the Chinese Communist and Nationalist Parties created a "United Front," which was mirrored in a Malayan "National Salvation Association." Its creation gave the Malayan Communist Party a sort of legitimacy that was exploited by Lai Tek, an intriguing character who became secretary general of the MCP in 1939. There is substantial evidence that Lai Tek, certainly a Communist, was also in the employ of the British and of the Japanese army after its invasion of Malaya in 1941.[9]

On 18 December 1941, Lai Tek met with British officers in Singapore to coordinate the training of some 200 Chinese guerrillas before the fall of Singapore. Moving into the jungle behind the advancing Japanese army, these men were the core of the Malayan People's Anti-Japanese army (MPAJA), which was to grow to a force of 7,000 men organized in eight regiments. It was to have remarkably little effect on the Japanese occupation and control of Malaya, instead focusing on building itself up for eventual action against the British after the war. Lai Tek was almost certainly responsible for a Japanese attack on an MCP/MPAJA conference held at the Batu caves outside Kuala Lumpur on 1 September 1942. "Unavoidably detained" in Kuala Lumpur, Lai Tek was one of very few high MCP officials who survived the attack, which consolidated his personal hold on the organization.[10]

Lai Tek controlled both the Central Executive Committee and the Central Military Committee of the MPAJA and devised a means of communicating with his subordinate regiments by sending messengers along jungle trails. After an initial series of poorly planned and executed confrontations with the Japanese Army of Occupation, the MPAJA settled deep inside the jungle and began political indoctrination and recruitment.

In 1943, the British were able to organize Force 136, the South-East Asian Division of the Special Operations Executive, which was to grow to a strength of 40 officers and 250 noncommissioned officers. Force 136, led by Colonel John Davis, was intended to organize the support of the MPAJA for the landings planned to expel the Japanese from Malaya. Force 136 equipped the MPAJA with weapons and supplies by air and submarine delivery. The MPAJA's liaison to Force 136 was the young party secretary of the state of Perak, Chin Peng.[11]

For the remainder of its supplies the MPAJA relied upon a loosely organized body of Chinese squatters on the jungle fringe known as the Malayan People's Anti-Japanese Union (MPAJU). The squatters were Chinese who had lost work during the economic downturns of the 1930s or been intimidated by the Japanese. They were to provide an essential reservoir of support, both material and human, to the MPAJA and to its successors;

their numbers were estimated at 400,000—half of the rural Chinese population.[12]

The sudden end of World War II left the Japanese Army undefeated in Malaya and the MPAJA the most coherent center of organization in the country. The Force 136 veteran Richard Broome recalls, "The Chinese Communists immediately spread the rumor that they were responsible for the whole victory and went out all over the country and made themselves extremely unpopular and unpleasant."[13] The war exacerbated the ethnic tensions that had already existed in Malaya, as the Malays had largely cooperated with the Japanese occupiers. The British forces that arrived to reoccupy the country in September 1945 had lost their aura of invincibility after their defeat four years earlier; they found a very different Malaya than the one they had left behind. Riots, racial violence, and MPAJA attacks on police stations caused hundreds of deaths and incited further ethnic conflict.[14]

After some initial hesitation, the MPAJA decided to hand over its weapons to the British; Chin Peng was the liaison officer between the two forces. Each member of the MPAJA who turned in a weapon was given a campaign medal and $350 at a ceremony in early December 1945.[15] Chin Peng was awarded the Order of the British Empire (OBE) and took part in the Victory Parade in London by invitation. While the MPAJA was disbanded, the MPAJA Ex-Comrades Association, ostensibly a fraternal organization, kept alive both the formal military organization and its support structure in the squatter population.

The British decision to create a Malayan Union in 1946 was opposed by nearly the entire Malay population of Malaya.[16] Violently opposed to giving the Chinese and Indian minorities the vote and equal rights, not a single Malay ruler or government officer attended the inauguration of the new Constitution in April. Law and order broke down almost immediately; the Malayan Communist Party played on the racial and political tension to reunite and improve its organization.[17] The disorganized government of the Federation made this revolt easier; Hugh Fraser described it as "a caricature of government not dissimilar to a cartoon of a constitutional monarch and of an unelected House of Commons attempting to administer through eleven suspicious Houses of Lords, led by eleven more or less recalcitrant Lord Mayors. Frustration results locally and at the centre."[18]

OUTBREAK OF INSURGENCY

There is still a great deal of historical debate about the impact of the Calcutta Youth Conference of February 1948 on the decision of the Malayan Communist Party to resort to open violence; Anthony Short suggests that Lawrence Sharkey, president of the Australian Communist Party, conveyed instructions for the insurrection to the MCP from Cominform representatives in Calcutta between 9 and 20 March 1948.[19]

Transcripts of the Fifth Plenary Session of the Central Committee of the MCP, held in Singapore on 10 May 1948, speak of a revolution that has already started. "Under the increased exploitation and oppression and even the use of violent attacks of the British imperialists, the working classes launched a violent strike struggle, followed also by an outbreak of peasant struggle in certain places."[20]

The newly formed Malayan People's Anti-British Army (MPABA), hearing the call to arms, resorted to arson and murder. On 16 June 1948 three European planters in Northern Perak were murdered by the MPABA, while Chinese workers were killed in Perak and Johore Bahru. Sir Edward Gent, high commissioner of the Federation of Malaya, declared a federationwide State of Emergency on 17 June, imposing "liability to death penalty for unlawful possession of arms, power of detention of any persons, search of persons and premises without warrant, and power to occupy properties."[21]

The Declaration of Emergency, though not quite imposing martial law, placed serious restrictions on the ability of the MCP to carry out its program of terror while maintaining a framework of legitimacy within which the government forces were compelled to act. Sir Robert Thompson, who played a large role in the writing and implementation of the Emergency Regulations, notes the necessity for government agents to act within such guidelines in order for their actions to be accepted as legitimate by local populations.[22]

Under the Emergency Regulations, the police immediately arrested some 1,000 known MCP members or sympathizers; 1,779 had been detained and 637 deported by the end of the year. Many more had taken to the jungle to continue the struggle against the British.[23] On 23 July the Malayan Communist Party and its subsidiary organizations—including the Min Yuen, its supporters in the Chinese population—had been proscribed by the government of the Federation of Malaya.

THE STRATEGY OF THE MALAYAN COMMUNIST PARTY

The Malayan Communist Party fully intended to use the example of Mao's Chinese Communist Party to defeat the will of the British to maintain control of their colony through a strategy of protracted insurgent warfare. They believed that the campaign of terror and violence against mines and estates would force European managers to desert their posts; without the income from these sources, the British would quickly tire of the counterinsurgency effort and hand over the country to the Communists.[24]

The MCP recognized that the people—and particularly the Chinese squatters on which it would depend for logistical support—were the key to the success of their insurgency. Richard Clutterbuck argues:

The Communists could have brought in as much as they wanted across the Thai border. . . . But they found it better to follow the normal Mao Tse-Tung doctrine of getting it from the local people. It was much easier to get ammunition or food by raiding a police post two miles away than by land or sea from Peking. . . . They never really tried. They obtained all their material internally. The same holds true for recruits. Local people were far better and more effective as guerrillas than any imported from outside.[25]

Communist tactics initially focused on the destruction of the means of production, but the MCP quickly realized that these were as important to the Chinese peasants as they were to their supervisors. The Fifth Plenary Meetings' transcript, entitled *Regarding Decision on Struggle Strategy*, therefore warned, "When using the tool of violent destruction of enemy production, natural resources or commodities, consideration would be given to the workers' support (to be carried out only when workers participate spontaneously or express sympathy . . .), the repercussions on the livelihood . . . of the general masses (mainly the workers and peasants) and politics."[26]

The liberated areas would be linked into base areas from which more recruiting and training could be done until the climactic phase III battle of conventional military attacks finally drove the British from the federation—if they had not already departed, fed up with the losses and expense of the protracted counterguerrilla struggle.

To accomplish the goals of this long struggle, Chin Peng organized his fighters into eight regiments composed of some 3,000 guerrillas in the jungle and another 7,000 in the Self-Protection Corps outside the jungle. During the first year of the insurgency, the MPABA lived in the jungle in large camps of up to 300.[27] From these base camps, what was now called the Malayan Races Liberation Army (MRLA) in a vain attempt to garner Malay and Indian support for the uprising emerged in bands of up to fifty. They aimed at ensuring support from the Chinese villages through the use of terror and encouraging the departure of the imperialist "running dogs" by sabotaging mine equipment, slashing rubber trees, and murdering planters and mine managers. Between June and October 1948 the MRLA killed 223 civilians (almost all Chinese; only 17 were European). A document captured in the home of one insurgent in early July suggests that the MRLA believed the strategy to be succeeding: "The main production of the British imperialists, rubber and tin, have already become stagnant. Most of the rubber estates and tin mines, especially rubber estates, have stopped work on a general scale, and workers have run to the farming villages. There is a shortage of labor, and this threatens the economic resources of British imperialism."[28]

The planters and mine managers bore the brunt of the emergency. Norman Cleveland, a tin miner stationed just outside Kuala Lumpur, noted that initially:

the confusion between the services and the civilians and between the state and federal government was almost unbelievable. . . . Immediately violence broke out we were told that we were on our own. I asked what would be available to us in the way of weapons and they said, "Nothing." The Chamber of Mines sent a signal of distress to London to get the Colonial Office to take action and the Colonial Office came right back and said that . . . their records showed that there were plenty of guns and ammunition in Malaya. We returned a message saying they were dead right; there were plenty of guns and ammunition in Malaya but they happened to be in the wrong hands.[29]

EARLY BRITISH COUNTERINSURGENCY

To protect the population of Malaya against this campaign of terror, the Federation had just ten battalions of troops (two British, five Gurkha, and three Malay) on which to draw and some 9,000 police officers. The army battalions were substantially under strength and remained so for some time; the Gurkha battalions were heavily occupied with training new recruits.[30] Richard Clutterbuck points out that, after accounting for the support staff who made up nearly half of a 700-man infantry battalion, insurgent and Federation fighting forces were approximately equal in 1948: "the 10 battalions in Malaya in 1948 could field at the most 4,000 riflemen for patrols and operations against the 4,000 guerrillas in the jungle."[31]

The Cabinet Defence Committee in London met on 13 August to consider telegrams from the Commissioner General, South East Asia and from the acting high commissioner, Malaya, requesting reinforcements. Although Chief of the Imperial General Staff Field Marshal Montgomery acceded to the request for an additional brigade to be dispatched to Malaya "as urgently as possible," he warned:

The arrival of the brigade would help stabilize the position and improve morale but it was not the long term solution. This would require a thorough reorganisation of the internal security forces of the Colonies in the Far East, including such measures as the establishment of a Home Guard, reinforcements and reorganisation of the police, and in addition it would probably require three or four divisions to clear up the whole situation.[32]

Despite the shortage of troops, the other steps suggested by Montgomery were quickly implemented. During the first three months of the insurgency some 24,000 Malays were enrolled into a special Constabulary and used for static guard duties, freeing troops for mobile patrols as the constables were trained. Passive defensive measures and several hundred policemen from Palestine were also used to stiffen local defenses. The former inspector-general of the Palestinian Police, Colonel W.N. Gray, became the commissioner of Malay Federation Police and further strengthened resolve by improving training and organization and by creating reaction units to respond to MCP attacks on police stations.[33] Unfortunately, in order to emphasize the fact that the armed forces were acting in support of the civil authority, Colonel Gray was placed in overall command of the counterinsurgency effort, diminishing the effectiveness and unity of combined army-police operations.[34]

Sir Edward Gent, the high commissioner, had strongly supported the use of police constables for local security and of an active search-and-destroy strategy by the army. In a conference in Kuala Lumpur on 22 June 1948, Gent argued, "The police and the army should continually be on the offensive in as large numbers as possible, and available fully-trained police and troops should be used to the least extent necessary on static jobs. The main campaign must be directed to an active, offensive routing out of suspects."[35]

Although Gent's proposal was in keeping with the army's own attitude on how best to defeat the insurgents, by failing to take action earlier he had lost the confidence of the European portion of the population. After Gent was recalled to offer his resignation, his plane crashed outside London on 4 July 1948, killing him.

Gent was replaced by Sir Henry Gurney, formerly chief secretary of Palestine, his installation delayed until 8 October by local optimism that "the worst of the emergency may be definitely behind us by the end of September."[36] This was certainly not the case: Gurney noted that the second week of his appointment had seen "seventy-three attacks of all kinds, which is thirty more than the preceding week and only three short of the highest recorded."[37]

Gurney recognized that the Chinese squatters who were "providing bases from which bandits operate and . . . helping them, in some cases under duress and in many others willingly with food, arms, money and other means of resistance . . . [were] a positive and formidable menace to security." As a result, Gurney added tougher Emergency Regulations, including 17C, providing for deportation of detainees; 17D, providing for collective punishment; and 17E and F, allowing compulsory resettlement of individuals or whole villages. The use of the collective punishment regulations led to opposition from the Chinese people, and they were eventually shelved.

The failure of the initial revolt against the British had temporarily dampened the ardor of the Communist Terrorists (CTs),[38] provoking a strong British military desire to hunt down and finish off the insurgents quickly. Two competing schools of thought governed the response of the Security Forces to the insurrection. These were the belief that the MRLA presented a military problem to be overcome by means of a military solution and a less conventional appreciation that placed the main emphasis on the economic and political factors that created and sustained the will of the insurgents. Although the British army had substantial experience in fighting small-unit jungle actions against the Japanese during World War II, the rapid demobilization of the Far Eastern Forces after the war combined with the dominance of the Western European experience in the careers of most regular soldiers to promote a "conventional" attitude to the war. Richard Clutterbuck explains:

The predilection of some army officers for major operations seems incurable. Even in the late 1950s, new brigade commanders would arrive from England, nostalgic for World War II, or fresh from large-scale maneuvers in Germany. On arrival in Malaya, they would address themselves with chinagraphs to a map almost wholly green except for one red pin. "Easy," they would say. "Battalion on the left, battalion on the right, battalion blocking the end, and then a fourth battalion to drive through. Can't miss, old boy." Since it took the better part of a day, with more than a thousand soldiers, to get an effective cordon even a half-mile square around a jungle camp, the guerrillas, hearing the soldiers crashing through the jungle into position, had no difficulty getting clear before the net was closed. Except for a rare brush with a straggler, all the soldiers ever found was an empty camp, but this enabled the officers to claim they had "cleared the area of enemy." This would be duly marked on the maps, and the commanders would go to bed with a glow of satisfaction over a job well done. The soldiers, nursing their blisters, had other words for it.[39]

Clutterbuck's parody seems only a slight exaggeration of the initial tactics of General Boucher, General Officer Commanding Malaya, who described his program to the Legislative Council on 27 July 1948:

My object is to break the insurgent concentrations, to bring them to battle before they are ready, and to drive them underground or into the jungle, and then to follow them there, by troops in the jungles, and by police backed by troops and by the [Royal Air Force] RAF outside of them. I intend to keep them constantly moving and deprive them of food and recruits, because if they are constantly moving they cannot terrorize an area properly so that they can get their commodities from it; and then ferret them out of their holes, wherever these holes may be.[40]

At this same conference, responding to press criticisms such as "Large sweep in Jahore—no success," General Boucher pointed to the training value of such operations for his troops and argued, "These areas were at least cleared . . . [and] it was now known that there were no insurgents in them, nor had any insurgent camps been left behind."[41] The CTs were not impressed; captured documents indicated that large, short-duration jungle sweeps "neither harried or worried [the CTs] particularly, but surprise raids and ambushes by small parties were greatly feared."[42]

British attitudes left little room for any appreciation of the political nature of the struggle, of the ability of the guerrillas to return and reuse these deserted bases, or of the necessity to limit the use of force to maintain the legitimacy of the security forces in the eyes of the populace. The issue quickly came to a head between police and army forces handicapped by the lack of a clearly defined hierarchy. The chief police officer of the state of Pahang reported his concern about restrictions on the use of force to the commissioner of police on 9 November 1948:

I am afraid we shall have a lot of trouble regarding this question of burning down of buildings by the military. OCPDs [Officers in Charge of the Police District] are the only people allowed to seize and or burn down buildings, and the military know this, though it has come to my knowledge that the military fully intend to burn down any buildings which they consider are being used or have been used by bandits without waiting for the instructions of the OCPD. In a recent conference . . . General Boucher mentioned that it was not proposed to obey this law, and that you would fully support him in this. It is going to cause a lot of trouble if the military fail to obey the law in this respect.[43]

With this sort of military attitude at the head of the chain of command, a confused organizational structure in which the army was nominally under the command of the police, and no clear strategy for bringing the conflict to a conclusion, a series of atrocities marred initial efforts of the British army to defeat the insurgents. Anthony Short notes the cases of the torching of the village of Kachau on 2 November 1948—a reprisal for the destruction of rubber stores at a nearby plantation earlier that morning—and the massacre of twenty-four Chinese by a Scots Guards patrol on 12 December after the ambush and killing of a second lieutenant and a police constable.[44]

Lacking strategic direction, frustrated by fruitless and dangerous "beating the bush" jungle sweeps, and without any clear intelligence about insurgent locations or strategy, the military effort to defeat the insurgents had an inauspicious beginning. It is not surprising that Colonial Secretary James Griffiths, handing his portfolio to Oliver Lyttelton on 27 October 1951, confessed to his successor, "At this stage, it has become a military problem to which we have not been able to find the answer."[45]

LEARNING IN PROGRESS: TACTICAL INNOVATIONS

Not all of the relevant World War II and colonial experience was lost. Lieutenant Colonel Walter Walker, a veteran of the Burma campaign from the sixth Gurkha Rifles, received permission to organize a unit composed of veterans of Force 136, the Special Operations Executive unit that supported the MPAJA during World War II. "Ferret Force" was organized in July 1948 at the Malayan Regiment's depot at Port Dixon.[46] The commanding officer was John Davis, who had been good friends with Chin Peng in Force 136; the training officer was Walter Walker. Walker had served as a General Staff officer on the staff of Field Marshal Sir William

Slim when the latter commanded the First Burma Corps after extensive service on the North West Frontier in the Eighth Gurkha Regiment.

Tom Pocock describes the composition of Walker's teams: "A typical Ferret Force group, led by a British volunteer with local knowledge, would consist of four teams, each consisting of a British officer, twelve volunteers from British or Gurkha regiments, the Malay Regiment, a detachment of the Royal Signals, Dyak trackers and a Chinese liaison officer." It was designed for traveling light and living off the land—field rations included fried iguana and python soup.[47] After viewing a demonstration of Ferret Force operations, General Sir Neil Ritchie, then serving as the commander in chief of Far East Land Force (FARELF), ordered Walker to establish a jungle training school to pass on the innovative tactics he had devised. Ferret Force was disbanded shortly thereafter,[48] but it had served to introduce such innovations as native trackers, small patrols, and the inclusion of interpreters and local natives in army operations.[49]

Walker established what became known as the Far Eastern Land Force Training Center (FTC), called by soldiers the Jungle Warfare School, in an abandoned lunatic asylum northwest of Singapore. Walker described the school's mission as "studying, teaching and perfecting methods of jungle fighting, [and to] raise the standard of jungle warfare among the Armed Forces in FARELF, and thus contribute in some measure to a speedier conclusion of the hostilities against the bandits in this country."[50]

Separate courses were run for officers and noncommissioned officers (NCOs); once they had completed a course, these leaders returned to their battalions to train their subordinates in what they had learned. Much of the course was spent in the jungle; the concluding four-and-a-half-day exercise was spent in actual counterguerrilla patrols, several of which made contact with CTs. Walker was concerned at the conventional warfare attitude he saw in his students, noting in March 1949: "An unfortunate term called 'jungle bashing' has crept in. The qualities required of the real jungle fighter are not those of the elephant but rather of the poacher, gangster, and cat-burglar."[51] There was apparently a split in attitudes along generational lines; Walker observed that "the majority of junior officers appeared to be in favour of smaller patrols, whereas more senior officers were divided in their opinion, those against stating that the advantages were outweighed by the danger of smaller patrols being lost or outnumbered."[52] Walker's determined personal leadership overcame this attitude, and the Jungle Warfare Training center soon spurred the creation of more effective counterinsurgency doctrine and practice.

Despite the successes of the Jungle Warfare School, Walker did not share the enthusiasm of the High Command that the war would be over quickly. In a private talk with Malcolm MacDonald, the commissioner-general for South East Asia, Walker said that the fight would take a long time. Tom Pocock explains why: "For a start, the British Army was geared to fight a nuclear, or conventional, war in Europe and all the thinking at the Staff College and the School of Infantry was in that direction. Moreover, it seemed to Walker that all the skills learned and equipment developed in the long struggle with the Japanese had been lost. The Army would have to learn all over again."[53]

MacDonald and Walker arranged a demonstration of jungle-fighting techniques. One demonstration was of the ambush of troop-carrying trucks; spectators watched a convoy of soft-skinned vehicles trapped and destroyed by guerrillas. As Pocock relates:

Walker pointed out that troops were being asked to travel long distances in un-armed trucks and were not equipped with the portable flame-throwers or grenade-dischargers for rifles: both weapons used with success against the Japanese. . . . After the demonstration, General Boucher and Colonel Nicol Gray, the Commissioner of Police, complained to Walker. Putting troops in armoured vehicles was, said Boucher, too "defensive minded." Gray agreed, adding that if he thought Walker meant what he was teaching he would send no more police officers to the Jungle Warfare School. In vain, Walker explained that these were the tactics that had been learned so painfully in Burma but seemed to have been forgotten since 1945.[54]

That night a police party in a soft-skinned vehicle was ambushed and wiped out.

Walker went to General Sir John Harding, then commander in chief, Far East Land Forces, to get reliable cartridges for flame throwers. Until then they had been using cartridges marked "For Training Only."[55] After thirteen months in command of the Jungle Warfare Training Centre, in November 1949, Walker returned to England to attend the Joint Services Staff College, where he studied the Russian threat to Europe and Berlin.[56] Walker took command of the Sixth Gurkha Rifles in October 1950.[57]

Another Burma veteran, Brigadier "Mad Mike" Calvert, reformed the Special Air Service Regiment in 1950 for deep jungle operations.[58] As the MRLA moved farther from populated areas, receiving support from the aborigines in the deep jungle, the Malayan Scouts (SAS) endured long jungle marches to reach likely areas of MRLA base camps. Their effectiveness was limited by the number and capability of helicopters for transport of personnel and supplies.[59]

These tactical innovations, important as they were, were limited in their effectiveness by the lack of a coherent strategic plan for the defeat of the insurgency and by the continuing attraction of large battalion sweeps to eradicate the insurgents quickly. The same history of colonial warfare that allowed and encouraged tactical innovation was beginning to make inroads on the strategic direction of the counterinsurgency effort in the person of Harold Briggs.

STRATEGIC DIRECTION: THE BRIGGS PLAN

An appreciation of the political nature of the counterinsurgency effort can be seen in a discussion in the Cabinet Malaya Committee of a captured MCP document, "Present Day Situation and Duties of the Malayan Communist Party." A note from J. Strachey, the secretary of state for war, affirms: "The struggle is, in one important aspect, a struggle for the support of the Chinese rural squatters. This seems to suggest that we ought to be exceedingly careful to avoid punitive measures that hit the Chinese squatter population indiscriminately. It suggests that it is of importance for us always to appear in the role of protectors of the population against the Communists and their destructive and terrorist activities."[60]

The same realization was being reached by Lieutenant General Sir Harold Briggs, appointed director of operations to assume overall direction of the counterinsurgency effort in April 1950. Briggs was another veteran of the campaign in Burma, having commanded the Fifth Indian Division there; he soon demonstrated an unusual grasp of the political nature of the insurgency and of the measures required to defeat it. In the words of a veteran of the emergency, "In the early days, we didn't grasp how important the support of the local people was. It wasn't until Briggs that we understood that the CTs got all of their support—food, supplies, intelligence—from the local people. Only about 1950 was the political nature of the war really grasped."[61]

One of the first steps taken by Briggs was the creation of the Federal Joint Intelligence Advisory Committee in May 1950. This committee coordinated the collection, analysis, and distribution of intelligence on insurgent locations, activities, and plans from whatever source—civil, police, or military. This same spirit of "jointness" in the counterinsurgency effort inspired the creation of a the Federal War Council to coordinate all civil, police, and military counterinsurgent efforts. The Federal War Council, whose members included the chief secretary of the federation, the general and air officers commanding in Malaya, the commissioner of police, and the secretary of defense, was replicated in District and State War Executive Committees throughout Malaya. The problem of efforts pulling in opposite directions had been solved.[62]

Having created an instrument to ensure the strategic direction of the war, Briggs now turned to the question of what that direction should be. The formula Briggs designed focused on the need to separate the insurgents from their source of supply and recruits in the population.[63] He recognized that these objectives could not be achieved immediately but would have to be achieved in small sections of the country first. The plan explicitly instructs that the peninsula be cleared "step by step, from South to North" by:

(a) dominating the populated areas and building up a feeling of complete security in them, with the object of obtaining a steady and increasing flow of information from all sources;

(b) breaking up the Min Yuen within the populated areas;

(c) thereby isolating the bandits from their food and information supply organisation in the populated areas;

(d) and finally destroying the bandits by forcing them to attack us on our own ground.[64]

The priority placed on winning the support of the population rather than defeating the insurgents by force of arms is reinforced in the specific instructions to military forces, in which the army is again listed after the police and is ordered not only to deploy its forces "in close conjunction with the police" but also to "cover those populated areas which the Police cannot themselves adequately cover." Striking forces to take offensive action against the CTs are instructed to "establish headquarters in populated areas" to ensure close coordination with the people, recognized as the main source of intelligence on future insurgent operations. The value of intelligence is again emphasized in instructions to the RAF, which is given permission to take offensive action against the insurgents "as and when reasonably reliable information is received."[65]

The Briggs Plan reverberated in London; Strachey presented a memorandum to the Cabinet Malaya Committee that noted approvingly: "General Briggs is always emphasizing that we cannot expect any sudden or overnight transformation in the situation. The only possible policy is a highly integrated combined operation. The obvious thing to do is to take one state at a time and get it and keep it permanently dominated."[66]

Not only was the Government in Whitehall not pressing for a quick solution to the problem, it also understood what that problem was—and recognized that previous efforts to overcome it had in many ways been counterproductive. Thus, Strachey speaks of "a certain tactical distortion . . . because of the way we formulated our task as the clearing up of gangs of bandits. This may have lead to a concentration on jungle patrols, etc., which inevitably pay comparatively small dividends for the effort involved, rather than to concentrate on our real task. That task is to break the power of the M.C.P."[67]

That would be a substantial task. The guerrillas had reorganized themselves by early 1950 to the point that one observer believed their civil support was "probably equal to that of government in the matter of supplies and superior in the matter of intelligence." As a result, guerrilla incidents, which had dropped from over two hundred monthly in the second half of 1948 to fewer than a hundred by the middle of 1949, increased to over four hundred a month by mid-1950.[68] The military was hard pressed, unable to station sufficient forces to guarantee the safety of cleared areas; the victory of Mao Tse-Tung's Communists in China provided an important morale boost to the MCP and influenced the Chinese in Malaya to believe that the British would be overwhelmed by a rising tide of communism. The GOC, General Boucher, noted in a military appreciation on the eve of his departure in February 1950 that because of insufficient forces to meet all insurgent challenges, he had to pull forces out of subdued areas; experience had shown that Communist activity revived in the absence of the security forces. The problem would remain as long as the Min Yuen organization was intact.[69]

General Sir John Harding, Commander in Chief, Far East Land Forces, noted in April:

Our greatest weakness now is the lack of early and accurate information of the enemy's strength, dispositions and intentions. For lack of information an enormous amount of military effort is being necessarily absorbed on prophylactic and will o' the wisp patrolling and jungle bashing and on air bombardment. Information services must depend almost entirely on the police who in their turn must depend on the confidence of the people, especially the Chinese, and the civil administration generally and its power to protect them.[70]

The lack of intelligence collection and analysis was perceived as negating the need for more troops; Harding stated, "Additional troops will certainly not pay the full dividend of which they are capable until the civil administrative follow up resources are much stronger."[71]

A typical army operation of the period, code-named Operation WARBLER and involving eight infantry battalions plus four Police Jungle Companies, was intended to "destroy utterly the Communist organization" in Johore. Results were poor: "Contacts showed a marked increase but unfortunately these increased contacts did not result in an increase in bandit casualties." In fact, "in one area, the bandits concentrated in large gangs with, it is thought, the object of being able to strike back at Security Force patrols with more effect and to 'show the flag' to the civilian population. They did in fact have considerable success against Security Force patrols in North Johore."[72] General Lockhart concluded his assessment of the operation phlegmatically: "It became apparent that no major result can be expected inside six months. There should be no relaxation of effort."[73] Operation SPRINGTIDE, conducted with twenty-two rifle platoons in the Kampar area in December 1951, was slightly more successful, though a conventional approach showed itself in Lockhart's comment "Artillery support proved invaluable for night harassing attacks and to sustain pressure over a wide area."[74]

The real problem was convincing the Chinese population that their future was in an independent Malaya rather than one subordinate to the Chinese

Communists. Failure to convince them of this idea had resulted in the continuance of their support of the MCP—sometimes willing, more often coerced. Harding appreciated their situation, saying, "The Chinese population is generally content to get on with its business even if it entails subsidising the Communists; nor is it willing generally to give any information to the Police Force for fear of reprisals until it is given full and continuous security by our Forces."[75] As a result, "one of our most vital aims throughout the Emergency must be to commit the Chinese to our side," partly by making them feel "that Malaya and not Red China is their home. Without their co-operation it will indeed be difficult to bring the Emergency to a successful conclusion."[76] As part of his campaign to achieve this political goal, Briggs decided to give the Chinese some stake in their own security. In his Directive No. 3 on 25 May 1950, Briggs argued, "The time has come when selected Chinese should be recruited as Auxiliary Police and where necessary armed with shotguns to take their share in antibandit operations."[77]

The addition of two brigades to the military forces available led to a desire to stamp out the terrorists quickly. Almost two-thirds of the army's available strength was concentrated in the three southern states of Johore, Negri Sembilan, and Southern Pahang, but with little effect on the Communist Terrorists. The failure of the troops to come to terms with the enemy was largely a result of not being able to find him; the population refused, or was too frightened, to give the Security Forces information on CT whereabouts and activity. Briggs began to appreciate that the problem was more difficult than he had thought; without intelligence on the terrorists, "Malaya is like a sponge and would engulf any number of extra battalions."[78]

Briggs personally fought against the organizational culture of the British army (which he knew quite well, having risen in it to the rank of lieutenant general). Harry Miller, a journalist in Malaya during the emergency, describes an incident when he and Briggs were standing on a road in Selangor and the latter said with a grin:

You know, some brigadiers and battalion commanders aren't going to like what I'm going to tell them—that they won't be able to use battalions or companies in sweeping movements any more. They'll have to reconcile themselves to war being fought by junior commanders down to lance-corporals who will have the responsibility to make decisions on the spot if necessary. We've got to look for the Communists now, send small patrols after them, harass them. Flexibility of operations in the jungle must be the keynote.[79]

On another occasion, Briggs argued:

The problem of clearing Communist banditry from Malaya was similar to that of eradicating malaria from a country. Flit guns and mosquito nets, in the form of military and police, though giving some very local security if continuously maintained, effected no permanent cure. Such a permanent cure entails the closing of all breeding areas. In this case the breeding areas of the Communists were the isolated squatter areas. . . . Once these were concentrated there might be some chance of controlling the Communist cells therein. This showed clearly that a quick answer was not to be counted on.[80]

The answer to the problem was the creation of "New Villages," settlements for the Chinese squatters, estate workers, and villagers that protected them behind chain link and barbed wire fences lit with floodlights and patrolled by Chinese Auxiliary Police Forces. More than concentration camps, the New Villages would include schools, medical aid stations, community centers, village cooperatives, and even Boy Scout troops. As the locals gained confidence in the determination of the government to protect them, they would progress from serving in an unarmed Home Guard through to keeping shotguns in their homes, ready for instant action. These New Villages were the heart of the Briggs Plan, and they had a decisive impact on the course of the emergency.[81] By the end of 1951 some 400,000 squatters had been resettled in over four hundred "New Villages."

Short describes the impact on the Communist Terrorists: "For the guerrilla it meant that the tide was going out; that he could no longer move among the people as the fish moves through the water; and that when he was now forced to go close inshore he not only gave away his position but ran the risk of being caught in the shallows."[82]

Even with the creation and protection of the New Villages, the support of the population for the MCP continued. Sir Henry Gurney, the high commissioner, was downcast about the prospects for success in a memorandum he wrote on 4 October 1951:

Three years ago it was made clear to the MCA [Malayan Chinese Association] leaders that unless they provided an alternative standard to which local Chinese would rally, the Communists would win. The answer was that the rural Chinese, the peasants, who are the real target, must first be protected. With the help of the MCA the whole vast scheme of resettlement has now been almost finished and labour forces regrouped. Into these settlements and into trade unions and into schools the MCP are trying hard to penetrate and are succeeding. If they are allowed to continue thus unopposed by any Chinese effort whatever, the whole of the Chinese rural population will soon come under Communist domination.[83]

Just two days after writing this pessimistic report, Gurney was killed in an ambush en route to a weekend resort some sixty-five miles from Kuala Lumpur. Gurney's death marked the low point of the emergency; the loss was made worse by the fact that Briggs retired in December as a result of illness and died soon after, and Colonel Gray, the commissioner of police, was also relieved in December.

The MCP, despite its assassination of Gurney, was going through a period of adjustment of its own. In October the Central Committee of the MCP met in the Mentakab area of Pahang to discuss its policy; the committee decided to assign equal priority to political subversion and military action and to decrease attacks on peasants and on their sources of livelihood to ensure their continued support for the struggle. That struggle was about to get much more difficult.[84]

A CHANGE OF GOVERNMENT AND AN ASSESSMENT

The new Conservative government in Britain, which was elected on 25 October 1951, named Oliver Lyttelton to the post of colonial secretary. Lyttelton spent most of December in Malaya; it was he who asked Police Commissioner Gray to resign after learning of Gray's dispiriting leadership of the Police Force in Malaya. Lyttelton wrote an appreciation of the situation in Malaya based on impressions gained during his visit; the report was drafted in Kuala Lumpur and dated 21 December 1951. It is an impressive document of nine sections with fifteen appendixes for which he apologized, "Their range and detail demonstrate how inadequate are the instruments of our policy."[85]

Despite Gurney's murder, Lyttelton appreciated the primacy of politics over military action in the campaign, noting that if the situation had to be summed up in a sentence, it would be "You cannot win the war without the help of the population, and you cannot get the support of the population without at least beginning to win the war."[86] This is an unusual kind of war, for it is "waged with two instruments, propaganda and armed forces," and presents a real challenge. "Communist efficiency has greatly improved and . . . a formidable instrument, both for propaganda and for war, has been forged." As a result, even "if we are successful in increasing our victories over the bandits, the Communists may well elect to go underground. Thus . . . we must quickly forge more effective weapons for the warfare of ideas."[87]

Lyttelton praised the "efficiency and bearing" of the British army forces in the theater, but despite their efforts noted: "It must be recognized that the war has now nearly reached a deadlock. In spite of the considerable casualties inflicted upon the bandits their operational strength remains virtually constant." Rather than commit more troops to the fight, Lyttelton supported the "creation of trained Police Forces and Home Guards. For this training, Police and Special Constables will have to be withdrawn; and during their absence the Army will have to bear a serious additional burden of static defence." The Commander in Chief, Land Forces, Far East, "who combines outstanding military ability with a firm grasp of the political situation," he said, supported the plan and encouraged Lyttelton's belief that "once the training and re-training of the Police and para-military forces have been completed, police action, including the better provision of information, will render military action gradually more effective and, I hope, ultimately unnecessary."[88]

Lyttelton turned next to the question of effective government, arguing, "The most effective single measure to be taken is the unification and concentration of command and responsibility in one man." In the same vein, "a Director of Intelligence and an intelligence staff (as far as possible drawn from military and police headquarters) should be added. Through them the Deputy Director of Operations would be able to direct, co-ordinate and distribute intelligence derived from the two main sources—the police and military intelligence branches."[89]

On the issue of police, Lyttelton states: "Urgent and drastic action is called for. The Emergency is in essence a Police rather than a military task. More troops would add little to the impact. . . . In short, I do not recommend any increase in tropps [sic]."[90] Lyttelton believed that the police were in vital need of more training and better officers, and it was for this reason that he relieved Police Commissioner Gray, whom he described as "a gallant officer but without the necessary grasp of organisation in these exceptional circumstances."[91]

Concerned with ethnic divisions in the Home Guard—only 1,860 of 38,466 Special Constables were Chinese, whereas 2,409 of the 2,578 Communist Terrorists killed to that date were—Lyttelton pushed for the creation and arming of a Chinese Home Guard, which "should, however, be looked upon only as a first step to trying to gain much more Chinese support and to enlisting much larger numbers of them in the police."[92] Part of that effort was to begin in the schools, for "children coming back from school convert their parents to our way of thinking . . . [in] the long-term war of ideas, which we must win if we are to see a peaceful country and one which can some day be entrusted with self-government within the British Commonwealth."[93]

Lyttelton's assessment is a remarkable document, one that reveals as much about the British government's concept of countering Communist insurgency and building a stable government as it does about the situation in Malaya at the low point of the Emergency.

ORGANIZATIONAL LEARNING IN MALAYA, 1948–1951

Did the British Army Develop a Successful Counterinsurgency Doctrine?

An assessment of the British army's success in developing a doctrine and techniques to defeat the insurgency in Malaya through the end of 1951 reveals markedly mixed results. As Lyttelton's report makes clear, there was no certainty that victory was closer or that "the objective of one day building a united Malayan nation within the British Commonwealth and Empire" would be achieved.[94] General Lockhart noted in early 1952: "The bandits are certainly holding their own and replace gaps in their ranks without difficulty. There is nothing to indicate that their supporters, the Min Yuen, are any fewer in number."[95] In fact, to this point in the emergency the army had failed in its pursuit of the objective, preferring to mount battalion sweeps in pursuit of the terrorists rather than contribute forces in static long-term pacification support programs. Typical was Operation LEO in Johore State, a ten-day operation in October 1949 involving twenty-four platoons of the Gurkha Rifles. Intelligence was poor, and the operation featured standard World War II tactics. The result was predictably inconclusive: "Looking back on LEO, the Gurkha commander felt that the air strikes had alerted the guerrillas, and that the troops, who moved in a line of small columns, were simply too thin on the ground to catch the enemy. Twenty-four platoons spread over an area of 74,000,000 square yards were not enough for the task, even if the operation order enjoined them to 'search carefully.' "[96]

Part of the problem in the army's lack of direction was disunity of command: the police commissioner was nominally in command of all army forces, and there was no overall integration of the civil and military efforts. As one colonial policeman remembers, "At no time in those dark days did anybody say, 'Don't forget that the police are supposed to be the friends of the people and it is essential that there should be a common understanding of this between population and police.' "[97] Although a commendable economy of force was exercised in pursuit of the CTs in the jungle, this was largely because there was little military force available to the British army at this time. In the words of a veteran of the campaign: "It seems strange now. You always saw films of Americans going on beaches in huge waves out of landing craft. And there was us being rowed ashore by Malay sailors in little rowing boats, one rowing boat at a time."[98] Despite efforts to create small counterguerrilla teams like Ferret Force and the Police Jungle Companies, the desire of British brigade and battalion commanders to mass their forces in large unproductive sweeps remained. "Typical, by contrast, was the experience of the North Malay Sub-District, whose large operations in the second quarter of 1949 yielded one kill, no surrenders, and no captures, whereas its routine patrolling resulted in nineteen kills and twenty-six arrests."[99]

To the end of 1951, then, it is difficult to argue that the British army developed a successful counterinsurgency doctrine as part of a comprehensive British effort to defeat the Communist Terrorists (see Figure 4-1).

Figure 4-1
Did the British Army Develop a Successful Counterinsurgency Doctrine in
Malaya, 1948–1951?

Victory: the achievement of national goals	Doubtful
Objective: the setting of realistic national goals	No
Unity of command: military subordination to political objectives	No
Economy of force: minimum necessary force	Yes
Mass: appropriate structure for threat	No

Was the British Army in Malaya a Learning Institution from 1948 through 1951?

The performance of the British army as a learning institution is similarly mixed through the end of 1951 (see Figure 4-2). Although there was a substantial degree of bottom-up input, particularly from Walter Walker in the guise of the Ferret Force and the Jungle Warfare Centre, suggestions from the field were not collated by intermediate headquarters, endorsed, and sent to the head of the chain of command for approval; instead, Walker demonstrated a great ability to bypass intermediate commanders to appeal directly to high command for change. Other officers were similarly oriented toward change: "Writing in 1949, Major E.R. Robinson, a rifle company commander, spoke out bluntly against the large operation. The bigger the operation, said he, and the higher the level at which it was planned, the less its chance of success; the buildup and the preparations were impossible to conceal; it was difficult to control troops in the jungle, and the guerrillas simply vanished."[100]

Superiors did make themselves available but were not particularly open to analytical thinking; witness Walker's pleas for armored vehicles for convoy work, which were ignored by Grey and Boucher. Although a local training center was established to devise and promulgate effective measures to combat insurgency, no overall doctrine was developed in the theater, and thus there was not standardization at the tactical and operational level. The army did not rise to the challenge of coordinating an effective political/military campaign; Director of Operations General Lockhart noted: "The Federal Government, although keenly interested in the Emergency, has tended to regard it as the concern of one department. The result has been that other departments have continued to be absorbed to a large extent in their normal activities and to adhere to normal peacetime methods and procedures."[101]

Higher-level staffs seemed to insulate the high command from the field,

Figure 4-2
Learning in Malaya, 1948–1951

Bottom-up input: Suggestions from the field	Irregular Channels Only
Superiors questioned	No
available	Yes
Theoretical thinking	Low Level Only
Local doctrine development	No
Local training centers	Yes
Small, responsive staff	No

rather than pass on the innovative techniques and requests for change from below. "The response to available information in the military headquarters most directly concerned with operations—battalion and brigade—varied with the imagination, skills, and personalities of individuals. In general, headquarters staffs tried to apply the familiar intelligence and operational procedures of World War II. They kept records, looked for patterns, and puzzled over the results."[102]

A colonial policeman summarizes the extent of learning required in the situation that confronted the British military and civilian leadership at the start of the emergency:

When I first arrived in August 1948, the police and the military forces in Malaya at that time, the Malay Regiment, were facing an armed insurrection, this very difficult task of first of all finding the enemy in the jungle and then eliminating him, countering the Communist propaganda in the populated areas, in both cases having had no experience of it before. However, as always happens in these situations— it happened in Palestine, it happened in Malaya, it happened in Kenya, it happened in Cyprus—there was a lot of reorganization, training and retraining to be done, new equipment to be acquired, new brains to be acquired, new systems to be worked out and applied and of course the basic method of correlating the activities of administration, army, and police so that there was a maximum push against the adversary. The three-legged stool system, it's called by so many so often. All these things had to be learnt the hard way.[103]

Whereas there were encouraging signs of learning from below—many emerging from junior officers who had extensive jungle experience gained fighting the Japanese in Burma during World War II (see Figure 4-2)—the middle and high levels of command demonstrated marked resistance to change, remaining entrenched in their desire to fight in Malaya as they had in Europe. As David Lloyd Owen notes, "They were flogging the jungle with enormous sweeps and that kind of thing, which is completely useless in this sort of war, and wasting a tremendous amount of effort."[104] The result, in the eyes of Derek Blake of the Royal West Kent Regiment, was that "I could see it being stalemate, that was the kind of situation that I envisaged, the way things were it was—it just arrived at the stage where things were a complete stalemate. And I could never ever see them giving up or surrendering or whatever. I could never see an end to the Emergency."[105]

Overcoming this organizational resistance to change would require the dramatic intervention of a single man who held absolute civil and military power to defeat the insurgents and would use that power and his personality to ensure that everyone concerned with the emergency adopted and implemented the lessons learned at such cost during its worst years.

NOTES

1. The island of Singapore was not part of the Federation of Malaya and is not included in the use of the word *Malaya* except where indicated.

2. Richard Clutterbuck, *Riot and Revolution in Malaya and Singapore* (London: Faber & Faber, 1973), 32–33. A very useful short history of the British involvement in Malaya is A.J. Stockwell's "Introduction" to *British Documents on the End of Empire: Malaya*, Part I, *The Malayan Union Experiment 1941–1948* (London: HMSO, 1995). The *British Documents on the End of Empire* (*BDEEP*) project is an excellent compilation of primary source documents on the emergency.

3. CO 537/3746, no. 9, enclosure [March 1948], "On the prospects of the emergence of a strong independence movement in Malaya in the near future," reprinted in A.J. Stockwell, *British Documents on the End of Empire: Malaya*. Part II. *The Communist Insurrection, 1948–1953*, 2–4; quotation is from p. 3. See also CO 537/3758, 75. Commenting on the causes of ethnic tensions, Richard Broome, who served in military and civilian positions in Malaya from 1942 through 1958, remembered, "And the Chinese were apt to let their pigs roam into mosques and that sort of thing and that always started riots straight away." Richard Broome OBE MC, "Special Operations Executive," Imperial War Museum Department of Sound Records Accession No. 008255/06 (no date) CXW. Dr. Conrad X. Wood of the Imperial War Museum has collected an impressive series of taped interviews with both military and civilian veterans of the emergency, a number of which have been transcribed. They are hereafter cited as IWM DSR [Number].

4. Clutterbuck, *Riot and Revolution*, 35–37. Charles Allen, ed., *Tales from the South China Seas: Images of the British in South-East Asia in the Twentieth Century* (London: Futura, 1984), is a very relevant oral history of the lives of Europeans before and during the emergency.

5. Anthony Short argues that the MCP, although not exclusively Chinese, was always at least 90 percent so. *The Communist Insurrection in Malaya, 1948–1960* (London: Frederick Muller, 1975), 19. This book, written with full access to the Malayan government's confidential and secret papers, remains "unquestionably the most authoritative and balanced book on the Communist Insurrection in Malaya" (John Bastin's "Foreword," 7).

6. Richard Clutterbuck, *The Long, Long War: The Emergency in Malaya 1948–1960* (London: Cassell, 1966), 14.

7. Edgar O'Ballance, *Malaya: The Communist Insurgent War, 1948–1960* (London: Faber & Faber, 1966), 24

8. Ibid., 25.

9. Short, *The Communist Insurrection in Malaya*, 22.

10. Ibid.

11. Clutterbuck, *The Long, Long War*, 16–17.

12. Ibid., 21.

13. IWM DSR No. 008255/06, Broome, 54. These problems were already becoming evident during World War II; Broome recalls Chin Peng's telling him while both were serving in Force 136, "You know that our objectives are not the same. . . . Your objective is to re-establish the British colonial rule in this country and we don't want it but we want a Communist rule in this country" (8).

14. Clutterbuck, *Riot and Revolution*, 40.

15. Richard Clutterbuck states that 5,497 weapons were handed in, as against 4,765 that had been issued by Force 136 over the course of the war; many more, captured during the British retreat in 1941, were already concealed in the jungle. Ibid.

16. For the context of British attitudes toward the end of empire within which the Malayan Emergency took place, see J.P.D. Dunbabin, *The Post-Imperial Age: The Great Powers and the Wider World* (London: Longman, 1994), 13–14, 52–53.

17. See Lucian W. Pye, *Guerrilla Communication in Malaya: Its Social and Political Meaning* (Princeton, NJ: Princeton University Press, 1958). Pye interviewed sixty Surrendered Enemy Personnel in Malaya from September 1952 through January 1953, examining their political life, the factors that drove them to join the MCP, and their decisions to leave the MCP.

18. Hugh Fraser, *Papers on the Emergency in Malaya* (16 January 1952), 1, in *Templer Papers* (National Army Museum, Chelsea), Box 9.

19. Short, *Insurrection in Malaya*, 43–53. A good summary of the British government's perspective on the leadup to the Emergency is CO 537/3753, no. 53 [15 August 1948], reprinted in Stockwell, *Documents* Vol. II, 53–65.

20. Quoted in Short, *Insurrection in Malaya*, 56.

21. CO 717/167/52849/2/1948, f 302 "Declaration of Emergency," in Stockwell, *Documents* Vol. II, 19–20.

22. Robert Thompson, *Defeating Communist Insurgency: Experiences from Malaya and Vietnam* (Westport, CT: Praeger, 1966), 53–54.

23. Clutterbuck, *Riot and Revolution*, 169.

24. Short, *Insurrection in Malaya*, 95.

25. Clutterbuck is quoted in A.H. Peterson, G.C. Reinhardt and E.E. Conger, eds., *Symposium on the Role of Airpower in Counterinsurgency and Unconventional Warfare: The Malayan Emergency* (Santa Monica: RAND, 1963), 18.

26. Short, *Insurrection in Malaya*, 58.

27. Short describes one, discovered through a captured MCP member, that despite being invisible from five yards away in any direction included accommodation for over one hundred men, running water delivered through hollowed out bamboo pipes, an elaborate security system, and even bamboo-seated toilet facilities (ibid., 97–98). William James Spearman, of the Malaya Special Police Constabulary, says that the MCP "were very jungle-expert. Nobody could touch them and

they were really good soldiers at this time." He recalls an MCP camp with a swimming pool. IWM DSR 009797/07, 3–4, 6.

28. Short, *Insurrection in Malaya*, 105.

29. Allen, *Tales from the South China Seas*, 295–296. Ken Annakin's 1952 movie *The Planter's Wife* (*Outpost in Malaya* was the title in America), although a very poor reflection of CT tactics and British army COIN tactics, does provide an interesting perspective on the lives and defense measures adopted by the planters in response to CT terrorism. *The Planter's Wife* is criticized by Oliver Lyttelton in his 18 September 1952 letter to General Gerald Templer. *Templer Papers*, Box 7.

30. Short, *Insurrection in Malaya*, 113–114.

31. Clutterbuck, *The Long, Long War*, 42–43.

32. PREM 8/1406/1, DO 16(48)3 [13 August 1948] "Malaya—present situation," reprinted in Stockwell, *BDEEP*, II, 51–53. Cognizant of the many demands on British forces at the time, Montgomery notes dourly, "The latter reinforcement was clearly out of the question."

33. O'Ballance, *Malaya*, 83–84.

34. This was, however, in keeping with the British tradition that "the civil authority represented by the constable took precedence over the military. The military was there merely in aid if necessary of the civil power, which of course is always the situation in my experience when in colonial territories the military are called out." Colonial Policeman Eric John Linsell, IWM DSR 10672/4 (1989), 10.

35. Gent's position paraphrased by Short, *Insurrection in Malaya*, 116.

36. CO 537/3687, no. 52 [1 September 1948] "Appointment of Sir Henry Gurney," reprinted in Stockwell, *Documents* Vol. II, 70–71.

37. CO 717/167/52849/2/1948, ff 108–110 [25 October 1948] "Inward telegram from Sir H. Gurney to Mr. Creech Jones on measures to deal with alien Chinese squatters." Reprinted in Stockwell, *Documents*, Vol. II, 77–79.

38. For insurance purposes, the war in Malaya was officially referred to as an *Emergency* and the enemy as *Terrorists, Communist Terrorists*, or *CTs*. Most insurance policies would cover losses due to terrorism but had a clause precluding payments for damage caused by war.

39. Clutterbuck, *The Long, Long War*, 51–52.

40. Short, *Insurrection in Malaya*, 136–137.

41. Ibid., 138, footnote 37.

42. Riley Sunderland, *Army Operations in Malaya, 1947–1960* (Santa Monica, CA: RAND, 1964), 127.

43. Short, *Insurrection in Malaya*, 154.

44. Ibid., 163–169; see also 1 February 1970 issue of *The People* Sunday newspaper, which devoted three pages to an examination of the massacre after the revelation of the My Lai massacre in Vietnam.

45. John Cloake, *Templer: The Tiger of Malaya* (London: Harrap, 1985), 199–200.

46. For the creation, activities, and disbandment of Ferret Force, see WO 268/647, "RHQ The Malay Regiment—Quarterly Historical Report for Period Ending 30 Sep '48" and "Quarterly Historical Report for Period Ending 31 Dec '48."

47. Tom Pocock, *Fighting General: The Public and Private Campaigns of General Sir Walter Walker* (London: Collins, 1973), 87.

48. Brigadier Michael Calvert recalls that the dissolution was the result of po-

lice suspicion that Ferret Force members retained ties with Chin Peng as a result of their wartime service with him in the MPAJA. IWM (Department of Sound Records) 009989/08 "Malayan Emergency 1948–1960," interview of Brigadier J.M. Calvert MA, DSO by CXW (no date), 29.

49. Raffi Gregorian, "Jungle Bashing in Malaya: Towards a Formal Tactical Doctrine," *Small Wars and Insurgencies* 5/3 (Winter 1994), 338–359.

50. PRO WO 268/116, *FTC Quarterly Historical Report*, Quarter Ending March 1948, Appendix B, 2.

51. Ibid.

52. Ibid., 3.

53. Pocock, *Fighting General*, 89. This perspective is echoed in a private letter from General Walker to the author, 18 October 1996. In Appendix B to the *FTC Quarterly Historical Report*, Quarter Ending March 1948, Walker states, "When the standard of training [of units in Malaya] is compared to that of units in Burma in 1944 and 1945, it is abundantly clear that we still have a very long way to go" (2).

54. Pocock, *Fighting General*, 89.

55. Ibid., 89–90.

56. WO 268/116, *Quarterly Historical Report*, FARELF Training Centre (Quarter Ending 31 December 1949), 1.

57. Pocock, *Fighting General*, 90.

58. See IWM DSR 009989/08 "Malayan Emergency 1948–1960." Interview of Brigadier J.M. Calvert MA, DSO by Conrad X. Wood.

59. Gregorian, "Jungle Bashing in Malaya," *Small Wars and Insurgencies*, 348–349.

60. PREM 8/1406/2. MAL C(50)12 [12 May 1950], reprinted in Stockwell, *Documents*, Vol. II, 214.

61. David Lloyd Owen interview, 11 November 1996.

62. Robert Jackson, *The Malayan Emergency: The Commonwealth's Wars 1948–1966* (London: Routledge, 1991), 19–21.

63. CAB 21/1681, MAL C(50)23 [24. May 1950], "The Briggs Plan," reprinted in Stockwell, *Documents*, Vol. II, 217.

64. Ibid.

65. Ibid., 218.

66. CAB 21/1681, MAL C(50)21 [17 June 1950], "The Military Situation in Malaya," reprinted in Stockwell, *Documents*, Vol. II, 236.

67. Ibid.

68. Short, *Insurrection in Malaya*, 211.

69. Ibid., 225–227.

70. Ibid., 229–230.

71. Ibid., 233.

72. "Precis of Operations carried out between 16 Jun 1951–2 Jan 1952," *Lockhart Papers* 9501-165-33, 1–2.

73. Ibid.

74. "Operation Springtide," *Lockhart Papers* 9501-165-33, 1–2.

75. Short, *Insurrection in Malaya*, 240.

76. Ibid.

77. Ibid., 241.

78. Lieutenant General Sir Harold Briggs, *Report on the Emergency in Malaya from April, 1950 to November, 1951* (Kuala Lumpur: H.T. Ross, 1951), TDRC Index No. 953, 16.

79. Harry Miller, *Jungle War in Malaya: The Campaign Against Communism, 1948–1960* (London: Arthur Barker, 1972), 72.

80. Briggs, *Report on the Emergency*, 17–18.

81. Short, *Insurrection in Malaya*, 293; Briggs's Directives No. 13, February 1951, and No. 17, October 1951. See "The Story of Permatang Tinggi New Village," *Templer Papers*, Box 30.

82. See Short, *Insurrection in Malaya*, 295.

83. Ibid., 302. The Malayan Chinese Association (MCA) was, as its name suggests, a political organization of the most influential Chinese members of Malayan society; its support was crucial to the defeat of the insurgents.

84. The change in MCP tactics is evaluated in General Sir Robert Lockhart, *Federal Government Press Statement*, Part Two (27 October 1952) *Lockhart Papers* 9501–165–77. This statement, jointly issued by the deputy director of operations and the press secretary, Alec Peterson, includes a very open question-and-answer session and is a model of military-press relations.

85. CAB 129/48, C(51)59 [21 December 1951], "Malaya: Cabinet memorandum by Mr. Lyttelton," in Stockwell, *Documents*, Vol. II, 318–353; quotation is from p. 319.

86. Ibid., 322.

87. Ibid., 322–323.

88. Ibid., 323–324.

89. Ibid., 324–325.

90. Ibid., 326.

91. Ibid., 328.

92. Ibid., 328–329.

93. Ibid., 329.

94. Ibid., 330.

95. General Robert Lockhart to Field Marshal Sir William Slim, CIGS (14 January 1952), *Lockhart Papers* 9501–165–49, 7.

96. Sunderland, *Army Operations in Malaya, 1947–1960*, 129–30.

97. British Colonial Police Officer Sir Richard Catling, IWM DSR 10392/9, 30.

98. John Marsh of the Queen's Regiment, IWM DSR 009589/06, 49.

99. Sunderland, *Army Operations in Malaya, 1947–1960*, 131.

100. Ibid., 133.

101. Sir John Lockhart, *The Situation in the Federation of Malaya from the Point of View of the Director of Operations* (26–27 November 1951), *Lockhart Papers* 9501–165–28, 2.

102. Riley Sunderland, *Antiguerrilla Intelligence in Malaya, 1948–1960* (Santa Monica, CA: RAND, 1964), 13.

103. British Colonial Police Officer Sir Richard Catling, IWM DSR 10392/9 (1988), 35–36.

104. David Lloyd Owen interview, 11 November 1996.

105. IWM DSR 008943/7, Blake, 55.

5

The Empire Strikes Back: British Army Counterinsurgency in Malaya, 1952–1957

TEMPLER TAKES OVER

On his return from Malaya, Colonial Secretary Oliver Lyttelton met with Prime Minister Winston Churchill and Field Marshal Montgomery on 23 December 1951. Lyttelton notes in his memoirs that at the end of the meeting, "I summed up by saying that we could not win the war without the help of the population, and of the Chinese population in particular; we would not get the help of the population without at least beginning to win the war." Afterward, Montgomery sent Lyttelton a note:

Dear Lyttelton,
Malaya
We must have a plan.
Secondly we must have a man.
When we have a plan and a man, we shall succeed: not otherwise.
Yours Sincerely,
Montgomery (F.M.)

Lyttelton notes in his memoirs, "I may, perhaps without undue conceit, say that this had occurred to me."[1]

The man Lyttelton selected was General Sir Gerald Templer, who had commanded the Fifty-sixth Division and the Sixth Armoured Division in Italy in World War II and served as the director of military government in the British zone of occupied Germany after the war. Because of an injury he suffered in an accident involving a minefield and a piano owned by the

Guards Brigade, Templer was not personally involved in the campaign against Germany. He had also served as director of military intelligence and in the intensely political jobs of vice-chief of the Imperial General Staff and commander of Eastern Command prior to his Malaya appointment.[2] His brief from the Government began with the statement that "The policy of Her Majesty's Government in Great Britain is that Malaya should in due course become a fully self-governing nation." Before that could happen, the terrorists had to be defeated; to accomplish that task Templer was instructed that "not only will you fulfill the normal functions of the High Commissioner but you will assume complete operational command over all the Armed Forces assigned to operations in the Federation."[3] Templer was thus granted exceptional civil and military powers to defeat the insurgency. After a meeting with Churchill in Canada in January, Templer arrived on 7 February 1952 in Kuala Lumpur, where he made a statement to "the Malayan peoples of all communities that they can count on the powerful and continuing assistance of His Majesty's government not only in the immediate task of defeating the terrorists but in the longer term objective of forging a United Malayan nation."[4]

He traveled to his official residence in the same car in which Gurney had been assassinated; it was still marked with bullet holes.

Each of the states of Malaya had a British adviser to assist in the direction of the counterinsurgency and the move to independence. Mervyn Sheppard, the British adviser in Negri Sembilan, wrote: "Within a week he had invited all the British Advisers to spend a night in King's House. . . . After dinner Templer took the four BAs [present at one dinner] to one end of the drawing-room and asked us what was wrong with the Government machine and what remedies we could suggest."[5]

Sheppard noted, "None of us scored many marks." In fact, Templer told Lyttelton that the British advisers were "on the whole an uninspiring lot. The tragedy is that there are so many good younger people about. . . . If only we could get some of these younger types into these positions without endless friction from the Rulers and so on, we'd get on so much quicker."[6] Some of those younger types were serving as district officers; Templer told Lyttelton: "I am assembling a committee of experienced DOs to get around a table and write for themselves the charter they would like to have. I expect it will turn out to be a very good document."[7]

All of these efforts were guided by Templer's vision of fulfilling the British government's intention that Malaya should become self-governing once the emergency had ended. He made the point quite plain in his first speech to the Legislative Council of Malaya on 19 March 1952. Templer had been accused of saying that he would confine political progress to the local level but denied that this was his primary objective:

But, I am a firm believer in first things first. . . . I believe it right to ensure that truly responsible local government at Rural Community and Municipal Council levels is firmly established, and as quickly as possible. Not for one moment would I suggest that this should be postponed in any way at all because the so-called "emergency" is upon us. On the contrary, it is all the more necessary because of the emergency to press on with this measure.[8]

Templer immediately began touring the country and soon set the tone for the counterinsurgency effort he would lead.

Three weeks after his arrival he had already decided to reorganize the headquarters of the counterterrorist effort, merging "the functions of the Federal War Council with those of the Federal Executive Council, which will then become the sole instrument of the expanded membership of the council." To the council he added Raja Uda, the Mentri Besar of Selangor; Tunku Abdul Rahman, the president of the United Malays National Organization [UMNO]; and Leong Yew Koh, a leader of the Perak Chinese Chamber of Commerce and of the Malayan Chinese Association. Templer thus drew national leaders of both the Malay and Chinese communities together in the responsibility for directing the war effort. A smaller eight-member Director of Operations Committee, including a director of intelligence, "when I get him," would meet at least three times weekly to direct actual military operations.[9]

A CT attack resulted in Templer's displaying personal leadership as well as organizational ability. On 25 March 1952 a repair party led by the assistant district officer moved out to repair the water supply of Tanjong Malim, a town about fifty-five miles north of Kuala Lumpur. The repair party was ambushed by terrorists; twelve of the party were killed and five wounded. Templer decided to impose collective punishment on the town as a reprisal for the lack of information on the insurgents from the inhabitants.

After haranguing the town's leaders, assembled in the town hall for that purpose, Templer imposed a twenty-two-hour daily curfew, cut the rice ration in half, and closed the schools. After listing the many attacks of the terrorists in the district, Templer declared: "This is going to stop. It does not amuse me to punish innocent people, but many of you are not innocent. You have information which you are too cowardly to give." In addition, Templer required every household in Tanjong Malim to submit a ballot providing information on Communists or their supporters. The resulting information led to the arrests of some forty Communist supporters in the town; the curfew was lifted. The idea to collect information on secret ballots was a junior Irish police officer's.[10]

It is difficult to overstate the impact that Templer's energetic personal leadership and desire to solve problems in Malaya had on the course of the emergency. Oliver Lyttelton states: "In short, he dominated the scene. . . . In a few months I had almost dismissed Malaya from its place in my mind amidst the danger spots. My role had become simple: it was to back him up and support him."[11]

John Cloake describes Templer's technique as follows:

1. Get the priorities right.
2. Get the instructions right.
3. Get the organization right.
4. Get the right people into the organization.
5. Get the right spirit into the people.
6. Leave them to get on with it.[12]

It is perhaps for the fifth of these techniques, getting the right spirit into the people, that Templer is best known. Police Superintendent Dick Craig recalls that during Templer's frequent visits to his district, "You'd meet him at the edge of your area, drive with him right through to the edge, then get out and the next man would get in." He also recalls when working at his desk one morning finding Templer's boots—with Templer in them— suddenly standing on the paperwork atop his desk. Photos in Cloake's biography show Templer on a jungle patrol with the Gurkhas, on the firing range with the Gordon Highlanders, and on an elephant in Perlis. Anthony Short sums up Templer's impact: "In a word, Templer can be said to have energised the situation."[13]

Just as important as Templer's energy and demands for innovative thinking was his understanding of the political change necessary for Malaya to move toward a stable independence. In a telegram to Oliver Lyttelton dated 27 July 1952, Templer notes:

The country lacks political leader [sic] with real political experience and, with the possible exception of M.C.A., there is no properly organised responsible political party with a coherent political programme. The first step necessary to political advancement, and so to independence is political education; this I believe can best be begun by experience in local politics. . . . The political parties which will emerge from this more active political life, will themselves largely determine to [sic] time of independence.

This healthy political life, from which independence would flower, would first require "the uniting of all races and classes in a common effort by the creation of a greater sence [sic] of Malayan loyalty and unity."[14]

That sense of unity was already developing in the shape of the Alliance Party. The United Malay National Organisation and the Malayan Chinese Association joined forces in January of 1952 while contesting municipal elections in Kuala Lumpur; the alliance won nine of eleven seats and became a national organization in 1953. By meeting the primary British requirement of a multiethnic society, the alliance allowed an increasing transfer of power to the local people and transformed "a colonial struggle in which the people could have been united against an alien government to a struggle for independence in which the colonial government had become an accessory to an emergent nation."[15] Harnessing nationalism as an issue for the government against the insurgents was the single most vital part of winning the "hearts and minds" of the population.

OPERATIONAL AND ORGANIZATIONAL INNOVATION

Although the political direction of the campaign toward full independence was necessary for the defeat of the insurgents, it was not sufficient; both organizational and operational changes were required to bring the insurgents fully to heel. A large number of these changes sprang from Templer personally, including changes in the organization of the Intelligence Service; reorganization of the Police Force and the Special Branch; changes to the role of the Information Services, the Military, and the Home Guard; and the overall coordination of the efforts of all of these organizations.[16]

The Intelligence Services and the Special Branch

Templer told Harry Miller, a journalist for the *Straits Times*, "The Emergency will be won by our intelligence system—our Special Branch."[17] Templer had experience with Colonial Intelligence services, as he writes,

when I was Director of Military Intelligence in the War Office, and also when I was VCIGS. All of us on the Operational and Intelligence sides in the three service Ministries took a very serious view of the whole business and took it up, as far as I remember, on a good many occasions, and in a big way, with the Colonial Office, pointing out where we were heading. . . . There must be other Malayas and Kenyas as possibilities in the future.[18]

Templer placed Jack Morton in the role of director of intelligence. Guy Madox, who later filled this position, analyzed Templer's "innovations of importance" in a letter to Anthony Short:

(a) Templer created a Director of Intelligence. The latter was responsible for Intelligence, but was not in charge of the Intelligence collecting machine—the Special Branch of the Police. (This sounds clumsy, but it worked awfully well. The Director of Intelligence and his CIS could "field" the many questions descending from on high, most of them requiring research. Thus Special Branch often was protected from problems that would have diverted it from its main task of collecting and collating intelligence.)

(b) The Director of Intelligence was a full member of the D. of Ops. Cte., ranking with the service commanders. (I heard many times that this was the first instance of the absolute importance of Intelligence being given full recognition. I know that it was true of Malaya.)

(c) A highly efficient Intelligence (Special Branch) Training School was established for the first time in Malaya. Not only did it train Special Branch personnel; it provided short courses for some executive officers of the Army, "General Duties" Police Officers, and certain civil departments of Government.[19]

Short notes that successful intelligence is largely cumulative and is the first step to any real progress in counterinsurgency.[20] Clutterbuck argues that the Special Branch did not begin to obtain effective intelligence in the Chinese villages of Malaya until police posts in those villages had themselves been made secure: "This must be the first step to any real progress in counterinsurgency."[21] In fact, one of the most remarkable features of the insurgency in Malaya was the willingness of Communist Terrorists to surrender themselves, becoming Surrendered Enemy Personnel (SEPs) and earning bounties for doing so; SEPs in turn often led army and Special Branch patrols on raids against their own recent comrades in Communist base camps, thus earning greater rewards. Chin Peng carried a $250,000 price on his head. Harry Miller tells the story of the murder of Ah Kuk, an important Communist leader, by three members of his gang who surrendered themselves with Ah Kuk's decapitated head to claim a reward they had read about in leaflets dropped by the RAF.[22] In Ah Kuk's possession were important MCP documents that provided valuable information including codes used by the Communist Central Committee and the location and commanders of new jungle bases.

The Special Branch continued to play an essential role through the end of the Emergency. Dick Craig noted in 1964:

As the Emergency progressed, and as the Communist targets grew smaller and more difficult to locate, the need for precise advance information increased. More and more stress was placed on the expertise and level of performance of individual SB officers. Courses of specialised training were given; up-to-date techniques of investigation and equipment were introduced. In this way SB was geared to provide Government with a broad range of political, security, and subversive information, not only on the current threats from militant communism but on possible long-term dangers as well.[23]

The value of intelligence to Security Forces is difficult to overstate. "Deep jungle patrolling, as the experience of the Special Air Service was to show, was of very little use when there was no specific information to go on. Even where troops and police were deployed in areas where there was a good chance of making contact—for example in the approaches to new villages—there was danger of a vicious circle developing: no intelligence meant no contacts and no contacts meant no intelligence."[24]

The Special Branch was revitalized under the leadership of Colonel Arthur Young, formerly commissioner of the City of London Police, who replaced Nicol Grey. Young gave the Special Branch to Guy Madoc, who improved an existing Special Branch school, personally teaching tactics and techniques to the heads and deputy heads of every state in Malaya. Madoc believed in the product: "The school was the sluice valve of the Emergency. Defeating the Emergency depended on intelligence. Intelligence capacity depended on the output of the school."[25]

The Information Services

In a battle against insurgents, persuading fighters to surrender and provide information on their comrades is much more effective than killing them; persuading the masses of the people that the government is capable of providing essential services—and of defeating the insurgents—is just as important. These two aspects of the battle for the hearts and minds were directed by the Psychological Warfare, or "Psywar," section of the Information Services. Never exceeding thirty in number, mostly Chinese ex-terrorists, the Psywar section played a large role in the success of the counterinsurgency effort.[26]

Wing Commander A.F. Derry notes: "Psywar policy evolved largely as the result of trial and error. Apart from those who had gained experience in the Political Warfare Executive during World War II (an entirely different political and military situation from that obtaining in Malaya from 1948 onwards), there was no one who had any previous experience of conducting propaganda or psywar operations."[27] At first, revenge motivated all counterterrorist efforts, and the idea that CTs should be allowed to surrender—or even encouraged to do so—was not welcomed. Hugh Carleton Greene, director of Emergency Information Services, Malaya (and later director general of the British Broadcasting Corporation [BBC]), only persuaded Briggs to accept the concept of rewards for surrendering by threatening to resign in 1950; he argued that "the policy of 'stringing them up, no matter what' gave him nothing to offer and left the insurgents with no choice but to fight on, whereas a surrender policy gave the only hope of acquiring the information which our intelligence so urgently needed."[28]

The Information Services used a number of techniques to communicate with the CTs; Derry ranks them by order of effectiveness; along with the years during which they were used (see Figure 5-1[29]).

In the campaign for the hearts and minds of the uncommitted population of Malaya, Radio Malaya and the vernacular press, especially the Chinese language newspapers, were most important in the early years of the emer-

Figure 5-1
Relative Effectiveness of Information Services

(1) Leaflets. Throughout the whole campaign	1948-1960
(2) Personal appearance of ranking SEP	1951-1953
(3) Government films	1952-1954
(4) Voice aircraft	1953-1954
(5) Playlets by SEP (written by Information Service)	1951-1954
(6) Vernacular Press	1948-1960
(7) Ground (jeep-mounted) loudspeakers	1950-1952

gency. Later, films were made and shown in the villages, where they had a dramatic impact. The information director describes the field teams: "Many of the field officers, after a course of training under an officer who had watched the Chinese Communist propaganda teams at work in central China, became first-class comic actors and 'mob orators.' Often the cinema vans were accompanied by one or two former Communist warriors who spoke direct to the people of the life they had led in the jungle and their reasons for changing sides."[30]

The reference to traveling film crews emphasizes an important difference between the Malayan Emergency and later wars:

Television was almost unknown during the Malayan campaign. Few if any requests were received from international TV companies to record the events of the Emergency, and requests for radio coverage, even from the BBC, were few and far between. In the light of the authoritarian way in which the politico-military campaign was conducted at the highest level, it is doubtful whether unlimited facilities would have been granted, even if they had been sought.[31]

The pamphlets and loudspeaker aircraft showed signs of great imagination and creativity; personally directed at individual terrorists, they were based on captured information or reports of SEPs. One leaflet, a special message to CT soldier Lim Yook Kee, showed a picture of a baby in a hospital cot over the caption "How safe and comfortable is this baby in a government maternity hospital!" It offered Lim Yook Kee congratulations on her pregnancy and urged her, "For your own safety and especially that of your new impending baby, come out at once and self-renew and have your child safely delivered in the Maternity Hospital."[32] The pamphlets became so effective that the MCP imposed the death penalty on any of its members who had one in his or her possession.

Messages broadcast from voice aircraft (VA) were also aimed directly at individual MCP members; aircraft flew especially plotted flight paths to blanket the jungle with propaganda, and it was obviously impossible for the MCP to forbid its members to listen. Surrendered Enemy Personnel often recorded messages to their own comrades, urging their friends to surrender also. Templer borrowed the idea for the voice aircraft—and, literally, borrowed one DC-3 Dakota aircraft—from United States Army General Mark Clark in Korea, where they were not particularly successful. In Malaya, where there was no opposing air force or antiaircraft fire and where the jungle made even firing small arms at the aircraft difficult, the loudspeaker aircraft were extremely effective. Whereas only 10 percent of interrogated SEPs had heard voice aircraft in the first six months of 1953, by early 1955 100 percent had heard voice aircraft, and 91 percent of a sample of forty-four who heard VA broadcasts distinctly considered them highly effective in destroying CT morale and inducing surrenders.[33] At the end of a six-month area denial operation, voice aircraft led ten CT to surrender, three of whom became SEPs and managed to persuade the other twelve members of the branch to surrender.[34]

It was the Psywar section that in 1952 convinced the government that referring to the Malayan Races Liberation Army was counterproductive and urged the adoption of the name Communist Terrorist Organization (CTO). The Malaya Information Service was transferred to the direction of Inche Yaacob, the first Malay director general, not long after Templer's departure in 1954; he moved the headquarters to a building adjacent to the Director of Operations Staff building on Bluff Road.[35] The Security Forces were not the only users of psychological operations; Derek Blake of the Royal West Kent Regiment recalled, "They [the CTs] would, on occasion, get in touch with battalion headquarters at KKB [Kuala Kabu Bahru]. . . . And they would send messages to battalion headquarters to the effect that such and such, Sergeant so and so, or Lieutenant so and so, 'tell him to be more careful next time he was patrolling such and such an estate, we saw him and he was very careless.' "[36]

The Military Effort

Military innovation in the campaign against the terrorists was initiated both from the high command and from the field. One of Templer's personal innovations was the creation of the Combined Emergency Planning Staff (CEPS) under Lieutenant Colonel (later Major General) Napier Crookenden, consisting of an airman, a police officer, and a civil servant. They served as Templer's eyes and ears, making unannounced inspection tours based on his whims. Crookenden describes Templer as "spring[ing] out of his bath one morning" and sending off the CEPS to Johore to "find out why they aren't killing more communists down there."[37] A report on the visit, including quite negative comments, would be forwarded to General

Headquarters Malaya and to the military commander concerned for comments before going to Templer, who shielded the CEPS personnel from reprisals. Templer then followed up the reports by requiring district advisers to report monthly progress on points raised to the Director of Operations Committee; the DOs were kept honest by the knowledge that Templer bathed every morning, deciding where to send his CEPS spies while doing so.[38]

The other important addition Templer made to his staff was an Operational Research Team intended "to analyse incidents and contacts and extract from them not only statistics and patterns, but lessons to be applied in future operations, large or small."[39] He told Lyttelton: "One of the reasons why there are comparatively heavy casualties in security forces, is because there has never been any proper scientific analysis of what has happened in incidents. This has now been started on a set proforma designed by my small new operational research staff. I have no hesitation in saying that we will get results from it."[40]

For its raw data, the team relied on information from a new patrol report, Form ZZ. Written by the commander of every patrol, the form included a sketch map of the action, who saw whom first, who fired first, at what range, and with what weapon.[41] David Pike, scientific adviser to the commander in chief of the Far Eastern Land Forces, recalls that his operational research sections published their findings in "Notes and Information on Training Matters" (NITM) distributed to the troops, though it appears that most of the lessons learned through Operational Research had already been absorbed by the battalions.[42] Templer himself describes an unsuccessful operation:

We have recently carried out a big operation in the deep jungle in Pahang, . . . As things turned out, it beat the air as is so often the case with major operations in deep jungle. And so we tied up three or four Battalions and a whole lot of Air for a couple of months, to small purpose. . . . They were defeated throughout the operation by the activities of the aboriginal screen. Wherever they moved, they were conscious that they were being watched and that their movements were being reported to the CTs.[43]

Dick Craig describes the learning process within battalions: "The massive 'shoulder to shoulder' sweep was abandoned in favor of a coordinated and methodical search by sections. Battle drills for assault through jungle terrain were devised. More efficient wireless techniques to improve communications were found. The heavy 'administrative tail' was eliminated by better rationing methods. The Security Forces had to learn or suffer. They learnt."[44]

Some of the learning was not popular. Lieutenant Colonel Walter Walker, founder of the Jungle Warfare School, returned from the Staff College to take command of the First Battalion, Sixth Gurkha Rifles in October 1950. He found a battalion that had settled into the most "convenient" way of making contact with the Communist Terrorists, setting cordons along roads so that troops could be trucked in instead of walking and firing artillery at random into the jungle to harass and interdict CT operations. These procedures changed, with Walker's "not only demanding new and more difficult tactics but insisting that officers took part in evolving them."[45] From Walker's decision to send a surrendered CT to evaluate each of his companies on operations in Johore arose such innovations as crossing streams walking backward and purposely leaving footprints to throw CTs off the track.[46]

DOCTRINE AND FOOD DENIAL

In 1950, Major General Boucher, then the general officer commanding Malaya, had asked "if there was a requirement for a pamphlet on jungle warfare," but decided that the Jungle Warfare School made such a manual unnecessary.[47] Templer disagreed. "I have been impressed by the wealth of jungle fighting experience available on different levels in Malaya and among different categories of persons. At the same time, I have been disturbed by the fact that this great mass of detailed knowledge has not been properly collated or presented to those whose knowledge and experience is not so great. This vast store of knowledge must be pooled. Hence this book."[48]

"This book," *The Conduct of Anti-Terrorist Operations in Malaya,* sized to fit in the pockets of a soldier's jungle greens, became known as *ATOM* and as "the soldier's bible." A battalion commander of the Royal Australian Regiment sent a staff officer to Malaya specifically to obtain copies in preparation for his battalion's upcoming tour there.[49] Written by Walter Walker at Major General Sir Hugh Stockwell's request in just two weeks, it was based on the syllabus of the Jungle Training School and on Walker's own experience in command. *ATOM* included a history of Malaya and of the Organization and Armed Forces of the MCP, the Emergency Regulations, Methods of Searching, Platoon Organization and Equipment, Patrolling and Ambushing; and Intelligence and Training.[50] Despite its thoroughness, Templer noted,

The book is by no means perfect. Criticisms and improvement are invited by GOC Malaya, who will produce a revised edition in six months' time. In the meantime, the methods described are to be adopted not only by the Army, but also by the Federal Jungle Companies, the Jungle Squads and the Area Security Squads of the Federal Police. Many of the methods laid down for the movement of vehicles and convoys are also applicable to the Police.[51]

Despite Templer's desire for improvements, the second edition of *ATOM* was not published until 1954, the third in 1958. Walker had done his work well; the only major changes made in later editions resulted from the increasing use of helicopters in operations. Templer noted in his own copy, "It is largely as a result of the publication of this handbook, and of its subsequent revisions, that we got militant communism in Malaya by the throat."[52]

The CTs were beginning to be strangled through food denial operations, made much more far-reaching through the effective policing of the New Villages and by Templer's focus on expanding "oil spots" of security. These food denial operations, "accompanied by vigorous military activity, a properly planned SB attack, and compulsion of the civil population to cooperate with the Government . . . were standardized and were carried out throughout the country to an almost identical pattern."[53] Targets selected for food denial operations were always complete Communist Party Districts; branches were too small, and fighting platoons were too mobile. Either would simply attach itself to another branch in order to survive. Operations were carried out in three phases.

During phase I, which would last from two to six months, Special Branch officers attempted to infiltrate the Min Yuen support organization of a single village in a district, while military activity was "frozen" from those areas that had been infiltrated by Special Branch. Instead, military patrols and ambushes focused on New Villages that Special Branch had not penetrated, in order to push the MCP toward the "Frozen Areas." The Civil Administration simultaneously took measures to win over the population of the New Villages in the area. Blaxland notes that the army also played a role, making "the New Villages defensible by putting up wire and earthworks, by keeping watch on their surrounds, and by trying to sow the seeds of responsibility that might blossom into the formation of a home guard."[54]

Phase II lasted another three to five months after "D-Day," when strict food rationing was introduced, including a house-to-house search to remove food stores and arrest known members of Communist organizations that had not been penetrated by Special Branch. Rice was cooked centrally by government cooks in small and medium-sized New Villages; no raw rice was distributed at all. Information Services explained the restrictions and told the villagers that they would be lifted once the CTs had been destroyed or captured. The military "now switched their attention to the jungle, leaving the Police to patrol the cultivated areas and the New Villages. The military looked to SB to produce precise advance information of Communist Terrorist movement to mount ambushes. A concerted, highly coordinated effort to destroy the target of the operation had begun."[55]

During Phase III, which began when the pressure had collapsed CT Branch and District Organizations, "successes were often spectacular. . . . SB operational teams, masquerading as communist terrorist units and using

SEPs as guides, tracked down the higher formations and either tricked them into surrendering or eliminated them. . . . Once their lines of communications were known, they could be quickly traced back along them."[56]

These successes were achieved despite an army that was composed largely of National Service officers and troops.[57] Turnover in the battalions was dramatic: during a three-year tour, 77 officers and 1,646 soldiers served with the Green Howards; only 1 officer and 75 other ranks served with the battalion for the entire three-year tour.[58] The army was confronted with the challenge of integrating other units from the Commonwealth as well. By the end of 1952 Commonwealth forces in Malaya included two battalions of the King's African Rifles, a battalion from Fiji, a squadron from Rhodesia serving with the SAS, eight Gurkha battalions, and a squadron of the Royal Australian Air Force. From 1 January 1953 an Australian, Air Vice Marshal Scherger, served as Air Officer Commanding.[59]

Templer's focus was on the native Malay Regiment. He noted on 17 November 1952, "I am convinced that an essential pre-requisite to the grant of independence of Malaya is the formation of an adequate Malayan Army to support the civil authority and the foundations of that Army cannot be laid too soon. . . . It must be a balanced force and it must be composed of men of all races who have made Malaya their home."[60] Templer had already announced the creation of the Federation Regiment, open to members of all races, in his speech to the Legislative Council on 20 March 1952. He established the Federation Military College, modeled on and originally staffed by Sandhurst instructors.[61]

Other innovations directly sponsored by Templer included use of helicopters in an operational role; he had written to Lyttelton on 29 March 1952:

The possibility of using helicopters for operational as opposed to medical evacuation purposes out here has never been properly analysed, presumably because it was considered that we would not get the helicopters . . . by the last quarter of the year I hope we will have all the planters hooked up by wireless to the Police UHF stations and this will go a very long way towards setting their minds at rest. If we could then produce an immediate reinforcement on the planters' tennis court, so to speak, by using three or four helicopters they would have very little to grouse about.

In addition to this use of helicopters to reinforce small defensible enclaves, Templer believed that "there are many other straight operational uses for them." As a result of Templer's efforts, ten S55 helicopters were provided by the United States under the Defence Assistance Program; they were used to insert soldiers into the deep jungle.[62]

Other innovations included the creation of fighting platoons of Iban trackers from Sarawak, who had been used as guides since 1950 but were now employed "not only for tracking but in their traditional fighting role of head-hunters." Templer formed a regiment in March 1953, naming them Sarawak Rangers.[63] Even more daring was the formation of the "Special Operations Volunteer Force" composed entirely of Surrendered Enemy Personnel who had graduated from rehabilitation centers. Building on an experiment initiated by the Special Branch in Pahang in 1952, the SOV Force grew to twelve small platoons in strength. Although they had great problems in marching, Templer was unconcerned: "To hell with drill. We want them to handle weapons and lay ambushes."[64]

Less revolutionary but far more important in the long run was the creation of an effective Home Guard paramilitary popular militia, the need for reform of which had been noted by Lyttelton on his visit in December 1951.[65] In July 1951, there were 79,000 Home Guards under Major General Edward de Fontlangue, who had just retired from the British army. Under de Fontlangue, numbers expanded to nearly 250,000 by the end of 1953, by which time the Home Guard was responsible for the defense of seventy-two New Villages.[66] Training for this vastly expanded force was of paramount importance; Templer noted in September 1952, "All the States and Settlements have now completed the building of one big Home Guard training camp in each state/settlement and 200–300 instructors are now being churned out each month." The force was to be led by Commonwealth officers, whose recruitment and arrival were a constant concern: "We will never get any sense into the thing until we get the British and Australian officers for whom we have been striving so long."[67] Although there were instances of terrorist intimidation and murder of Home Guard officers, in general the "Chinese Army" resisted effectively; of 89,000 weapons issued to the Home Guard by November 1954, only 103 had been lost.[68]

Perhaps Templer's greatest contribution to the conduct of the counterinsurgency campaign was his ability to coordinate all of the efforts—social, political, economic, police, and military—to move Malaya forward to a position in which it would be ready for independence, thus removing the primary claim of the MCP for public support. The Federal Executive Council was mirrored by State and District War Executive Councils; it was the latter that were critical to the success of the effort. Templer reminded district officers of their general priorities in February 1953:

The District Officer must be the central and binding force in relation to all administrative, police, and military effort in his district. It is his responsibility to coordinate and encourage all measures taken by the police and the military, to sort out any differences which occur between these two and to provide the direction and advice which both need in their relation to the general aim of the Government. He must, therefore, continue to act as the Chairman of DWEC.[69]

The district officers' responsibilities extended far beyond direction of the police/military effort, to "the inauguration and guidance [sic] of elected local councils"; "the fostering of Civics Courses"; "improvements to Malay kampong life, e.g., in water supplies, bridle paths, the provision of electric lights"; and "land administration generally." Templer created and enforced a clear chain of responsibility for the winning and maintaining of the security, hearts, and minds of the Malayan people. Major Bill Tee of 1/6 Gurkha Regiment, who sat on a District War Executive Committee that Templer sometimes visited, remembers the district officer's chairing a committee composed of an army officer, a police officer, a Home Guard officer, and the district school administrator and public works officer. He notes, "Military force cannot change opinion. It can only create a framework in which economic reform and good government can take effect."[70]

ELECTIONS AND THE END OF THE INSURGENCY

Once that framework had been built, through a difficult learning process and largely as a result of Templer's leadership, desire for an independent government in Malaya grew rapidly. The British government supported this development and recognized its responsibility to assist in the process of creating multiracial institutions to further it. A Colonial Office Memorandum for the Ministry of Defence's Joint Planning Staff on 10 March 1953 noted: "We all aim at helping the colonial territories to attain self-government within the British commonwealth. To that end we are seeking as rapidly as possible to build up in each territory the institutions which its circumstances require."[71]

Some of those institutions were building themselves; for example, the United Malay National Organization and the Malayan Chinese Association collaborated on a blueprint for a new Federal Constitution and proposed elections to a new Federal Council in December 1954 that would meet for the first time in February 1955.[72] Templer was concerned that unless the British government quickly announced its own plans to study changes in the system of elections to the legislative council, "Her Majesty's Government would at least appear to have lost the initiative in the matter and it might later be represented that action had eventually been taken only under 'Nationalist' pressure."[73]

Templer had originally hoped to have state-level elections nationwide in late 1955 as preparation for elections to the Federal Legislative Council a year or two later. As was Sir David MacGillivray, he was concerned about the need for "a wider training ground for the Asian politicians who will, within the next decade, be required to play an increasingly prominent part in the government of Malaya" (the current native leaders were "none of them young" and were not adept at mentoring young leaders: "Like beech trees, they are stately, but nothing is growing under them").[74]

These developments were made possible by the increases in security and diminished threat from the insurgents, a consequence of the military and

Figure 5-2
Classification of Incidents, 1951–1954

	Total	"Major A"
July 1951	506	33
July 1952	310	14
July 1953	97	7
April 1954	101	0

political innovations of the Templer regime. The most notable sign of success was Templer's declaration of a large part of the State of Malacca as a "White Area" on 3 September 1953. Within the area, curfews and food controls were lifted, and no villagers were searched, although road checkpoints were maintained. Templer believed that this would "give the great fillip to morale . . . encouraging those people in areas where restrictions are still, of necessity, imposed, to co-operate more freely with Government to remove the CTs so that they could also reap the rewards of greater freedom."[75] This turned out to be the case; emboldened by the relative freedom in Malacca, local support for the counterinsurgency effort intensified. Over 13 million Malay citizens were enjoying life in White Areas by Templer's departure in mid-1954.[76] Although the Malayan Emergency continued for another seven years, its back had been broken during Templer's administration. He left Malaya on 31 May 1954, driving to the airport in an open car. By this time, the number of CT attacks had dropped dramatically, as Figure 5-2[77] shows.

The End of the Insurgency

Templer was replaced by Sir Donald MacGillivray, his deputy and a career member of the Colonial Service. The director of operations became the ranking military officer, filling that role along with the job of general officer commanding, Malaya; Sir Hugh Stockwell was thus Templer's military successor. After political unrest in Malaya over the extent of local representation on the Federal Legislative Council, a compromise was reached. Just before the first elections under the new agreement, Chin Peng sent an offer to negotiate a political solution to the emergency.[78] Tunku Abdul Rahman's Alliance Party won fifty-one of fifty-two seats in elections held on 31 July, making him the chief minister of the federation. He held negotiations with Chin Peng in December near the border of Thailand. There the Tunku refused Chin Peng's demand that the Communists be allowed to form a legal political party after their surrender, and Chin Peng returned to the jungle.[79]

Figure 5-3
The Reckoning

	Killed in Action	Wounded	Captured/Surrendered
Communists	6,698	2,819	2,675
Security Forces	1,865	2,560	None
Civilians	2,473	810	None

The British government granted independence to Malaya on 31 August 1957, although the insurgency dragged on for another three years. The Tunku declared it officially over on 31 July 1960. Final casualty figures are listed in Figure 5-3[80].

In its Special Edition proclaiming the end of the Emergency, the *Straits Times* commented, "Perhaps there is no great point in recalling all the tragic and idiotic blunders, all the false optimism, all the unrealism of the first phases of the war, but it is not possible to appreciate fully the heroism of the Security Forces unless the stupidities of some of those in command are remembered."[81] After an early period of uncoordinated and too-conventional military operations, the British army had played a major role in allowing independence to be granted to a stable, freely elected government through its successful counterinsurgency efforts, demonstrating remarkable tactical and operational innovation within a framework of political ascendancy over military requirements.

ORGANIZATIONAL LEARNING IN MALAYA, 1952–1957

Did the British Army Develop a Successful Counterinsurgency Doctrine?

A comparison of British army doctrine and techniques in 1957 with those it had previously developed at the end of 1951 demonstrates the evolution of a comprehensive doctrine for counterinsurgency (see Figure 5-4). *Victory* was achieved; the Colonial Office had informed the Malayan high commissioner on 14 September 1954:

A united Malayan Nation, self-governing within the Commonwealth, is the aim of United Kingdom policy in Malaya. . . . We are pursuing this aim because the people of Malaya want self-government, because without the kernel of nationhood self-government is an empty shell, and because in a multi-racial society nationhood is unattainable without unity."[82]

The British army had assisted Her Majesty's Government in setting this policy as its *objective*, as Templer emphasized the political development of

Figure 5-4
Did the British Army Develop a Successful Counterinsurgency Doctrine in Malaya?

	1948–1951	1952–1957
Victory: the achievement of national goals	Doubtful	Yes
Objective: the setting of realistic national goals	No	Yes
Unity of command: military subordination to political objectives	No	Yes
Minimum force: minimum necessary force	Yes	Yes
Mass: appropriate structure for threat	No	Yes

Malaya and the ability of local people to run the government as well as fighting against the insurgents. He noted:

The Army is doing a big job of work out here in the whole general sphere of the fight against Communism—I mean the non-shooting side, by such things as the adoption of Asian schools by units and teaching them games and boxing and so on and so forth, and giving them a general helping hand. Perhaps the R.A.M.C. are doing more than most, for all Army hospitals out here are now open to Asians, and I think this sort of thing probably turns a lot of people against Communism.[83]

Templer's appreciation of the role of indigenous military leaders in creating a stable nation and of the necessity of integrating all races into the Malayan Federation Army further contributed to this objective. The British government's selection of Templer as high commissioner *and* director of operations ensured unity of command at the highest levels; he himself insisted on unified direction of the counterinsurgency effort at the state and district levels and continually emphasized the political primacy of the task. In the words of British Colonial Police Officer Sir Richard Catling:

Templer introduced a means of planning the conduct of the campaign against the terrorists centrally in Kuala Lumpur and for consulting those on the ground, both army, administration, and police in the course of putting the plans together and giving these bodies, having seen the first thinking, time to what he called "belly-ache," in other words to offer criticism if they thought they wished to and to substantiate it, so that when the final papers were written as High Commissioner's Operational Directives the ground had had their opportunity to say what they thought and when the finished article reached them they knew perfectly well not only that those operational directives had to be carried into effect without deviation because the Director of Operations himself, General Templer, would shortly descend on them to make quite certain that that was what was happening.[84]

Gradually the army learned that "shoulder-to-shoulder" sweeps were not productive but actually counterproductive; instead of *massing* troops, the army developed small patrols that used the skills of native trackers and intelligence provided by Surrendered Enemy Personnel or Special Branch infiltrators into Min Yuen organizations to target selected terrorists with the *minimum force* required:

In the second year of General Briggs's period as Director of Operations, and, even more, in General Templer's time, the Army learnt a new approach. Now an Army unit—generally no more than a platoon or a couple of sections—goes into the jungle only on first-class information, and it goes in very quietly, with a screen of deception, accompanied by police, with Iban or aborigine trackers or with dogs or a surrendered bandit or two; and when it is inside it stays there for a week, two weeks, a month if need be; and if anybody is going to be ambushed, it is probably the bandits.[85]

Use of heavy firepower was minimized: "We concluded that given accurate information as to a target then there would be merit in considering bombing as a means for attacking it. But to use bombing on a random basis would really be far too costly. And could well perhaps do more harm than good," said Lieutenant Colonel Robert Ian Hywel-Jones.[86] Priority was placed on capturing rather than killing Communist Terrorists in order to capitalize on the information the SEPs could provide; small patrols were constantly standing by to take immediate advantage of information as it became available. The British army thus developed a successful counterinsurgency doctrine under Templer—and continued to follow it under his successors—as a critical part of the British government's comprehensive counterinsurgency efforts in Malaya from 1952 to 1957 (see Figure 5-4).

Crucially, the army learned that to be successful in counterinsurgency, it had to coordinate the activities of police and civil authorities as well as its own: "The secret of the change is not so much the new type of training as the integration of Army and Police together as a single anti-Bandit force and the close association with them of the District Officers and other civil authorities on the ground."[87]

Was the British Army in Malaya a Learning Institution, 1952–1957?

The British army demonstrated a remarkable openness to learning during the years from 1952 to 1957. Bottom-up input was welcomed, from tactical innovations, such as walking backward, through operational ones, such as food denial operations; district advisers, British army privates, and Surrendered Enemy Personnel were asked for ideas on better ways to accomplish the objectives of the organization. Not only were superior officers *available* for *questioning*; they also did a great deal of questioning themselves, as Templer directed his own spy network from his bathtub to ensure that the answers he received had close connection to the reality on the ground; in the words of his military assistant, "General Templer was smart enough to go out into the jungle with the Gurkhas to find out for himself."[88] *Theoretical thinking* was required, not only from district advisers but from junior officers in Walter Walker's Gurkha Battalion as well:

Intelligence was absolutely the most supreme requirement. Everything else that we did was geared to producing intelligence. . . . One developed instincts about where there would be terrorists and where there wouldn't—by studying the actual nature of the ground itself. By studying the nature of the vegetation on the ground, where there was water and where there wasn't, where there were people and where there were not. What sort of people they were. And the roads and the tracks and so on. And then by studying reports of terrorist incidents—and all of the papers that were available which were captured from terrorists up and down the peninsula—one developed really quite an understanding of what they were, and how they would do things.[89]

Walker played an important role in *local doctrine development* in writing *ATOM*, which was based on his personal experience of running the Jungle Warfare School and of commanding a battalion on operations; the *schools* (both police and army) and locally produced manuals ensured that the solutions advocated fitted the problem at hand. Templer reported to Lyttelton in late 1952, "We have just completed the fourth and last course for members of District War Executive Committees. We have put through 150 District Officers with their equivalent Policeman and Soldier. . . . They have all voted them a tremendous success, and we shall get results."[90]

An RAF veteran of the jungle course reported, "I had to do the jungle warfare course at Kota Tinggi and then I did a post-grad one after a successful engagement. We were brought back by selection, if you'd done something, so that it was really discussion and tactics and 'What had you done that had been successful?' Then you'd go out together and, as a patrol, see if you could do something."[91]

Finally, Templer's small staff fed him the true story of what was happening in the country:

The Director of Operations ran this war, directing the Army, the Air Force, the Police, the civil agencies, food control, the registration—everything, with a total staff of seven. The staff was never allowed to mushroom. It consisted of a brigadier, his principal staff officer, who stayed put; then a group of four, an Army lieutenant colonel, an Air Force wing commander, a superintendent of police, and a Malayan civil servant. Those four traveled most of the time, sometimes as a team and sometimes individually, seeing what was going on, finding out what was working and what was not working.[92]

Figure 5-5
Learning in Malaya

	1948–1951	1952–1957
Bottom-up input: Suggestions from the field	Improper Channels	Yes
Superiors questioned	No	Yes
available	Yes	Yes
Theoretical thinking	Low Level Only	Yes
Local doctrine development	No	Yes
Local training centers	Yes	Yes
Small, responsive staff	No	Yes

Templer himself was afraid of neither receiving bad news nor sending it back to London. Above all, the spirit of innovation he created in the British army in Malaya encouraged the taking of risks and the honest assessment of results—essential to improving the performance of the organization toward the accomplishment of its clearly defined objectives. Looking back, Templer thought the progress in learning should have been quicker: "Certainly the soldiers should have realized much earlier in the proceedings that 'jungle bashing' on false or no information was a complete waste of time and energy. I also think that all those concerned with policy (including myself) should have appreciated earlier the vital part which food control could play in that environment."[93]

Despite Templer's impatience, the learning experience of the British army in Malaya is a remarkable example of an organization's institutional culture's remaining open to innovation while retaining a clear sense of the objectives it was trying to accomplish (see Figure 5-5). It is a rare example of a military organization's adapting its organization, doctrine, and training during the course of a conflict in order to fulfill the desires of its parent government, and truly stands as "one of the finest achievements of the British Army since 1945."[94]

NOTES

1. Viscount Chandos, *Memoirs of Lord Chandos* (London: Bodley Head, 1962), 378–379.

2. The best source on Templer is John Cloake's *Templer, Tiger of Malaya: The Life of Field Marshal Sir General Templer* (London: Harrap, 1985). Templer's papers, stored in the National Army Museum in Chelsea, were opened to me by Templer's son Miles.

3. PREM 11/639, H 20–22 [1 February 1952] "Directive issued by Mr. Lyttelton on behalf of HMG," in Cloake, *Templer*, 457–458.

4. Message to the People of the Federation of Malaya from His Excellency Sir Gerald Templer KCB, CMG, DSO, *Templer Papers*, Box 9. King Edward VI had died while Templer was en route to Malaya.

5. Mervyn Sheppard (Tan Sri Dato Mubind), *Taman Budiman: The Memoirs of an Unorthodox Civil Servant* (Kuala Lumpur: Heinemann, 1979), 192, in Cloake, *Templer*, 213.

6. Cloake, *Templer*, 213.

7. Ibid.

8. CO 1922/298, no. 6 [12 March 1952] "Political Progress," in A.J. Stockwell, *British Documents on the End of Empire: Malaya. Part II, The Communist Insurrection, 1948–1953*, 377.

9. CO 1022/60, no. 3 [28th February 1952] "Reorganization of Government," in Stockwell, *Documents* Vol. II, 373–376.

10. Cloake, *Templer*, 220–221; 26 March 1996 inteview with R.J.W. Craig MC, described by Templer as "an absolutely first-rate policeman from Limerick" in a 29 March 1952 dispatch to Colonial Secretary Lyttelton. The thirty-nine letters between Templer and "Captain the Right Honourable Oliver Lyttelton, P.C., D.S.O., M.C., M.P." between 20 February 1952 and 25 May 1954 constitute a remarkable look inside this critical period of the Malayan Emergency. Their importance to any student of the period cannot be overemphasized. As Templer himself wrote on the file folder in which they are still housed, "They are important, and the only month by month record of my time in Malaya."

11. Chandos, *Memoirs of Lord Chandos*, 382.

12. Cloake, *Templer*, 227.

13. Interview 26 March 1996 with R.J.W. Craig in London; Anthony Short, *The Communist Insurrection in Malaya, 1948–1960* (London: Frederick Muller, 1975), 343.

14. CO 1022/81, no. 24 [27th July 1952], "Pace of Constitutional Advance," in Stockwell, *Documents*, Vol. II, 394–395.

15. Short, *Insurrection in Malaya*, 346.

16. This organization follows Cloake, *Templer*, chapter 10.

17. Harry Miller, *Jungle War in Malaya: The Campaign Against Communism, 1948–1960* (London: Arthur Barker, 1972), 90.

18. Templer to Lyttelton, 23 March 1953, 10, in *Templer Papers*, Box 7.

19. Short, *Insurrection in Malaya*, 360, footnote 19.

20. Ibid., 359.

21. Richard Clutterbuck, *The Long, Long War: The Emergency in Malaya 1948–1960* (London: Cassell, 1966), 100.

22. Miller, *Jungle War in Malaya*, 127–131.

23. R.J.W. Craig, *A Short Account of the Malayan Emergency* (unpublished manuscript, 1964), 8.

24. Short, *Insurrection in Malaya*, 364.

25. Cloake, *Templer*, 232.

26. Wing Commander A.F. Derry, *Emergency in Malaya: The Psychological Dimension* (Latimer, England: National Defence College, 1982). Wing Commander Derry served as an intelligence officer in World War II and during the Malayan

Emergency; his monograph includes a reprint of Hugh Carleton Greene's "Report on Emergency Information Services, September 1950–September 1951," dated 14 September 1951, and numerous reprints of Psywar pamphlets dropped in the jungle to induce surrenders. The author is grateful to Dick Craig for providing him with a copy of the monograph.

27. Derry, *Emergency in Malaya: The Psychological Dimension*, 2.

28. Ibid., 3.

29. Ibid., 4–2.

30. Alec Peterson, "Telling the People in Malaya," *New Commonwealth* (25 November 1954), 553–555, in *Templer Papers*, Box 30, quotation is from 555.

31. Derry, *Emergency in Malaya: The Psychological Dimension*, 4–1 to 4–2.

32. Ibid., 6–1.

33. Ibid., 6–1 to 6–4.

34. Wing Commander Charles O'Reilly, Imperial War Museum (IWM) Department of Sound Records (DSR) 10121/3, 1988, 8.

35. Derry, *Emergency in Malaya: The Psychological Dimension*, 4–1.

36. Blake, IWM DSR 008943/7, 42.

37. Cloake, *Templer*, 241.

38. Ibid.

39. Ibid., 242.

40. Letter from Templer to Lyttelton, 7 May 1952, *Templer Papers*, Box 3, 4–5.

41. Raffi Gregorian, "Jungle Bashing in Malaya: Towards a Formal Tactical Doctrine," *Small Wars and Insurgencies* 5/3 (Winter 1994), 351. A copy of the form is in J.B. Oldfield, *The Green Howards in Malaya (1942–1952): The Story of a Post-War Tour of Duty by a Battalion of the Line* (Aldershot: Gale and Polden, 1953), 129–131.

42. Gregorian, "Jungle Bashing in Malaya: Towards a Formal Tactical Doctrine," *Small Wars and Insurgencies* 5/3 (Winter 1994), 351 and 359, footnote 83.

43. Templer to Lyttelton, 22 December 1953, *Templer Papers*, Box 7, 1.

44. Craig, *A Short Account of the Malayan Emergency*, 5.

45. Tom Pocock, *Fighting General: The Public and Private Campaigns of General Sir Walter Walker* (London: Collins, 1973), 90–91.

46. Ibid., 93.

47. PRO/WO 231/38, 9, quoted in Gregorian, "Jungle Bashing," *Small Wars and Insurgencies* 5/3 (Winter 1994), 349.

48. Walter Walker, "Foreword to First Edition," *The Conduct of Anti-Terrorist Operations in Malaya* (Malaya: Director of Operations, 1952). Third Edition, 1958, archived at TDRC, Index Number 2369.

49. Gregorian, "Jungle Bashing," *Small Wars and Insurgencies* 5/3 (Winter 1994), note 72, 358.

50. Ibid., 349–350.

51. Walter Walker, "Foreword," *The Conduct of Anti-Terrorist Operations in Malaya*, xc.

52. Cloake, *Templer*, 242.

53. Craig, *A Short Account of the Malayan Emergency*, 16–17. "In the end, what won the Emergency was starving them out." Craig interview, 26 March 1996. This description of food denial is based on this inteview and on Craig's monograph,

pp. 16–20, and on Richard Clutterbuck, *Riot and Revolution in Malaya and Singapore* (London: Faber & Faber, 1973), 211–226. For a description of food denial operations by a soldier who conducted them, see David Kelly, "The Malayan Emergency 1950–1955," IWM DSR 010043/3 (No Date), CXW, 16–20.

54. Gregory Blaxland, *The Regiments Depart: A History of the British Army, 1945–1970* (London: Kimber, 1971), 93.

55. Craig, *A Short Account of the Malayan Emergency*, 19.

56. Ibid., 19–20.

57. Robert Jackson, *The Malayan Emergency: The Commonwealth's Wars 1948–1966* (London: Routledge, 1991), 45.

58. John B. Oldfield, *The Green Howards in Malaya, 1949–1952* (London: Gale and Polden, 1953), appendix.

59. Cloake, *Templer*, 244–245.

60. T 220/493, IF 242/23/01 B [17 November 1952], "Expansion of Malaya's land forces," in Stockwell, *Documents*, Vol. II, 414.

61. Cloake, *Templer*, 246–247.

62. Ibid., 245.

63. Ibid., 247.

64. Ibid., 248; Blaxland, *Regiments Depart*, 105. Templer's quotation is from Blaxland.

65. CAB 129/48, C(51) 59 [21 December 1951], in Stockwell, *Documents*, Vol. II, 324.

66. Short, *Insurrection in Malaya*, 412–413.

67. Cloake, *Templer*, 249.

68. Short, *Insurrection in Malaya*, 414.

69. "A good district officer is worth more than a battalion." Oliver Lyttleton, 21 December 1951. CAB 129/48, C(57)59, in Stockwell, *Documents*, Vol. II, 324.

70. Bill Tee interview in Oxford, 19 January 1996.

71. CO 1022/91, no.25 [10 March 1953] "Political Objective in British territories of South East Asia," in Stockwell, *Documents*, Vol. II, 441–442.

72. CO 1022/86, no.23 [17 April 1953] "Alliance constitutional plans," in Stockwell, *Documents*, Vol. II, 458–460.

73. CO 1022/86, no.27 [1 May 1953] "Federal Elections," in Stockwell, *Documents*, Vol. II, 461.

74. CO 1022/86, no.5 [14 March 1953] "Training Malayan Politicians," in Stockwell, *Documents*, Vol. II, 447–448

75. CO 1022/58, no.8 [28 August 1953], "White Area in Malacca," in Stockwell, *Documents*, Vol. II, 469.

76. Templer discusses the creation of "white areas," and their impact on the population's desire to rid itself of the restraints made necessary by the Emergency, in a letter to Lyttelton dated 21 April 1954. *Templer Papers*, Box 7.

77. Police Headquarters, *Classification of Incidents* (Kuala Lumpur, Federation of Malaya, 12 May 1954), in *Templer Papers*, Box 7. A "Major A" Incident resulted in loss of life, serious injury, or considerable damage to property with careful planning and demonstrated aggressiveness by the CTs.

78. Chin Peng's letter is reprinted in Stockwell, *Documents*, Vol. III, 126–128.

79. A detailed description of the negotiations is presented in chapter 18 of Miller, *Jungle War in Malaya*, 167–172.

80. "The End of the War," *Straits Times* (20 April 1960), 1, in *Templer Papers*, Box 30.

81. Ibid.

82. CO 1030/67, No.1 [14 September 1954], "United Kingdom Policy in Malaya," in Stockwell, *Documents*, Vol. III, 72.

83. Templer to Lyttelton (3 November 1952), *Templer Papers*, Box 7, 8.

84. British Colonial Police Officer Sir Richard Catling, IWM DSR 10392/9, 31–32.

85. J.B.P.R., "The Emergency in Malaya: Some Reflections on the First Six Years," *The World Today* 10/11 (November 1954), 480.

86. Lt. Col. Robert Ian Hywel-Jones MC, IWM DSR 009287/6, 18.

87. J.B.P.R., "The Emergency in Malaya: Some Reflections on the First Six Years," *The World Today* 10/11 (November 1954), 481.

88. David Lloyd Owen interview, 11 November 1996.

89. Hywel-Jones, IWM DSR 009187/6, 50.

90. Templer to Lyttelton (12 September 1952), *Templer Papers*, Box 7, 6.

91. Wing Commander Charles O'Reilly, IWM DSR 10121/3, 31.

92. Colonel Richard Clutterbuck, OBE, in A.H. Peterson, G.C. Reinhardt, and E.E. Conger, eds, *Symposium on the Role of Airpower in Counterinsurgency and Unconventional Warfare: The Malayan Emergency* (Santa Monica, CA: RAND, 1963), 9–10.

93. Script (30 March 1977), *Templer Papers*, Box 9, 30.

94. Michael Dewar, *Brushfire Wars: Minor Campaigns of the British Army Since 1945* (London: Robert Hale, 1984), 44.

III

VIETNAM

6

The U.S. Army in Vietnam: Organizational Culture and Learning During the Advisory Years, 1950– 1964

The American army's involvement in the Second Indochina War from 1950 to 1972 demonstrates the triumph of the institutional culture of an organization over attempts at doctrinal innovation and the diminution of the effectiveness of the organization at accomplishing national objectives. The United States Army had become reliant on firepower and technological superiority in its history of annihilating enemy forces; although political considerations may have governed the strategic conduct of war, they had little connection with the tactical-level management of violence. That was purely military—army—business. The concept that success in counterinsurgency consisted of separating the insurgents from popular support never took root. The U.S. Army proceeded with its historical role of destroying the enemy army—even if it had a hard time finding it.

The United States Army entered the Vietnam War with a doctrine well suited to fighting conventional war in Europe, but worse than useless for the counterinsurgency it was about to combat. The army did not allow learning to occur during the course of the conflict, neither from its own officers, the United States Marine Corps, nor the British Advisory Mission, invited to Saigon for the express purpose of imparting lessons learned from the Emergency in Malaya. The British Advisory Mission attempted to suggest more appropriate counterinsurgency techniques but was ignored. When some relatively junior U.S. officers protested that the American techniques were ineffective, their suggestions were quashed by the high command. The U.S. Marine Corps, proceeding from a different organizational culture and a history of small wars, developed some genuine innovations that showed promise in the counterinsurgency effort but were also discouraged by the army officers in command of the American effort in Vietnam. Even General Creighton Abrams had great difficulty in implementing change when he assumed command in Vietnam in 1968. Throughout the American experience in Vietnam, organizational learning foundered on what Andrew Krepinevich called "the Army Concept,"[1] a Jominian vision of the object of warfare as the destruction of the enemy's forces. This concept was so deeply ingrained in the army's leaders that they refused to listen to innovators from below who were convinced that the army's concept was not just ineffective but actually counterproductive in the new kind of warfare the nation faced in Vietnam.

The learning cycle was also ineffective in recognizing poor performance, suggesting doctrinal innovation, gaining organizational consensus behind new doctrine, and disseminating the changes throughout the army in Vietnam. Although there was substantial innovation from below, neither the personnel nor the organization of the Military Assistance Advisory Group (MAAG) and of its successor organization, Military Assistance Command—Vietnam (MACV), was conducive to counterinsurgency learning. With all doctrine and training emanating from the United States, there was little opportunity for doctrinal innovation; the conventionally bred army generals who ran MAAG and MACV were not the sort to encourage new ways of winning wars and in fact often actively discouraged innovation by their subordinates.

The history of the U.S. Army in Vietnam can be seen as the history of individuals attempting to implement changes in counterinsurgency doctrine but failing to overcome a very strong organizational culture predisposed to a conventional attrition-based doctrine. After a brief review of the history of the insurgency in South Vietnam, the following two chapters will evaluate the attempts of a number of individuals and organizations to convince the United States Army that its emphasis on exclusively military solutions to the insurgency was counterproductive.

INDOCHINESE WARS

Insurgency has a long history in Vietnam; the sisters Trung Tran and Trung Nhi led a successful revolt against Chinese rule in A.D. 40. Sporadic fighting between the Vietnamese and Chinese (and among the Vietnamese themselves) continued until the middle of the nineteenth century, when the French made Indochina part of their empire. Insurgency erupted against the French in 1859, the same year they captured Saigon; in 1862 the French commander in Saigon reported, "We have had enormous difficulties in enforcing our authority. . . . Rebel bands disturb the country everywhere. They appear from nowhere in large numbers, destroy everything, and then disappear into nowhere."[2]

Unlike the British, the French attempted to "assimilate" the Vietnamese, ruling directly themselves rather than through local rulers like the Mentri Besars of British Malaya. This inspired a strong and broad-based nationalism against both the French and those through whom they ruled, who often converted to Catholicism, studied in French schools, and preferred to use the French language. French desires to export rice led to the creation of huge farms worked by landless peasants; those who could not find work as sharecroppers labored in rubber plantations and coal mines. Economic grievances provided kindling for nationalistic fires in young men like Nguyen Sinh Cung, born in 1890 in central Vietnam. Filled with wanderlust, he left Saigon aboard a French freighter in 1911, working his way through menial jobs in Marseilles, Brooklyn, and the Carlton Hotel in London, where he labored as a pastry chef.

The young man went through a variety of noms de plume before settling on Ho Chi Minh, "Bringer of Light." He spent six years in Paris, where he became a founding member of the French Communist Party while retaining his nationalist fervor. In the pamphlet "French Colonialism" he noted, "The figure of justice has had such a rough voyage from France to Indochina that she has lost everything but her sword."[3] He met Stalin and Trotsky in Moscow and worked for Chiang Kai-Shek in Canton, mobilizing Vietnamese students in southern China. Ho created the Indochinese Communist Party in Hong Kong in 1929 (during a football match!) but did not return to Vietnam until after the Japanese occupation of his country. In 1941, thirty years after his departure, he created the Vietnam Independence League, the Viet Minh.

U.S. policy toward Indochina was "ambivalent' during World War II; President Roosevelt believed that the French had "milked it for one hundred years," leaving its people "worse off than they were at the beginning."[4] Nonetheless, the United States divided Vietnam for postwar occupation, the British accepting the surrender south and the Chinese north of the sixteenth parallel. Ho Chi Minh declared Vietnam's independence in Hanoi on 2 September 1945, quoting liberally from the American Declaration of Independence; nonetheless, the British government returned control of Southern Vietnam to the French, and the Chinese were persuaded to withdraw from the North.

The Viet Minh fought against the resumption of French control of South Vietnam until 6 March 1946, when Ho Chi Minh accepted recognition of the Democratic Republic of Vietnam as a "Free State" in the French Union, largely to expel the Chinese. Ho reminded those who criticized the surrender: "The last time the Chinese came, they stayed a thousand years. The French are foreigners. They are weak. Colonialism is dying. The white man is finished in Asia."[5] By December 1946 the agreement was in ruins, and the Viet Minh began guerrilla warfare against the French that would continue until the Europeans were finally defeated in 1954. John Carter Vincent in the U.S. State Department's Office of Far Eastern Affairs summed up the situation from a U.S. perspective in late 1948: "Although the French in Indochina have made far-reaching concessions to the Vietnamese desire for autonomy, French actions on the scene have been directed toward whittling down the powers and the territorial extent of the Vietnam 'free state.' This process the Vietnamese have continued to resist. . . . Given the present elements in the situation guerrilla warfare may continue indefinitely."[6]

The fall of China to Mao Tse-Tung's Communist forces soon changed American views on the importance of the conflict in Vietnam. In an urgent session, the U.S. National Security Council decided, "The extension of communist authority in China represents a grievous political defeat for us; if Southeast Asia also is swept by communism we shall have suffered a major political rout the repercussions of which will be felt throughout the rest of the world."[7]

The United States decided to take action to keep the dominoes of Southeast Asia standing.[8] Direct U.S. military involvement in Indochina began on 1 August 1950 with the creation of a four-man Military Assistance Advisory Group (MAAG); by 1954 the MAAG had increased to 342 advisers. U.S. Army Lieutenant General John O'Daniel visited the MAAG in August 1953, stating that the French would defeat the Viet Minh by 1955 and that "additions [to the Vietnamese military] other than in divisional organization would be in error since it is the divisional team, with its combat proven effectiveness, which is sorely needed in Vietnam."[9]

O'Daniel was wrong. The Viet Minh defeated the French after a brutal guerrilla war progressing through the three phases prescribed by Mao, finally destroying French will to resist in the battle of Dien Bien Phu. The French garrison surrendered on 7 May 1954. The next day peace negotiations began in Geneva.[10]

The United States, despite the hardening of the cold war, decided not to intervene with ground or air power to prevent the French defeat at Dien Bien Phu, largely because of British hesitancy to assist. The U.S. Army was particularly cautious about the prospect of intervention, estimating that seven U.S. divisions would be required to defeat the insurgents if the French withdrew and the Chinese did not intervene.[11] Ngo Dinh Diem, a Catholic Vietnamese nationalist, returned from exile in the United States to lead the Government of Vietnam (GVN) with U.S. support, landing in Saigon to a moderate welcome on 26 June 1954. The U.S. decided not to sign the Geneva agreement, concluded about a month later, until elections, planned for 1956, unified the country. The agreement partitioned Vietnam at the seventeenth parallel, with French forces withdrawing from the north and Democratic Republic of Vietnam (DRV) forces from the south.

One of the pillars of any new state is its army, but creating a viable Army of the Republic of Vietnam (ARVN) was a formidable task. It was not until late 1954 that the Vietnamese General Staff became all-

Vietnamese for the first time, without French officers and noncommissioned officers (NCOs). It was at the same time that Vietnamese rather than French became the official language of the armed forces. Lieutenant General O'Daniel was put in command of the Franco-American Training Relations and Instruction Mission (TRIM) in February 1955. TRIM saw its primary function as the creation of an army able to resist a conventional invasion from North Vietnam.[12] Profound cultural differences made the task of re-creating the ARVN in the image of the U.S. Army more difficult. The ARVN General Staff contended that an ARVN company commander needed only a .45 caliber pistol as an individual weapon, whereas their U.S. advisers demanded that company commanders carry rifles—and fight—as did the rest of the men in their commands.[13]

As defined in a memorandum published by the Vietnamese General Staff on 10 April 1955, the mission of TRIM advisers was "to assist and advise, on strictly technical aspects, Vietnamese military commanders to whom they were assigned, in order to rapidly and effectively rebuild the Vietnamese Armed Forces on a new basis." The insistence on "strictly technical aspects" set the tone and direction for the U.S. Army advisory effort which was to remain technically-oriented throughout its existence. The "new basis" for reorganization needed no clarification: it was understood to be the doctrine of the U.S. Army.[14]

The Army of the Republic of Vietnam with which TRIM was to work was primarily composed of light infantry and was badly lacking in leadership: "The majority of Vietnamese, still hungering for independence, had no side to join. They were opposed to both the Communist Vietminh and the French. . . . French paternalism was turning over the controls of self-rule too slowly and grudgingly to the Vietnamese to generate any enthusiasm among Vietnamese nationalists."[15]

Drawing down to meet a 100,000-man force (limited by financial constraints), the MAAG resisted the Government of Vietnam's (GVN's) desire to retain regional units for internal defense because they were not "strategically mobile."[16] This attitude ignored the lessons learned by the French army during its long involvement in the First Indochina War. As Ronald Spector notes, "Despite their trucks, planes, tanks, and helicopters, the French were less mobile in a practical military sense than were the Viet Minh, who could shift entire divisions across vast areas unimpeded and often undetected by the French."[17] O'Daniel's focus was on the creation of conventional forces: four light and five medium divisions, each composed of three regiments with three battalions each.[18]

This concept was in contravention of Secretary of State John Foster Dulles's position that "only relatively small military forces were needed; their principal purpose should be to promote internal stability rather than to guard against external aggression; nations acting in concert (under the umbrella of US nuclear superiority) would guard against external aggression."[19] Dulles wanted to defend South Vietnam against external aggression with the newly signed South East Asia Treaty Organization (SEATO) treaty, using South Vietnam's own forces in a counterinsurgency role, but the MAAG had another agenda. General Westmoreland notes in his memoirs: "In the first years of American aid beginning in late 1954, with the conventional invasion of Korea still fresh in mind, the Pentagon's thinking was to create a South Vietnamese army capable of resisting an invasion long enough to enable an international force to intervene in order to circumvent overt aggression. That led inevitably to the creation of a conventional force organized into divisions and corps."[20]

CREATING A MIRROR: THE U.S. ADVISORY MISSION

The U.S. Army advisors in Vietnam were unprepared by nature or training to do anything except build a Vietnamese army in their own image and likeness. Two participants agree: Major General John Tillson remembers, "We tried to build the ARVN into conventional divisions just like we were."[21] A former U.S. Marine Corps adviser to ARVN Marines notes, "The good ARVN units were only effective in conventional operations because that's how we'd taught them to fight."[22]

This organizational proclivity toward conventional armed forces was reinforced by "the generalized assumption that the ability to promote internal security was automatically provided for in the creation of forces capable to promote external security."[23] As a result:

The program of advice and assistance came to be dominated by conventional military conceptions. Insuring internal stability is a "lesser included capability" of armed force, the reasoning went; the principal purpose of such a force is to protect the territorial integrity of the nation.

It was such a conventional force that the small USMAAG attempted to produce from 1955 until about 1960. The Army of the Republic of Vietnam (ARVN) was made to "mirror image" the U.S. Army to the extent permitted by differences in equipment and locale . . . ARVN developed into a multi-divisional force oriented primarily toward conventional defense. The later transition to a force designed for counterinsurgent warfare was therefore made more difficult.[24]

In addition to creating a military force that was unsuited to the nature of the war it would have to fight, the U.S. Advisory team insisted that it and it alone was in sole charge of all matters military in South Vietnam. Thus MAAG Chief Lieutenant General John O'Daniel insisted that his chain of command was through the commander in chief Pacific (CINCPAC) rather than through Ambassador Elbridge Durbow, and refused to give Durbow any control over his dealings with President Diem. The disagreement led to a well-known personality conflict between the two that did little to further the cause of defeating the insurgency in Vietnam.[25]

Another result of the focus on creating the ARVN in the image of the United States Army was the parallel neglect of the paramilitary militia that would serve on the front lines in any struggle over control of the rural population in Vietnam. The Regular Army of the United States of that time treated the "weekend warriors" of its own National Guard and Reserve Forces with tolerance at best and condescension at worst; the Vietnamese militia was thought even less worthy of respect. The neglect resulted in a Self-Defense Corps (SDC) and Civil Guard (CG) that "were poorly trained and equipped, miserably led, and incapable of coping with insurgents; they could scarcely defend themselves, much less the peasantry. Indeed, they proved to be an asset to the insurgents in two respects: they served as a source of weapons; and their brutality, petty thievery, and disorderliness induced innumerable villagers to join in open revolt against the GVN. Nor was the ARVN much better."[26]

When MAAG did involve itself with the Regional Forces and Popular Forces (RF/PF):

the U.S. civilian advisors who had been called in to give assistance with police and internal security matters tended to favor making these paramilitary forces less military *per se* and more police intelligence–minded. MAAG tended to favor making them more consciously military and territorially oriented in order to free ARVN for mobile, offensive operations rather than tying its forces down in static defense duties. . . . Thus questions of local physical security would almost inescapably be decided with reference to the effect they would have on the functions of ARVN, itself created with an eye to external defense. This may be said to be an awkward structure from which to launch an effort aimed primarily at internal security. It was, however, the structure that existed.[27]

MAAG was concerned that, as a result of the poor state of training and readiness of the paramilitary forces designed to enhance local security, ARVN units were increasingly forced to interrupt their training cycles to respond to failures of pacification. Each such involvement of ARVN units in pacification operations, "though of some training value, in general interrupts the planned training of participation units and delays arrival at a satisfactory state of training readiness," argued a U.S. Army Command and General Staff College study for Lieutenant General Lionel C. McGarr prior to his assumption of command of MAAG.[28] Communist insurgency recommenced in the South in October 1957; over four hundred South Vietnamese officials were assassinated over the next two years.[29]

The American MAAG's insistence on instilling a conventional focus in the ARVN was enthusiastically received by Diem, who ignored the advice of some of his senior commanders in accepting and even encouraging the

American direction. "Diem involved himself with the equipping of his military forces showing a distinct proclivity toward heavy military forces of the conventional type. He wanted the Civil Guard equipped very much like his regular army—possibly with a view to assuring himself a check on army power. There were a few soldiers, like General Duong Van Minh, who sharply disagreed with the President on this point. Nonetheless, Diem persisted."[30]

Creating a conventional army, however, had little relevance to the insurgent war that was erupting in South Vietnam even as the ARVN prepared for a conventional cross-border invasion. In late 1959, the Draper Committee (The President's Committee to Study the United States Military Assistance Program) questioned the basic premise of the American advisory effort: that fighting insurgents was a "lesser included capability" of fighting a conventional war. Instead, the committee reported,

tailoring a military force to the task of countering external aggression—i.e., countering another military force—entails some sacrifice of capabilities to counter internal aggression. The latter requires widespread deployment, rather than concentration. It requires small, mobile, lightly equipped units of the ranger or commando type. It requires different weapons, command systems, communications, logistics.[31]

Not just the Draper Committee, but the advisers themselves had begun to question the American army's gospel that by preparing to defeat a conventional invasion of South Vietnam they were also building a capability to defeat insurgents.

The U.S. military advisors in Vietnam had learned—or at least thought they had learned—during this period of gradual disintegration the true nature of the battle in which they were engaged by proxy. This was an unconventional, internal war of counterinsurgency rather than a conventional struggle against an external foe. It was a battle for the "hearts and minds" of the indigenous (and especially the rural) population rather than a contest to win and hold key terrain features. It was an intermeshed political-economic-military war rather than one in which political and economic issues were settled by military victory.[32]

ARVN officers "found American training methods too constraining, too conventional and ill-suited to the war conditions in Vietnam."[33] As several noted later, "Whereas the French emphasized commando tactics, characterized by rapid movement and hasty raids with little or no combat support, the American way was methodical, careful and thorough, characterized by detailed planning and preparation. In a word, it was by the 'book.' Intermediate objectives were chosen, fire-plans prepared, and all moves were made step-by-step."[34]

Whereas such learning was taking place at low levels of the American advisory effort, it was not taking root at the higher levels of the MAAG. In fact, General Sam L. Meyers, deputy chief of the American military mission in South Vietnam, testified before the Senate Foreign Relations Committee in April 1959 that the guerrillas had been "gradually nibbled away until they ceased to be a major menace to the government."[35]

Less than three months after this assertion Viet Cong insurgents attacked a compound manned by a U.S. advisory team in Bien Hoa: "nibbled away" guerrillas killed two American soldiers in the attack on 8 July. This episode marked the escalation of the Communist offensive against the Diem government. There were 110 assassinations of local government leaders in the last four months of 1959.[36] The importance of the attacks was in their intent: to fill the political vacuum in the countryside left open by the ineffectiveness of local militias and RF/PF forces, who were ineffective largely because of the misplaced focus on conventional warfare of the ARVN instilled by the U.S. Army.

Efforts to change the system, both by some of Diem's officers and by American advisers and the recommendations of the Draper Report, foundered on the professional optimism and single-minded focus on the creation of an American-style army of the MAAG high command. Any attempt to reform the ARVN was bound to confront a problem of the Americans' own making:

These later efforts were faced with the reality of a sizable army—conventionally organized, trained, and equipped—which had been created under different circumstances and for different purposes. One is forced to wonder, if Vietnamese institutions are as difficult to remold as their American counterparts, whether the later advisory effort was not faced from its inception with an almost insurmountable task.[37]

The MAAG focused on the creation of an army that could resist an invasion from North Vietnam, rather than one able to defeat insurgents by protecting the population. To create an army capable of withstanding a conventional invasion, Lieutenant General O'Daniel centralized the ARVN units then engaged in pacification efforts for training in battalion and larger operations.[38] His successor, General "Hanging Sam" Williams, explicitly stated his belief that the role of the U.S. MAAG was to prepare for a repeat of the Korean conflict on 4 October 1960:

I am one of those that believe if we as Americans, either alone or as part of SEATO, become engaged in a hot war in [Southeast Asia] it will be against Chinese forces primarily and not against the Viet Cong of North Vietnam. The MAAG mission in Vietnam, then, after all the lesser issues are wiped aside, is to expand [sic] our last ounce of energy (mental and physical) to see that Vietnam is ready for the preliminary bout and can keep its back off the canvas for the longest possible time—a preliminary bout, incidentally, that could open with little warning.[39]

This conventional focus gave the insurgents freedom to recruit and create terror throughout the South. The insurgency quickly gained in ferocity. In 1960, 10,000 Viet Cong fighters captured 5,000 weapons from the security forces; in 1961, an estimated 16,000 Viet Cong captured another 6,000 weapons.[40]

KENNEDY AND COUNTERINSURGENCY

John F. Kennedy took a deep personal interest in counterinsurgency almost immediately on taking office in January 1961: the first question he asked his aides after his inauguration was reportedly "What are we doing about guerrilla warfare?"[41]

Kennedy was no stranger to the war in Vietnam, having visited the country as a congressman and as a senator. His understanding of the essentially political nature of insurgency—and of the dramatic changes in military tactics and operations required to defeat it—would present a substantial challenge to the U.S. Army's preferred method for fighting insurgents. Roger Hilsman remembers an early discussion he had with Kennedy on the subject during which the president stated, "The most likely and immediate threat from the communists was neither nuclear war nor large-scale conventional wars, as in Korea, but the more subtle, ambiguous threat of the guerrilla. To meet this threat new military tactics had to be developed, which he hoped the Special Forces would do. But new political tactics also had to be devised, and, most importantly, the two—the military and political—had to be meshed together and blended."[42]

The president almost immediately faced strong resistance from the army, which persisted in its belief that any soldier could handle insurgents. General Lyman Lemnitzer, Chairman of the Joint Chiefs of Staff (JCS), reportedly felt that the new administration was "oversold" on the importance of counterinsurgency. Lemnitzer warned in a story leaked to the press (and apparently reflecting the views of the Joint Chiefs) on 18 April 1961 that excessive emphasis on COIN could impair the ability of South Vietnam's army to resist a conventional attack of ten or more regular divisions from North Vietnam.

President Kennedy quickly and painfully developed a healthy skepticism regarding the quality of the military advice he was receiving; he created the Cuba Study Group on 22 April 1961 to discover why and how he had received such poor military counsel from the Joint Chiefs of Staff on the Bay of Pigs invasion. General Maxwell Taylor served as chairman of the high-level group, which included Attorney General Robert Kennedy, head of the Central Intelligence Agency (CIA) Allen Dulles, and Chief of Naval Operations Admiral Arleigh Burke; it was given the secondary purpose of determining the proper role of the United States in guerrilla and counter-guerrilla warfare.[43]

A successor, the Special Group (Counterinsurgency), was created in a charter signed by President Kennedy on 18 January 1962. Again chaired by Maxwell Taylor and including Chairman of the Joint Chiefs Lemnitzer, Director of the CIA John McCone, and Attorney General Kennedy, the group had a far-ranging agenda that included Latin America but focused on Vietnam. The Special Group reflected the president's personal interest in developing American capability for counterinsurgency operations. It was chaired by Taylor until he departed the White House to become Chairman of the Joint Chiefs in 1962.[44]

Kennedy worked very hard to get the army behind his counterinsurgency program, concentrating on the subject in his address to the West Point class of 1961, in which he warned the young lieutenants about

another type of war, new in its intensity, ancient in its origin—war by guerrillas, subversives, insurgents, assassins, war by ambush instead of by combat, by infiltration instead of aggression, seeking victory by evading and exhausting the enemy instead of engaging him. Where there is a visible enemy to fight in open combat, the answer is not so difficult. Many serve, all applaud, and the tide of patriotism runs high. But when there is a long, slow struggle, with no immediately visible foe, your choice will seem hard indeed.[45]

Kennedy's administration quickly picked up the theme; Hilsman gave a speech, "Internal War: The New Communist Tactic," on 10 August 1961.[46] Hilsman decried "the traditionalists' belief that well-trained regulars can do anything," calling it "ironic that we Americans have to learn this lesson again in the twentieth century." After recalling American counterinsurgency efforts in the Philippines in 1901–1902 and his own experience in Burma, Hilsman argued, "For effective counterguerrilla operations we need radical changes in organization, combat doctrine, and equipment."[47]

The military resisted this demand for change; instead, the Joint Chiefs of Staff requested that Kennedy approve a conventional intervention in Laos or, if this was "politically unacceptable," a "possible limited interim course of action" consisting of a deployment of 20,000 troops to the central highlands of South Vietnam near Pleiku to free ARVN forces for offensive action against the Viet Cong.[48]

Slowly, Kennedy managed to convince the military that he was serious in his demands for real change; as a result many army schools added COIN instruction. The Army Cooks and Bakers' School even added classes on counterinsurgency to its pie-making classes.[49] However, Kennedy did not trust the army: "I know that the Army is not going to develop this counterinsurgency field and do the things that I think must be done unless the Army itself wants to do it."[50]

THE ARMY RESPONDS

Unfortunately, the army had neither the knowledge nor the desire to change its orientation away from conventional war. The army had not yet recovered from the lean years of "massive retaliation" under President Eisenhower; in 1957, financial considerations led an army study to conclude: "The required forces, then, for the small war appear to be much the same as those for the atomic war against the Soviet Union."[51] An army historian notes the difficulties: "Perhaps the most difficult obstacle facing the Army as it attempted to prepare for counterinsurgency operations was the mental redirection and re-education required of its officers and soldiers, most of whom had only been exposed to nuclear or conventional tactical doctrine. . . . Attempts to redirect thinking, however, were hampered by the absence of any clear doctrine."[52]

William E. DePuy became the army's director of special warfare in the spring of 1962. "Needless to say, I didn't know anything about it," he later recalled. "The Army was trying to find, as were the other services, a role in this new and exciting high-priority national endeavor . . . We were rather mechanistic about the whole thing."[53]

The army attempted to create the doctrine very quickly without doing the deep analytical thinking required for a complete understanding of the changed nature of warfare: "The crash nature of the new entry into counterinsurgency caused the Army to focus much of its initial efforts on tactical methods. The elusive goal of identifying the goals of military action within counterinsurgency was thus overwhelmed by the more immediate task of developing tactical organizations, equipment, and doctrine."[54]

Operations Against Irregular Forces, a 1962 attempt at counterinsurgency doctrine, stated, "A defensive attitude . . . permits the guerrilla to concentrate superior forces, inflict severe casualties, and lower morale."[55] Offensive operations, in the mode of Korea and World War II, were the answer: "Most tactics for counterinsurgency remained extensions of, or resembled, small-unit tactics for a conventional battlefield."[56] FM 100–5, *Operations*, the army's warfighting bible, included a chapter on counterinsurgency for the first time in 1962.

Some officers recognized that the army was not doing a good job of establishing itself to defeat an insurgency. The Howze Board, set up at the request of President Kennedy, reported on 28 January 1962. "The tactical doctrine for the employment of regular forces against insurgent guerrilla forces has not been adequately developed, and the Army does not have a clear concept of the proper scale and type of equipment necessary for these operations."[57] The Howze Board also recommended the creation of air assault divisions and air cavalry combat brigades in its Final Report on 20 August 1962. These forces would be useful in both conventional and counterinsurgency warfare. The army as a whole made only paper changes to its doctrine, without fully training and equipping its officers and men for the challenges they would soon face in Southeast Asia.

The president wished to shake up the State Department as well as the army and considered replacing the American ambassador to South Vietnam with Edward J. Lansdale, an air force intelligence officer with CIA ties who had almost single-handedly (at least according to his memoirs) defeated an insurgency in the Philippines and installed a stable government under Ramon Magsaysay. Roger Hilsman describes the decision: "The new President all but decided to send Lansdale himself as the new American Ambassador [in early 1961], but the suggestion raised a storm in the Pentagon, where Lansdale was viewed as an officer who through his service with CIA had become too political. Since there was, of course, a certain amount of truth in the charge, McNamara was persuaded and Lansdale was put aside."[58]

The top decision makers in the Pentagon continued to insist that the U.S. military had solutions to the problems in Vietnam. General Earle Wheeler, later Army Chief of Staff and, under President Johnson, Chairman of the Joint Chiefs of Staff, said in a speech at Fordham University on 7 November 1962: "It is fashionable in some quarters to say that the problems in Southeast Asia are primarily political and economic rather than military. I do not agree. The essence of the problem in Vietnam is military."[59]

Wheeler had not been reading his own journals. A seasoned Australian journalist specializing in Southeast Asia had reported in the unofficial but highly respected magazine *ARMY* just over a year earlier that Lieutenant Colonel Arthur P. Gregory, a MAAG officer assigned to the southern Delta, did not agree with the chief's assessment. "Most of us are sure that this problem is only fifteen per cent military and eighty-five per cent political," said Gregory. "It's not just a matter of killing Viet Cong but of coupling security with welfare."[60]

Lieutenant Colonel Gregory was one of many junior army officers who would find that their understanding of the war on the ground differed substantially from that of their superiors in Saigon and Washington—and that their superiors were unwilling to listen to their advice.

CIA, CIDG, and SWITCHBACK

The Central Intelligence Agency, with a much shorter and more varied institutional memory than the U.S. Army, was correspondingly more open to experimentation in counterinsurgency techniques than was the older service. It had its roots in the Office of Strategic Services, placing guerrillas in occupied Europe during World War II. "The CIA had been involved in many operations, both political and military, in support either of insurgents against a hostile government (Indonesia, Guatemala) or of a government against such a challenge (Philippine Islands, Laos)," remembers William

Colby, who had himself fought as a guerrilla in France and Norway. "Uniquely in the American bureaucracy, the CIA understood the necessity to combine political, psychological, and paramilitary tools to carry out a strategic concept of pressure on an enemy or to strengthen an insurgent."[61] The CIA demonstrated the advantages of such an organizational culture by developing the Civilian Irregular Defense Group (CIDG) program in the early 1960s. One of the most successful innovations in counterinsurgency techniques, CIDG worked well until control over it was transferred to MACV, which changed the program to emphasize offensive operations rather than village security.

The experiment began in Buon Enao village in Darlac province in November 1961. Villagers were armed, organized, and given medical and agricultural assistance under the supervision of U.S. Army Special Forces soldiers. By April 1962, forty villages in the province had been pacified, and the oil spot of security was continuing to spread. In July, the CIA requested another sixteen Special Forces teams to join the eight who had arrived in May. By the end of the year, some 38,000 irregulars were participating in the program, and the Government of Vietnam declared the province secure.[62] But the CIDG experiment, far from initiating the learning cycle and changing U.S. Army counterinsurgency doctrine, was instead about to be gutted. General Rosson, after an inspection tour of the program in April 1962, reported to Taylor that the Special Forces were being used "improperly" and should engage in more offensive operations in keeping with the army's "find 'em, fix 'em, and finish 'em" philosophy.[63]

The conventionally minded powers who controlled the United States Army displayed a marked ambivalence toward the unconventional Special Forces, perhaps never better demonstrated than in General Harold K. Johnson's Senior Officer Oral History Project debriefing. Johnson, Chief of Staff of the U.S. Army from 1964 to 1968, stated:

Well, the Special Forces that were available at the time President Kennedy latched on to them as a new gimmick, were what I would describe as consisting primarily of fugitives from responsibility. These were people that somehow or other tended to be nonconformist, couldn't quite get along in a straight military system, and found a haven where their actions were not scrutinized too carefully, and where they came under only sporadic or intermittent observation from the regular chain of command. . . . Perhaps there is a desirability for this highly specialized effort, but I continue to really question it as such.[64]

Dr. Robert K. Wright, command historian of the Twenty-fifth Infantry Division in Vietnam, made the point even more tellingly: "The Special Forces were the only soldiers who had the knowledge and experience to point out the answer, but the Regular Army absolutely wouldn't listen to them. They'd have listened to the French before they listened to our own Special Forces."[65]

General Rosson's report led to a transfer of CIDG from CIA to MACV control in July 1963. The transfer, known as Operation SWITCHBACK, changed the nature of the program from a defensive orientation on population security to a more aggressive, offensive stance. Thus the U.S. Army deputy chief of staff for operations, Lieutenant General Barksdale Hamlett, instructed MACV on 15 August 1963, "We prefer to see Special Forces personnel used in conjunction with active and offensive operations, as opposed to support of static training activities."[66] Under MACV's leadership, the CIDG soldiers were integrated into the ARVN and used as mobile strike forces while U.S. Special Forces were withdrawn from the program to be placed in offensive roles; they were replaced by far less capable Vietnamese Special Forces. Brigadier General York commanded a special detachment to experiment with weapons and tactics in Vietnam; he had served as the U.S. Army's observer of the campaign in Malaya from 1952 through 1955.[67] York is quoted by Roger Hilsman as believing that the change would mean "a further step away from using guerrilla techniques against the guerrillas and another step toward regular, conventional tactics."[68] Wilbur Wilson, senior U.S. adviser in III Corps, warned that as a result of the changes, "the effectiveness of the Buon Enao concept will decrease sharply throughout all the highlands with the side effect of destroying the potential success of the Strategic Hamlet program in restoring law and order," but he was unable to penetrate the offensive-minded optimism at MACV Headquarters.[69] By 1 January 1965, General Westmoreland, then beginning his service as Commander of the Military Assistance Command—Vietnam (COMUSMACV), had redefined the mission of Special Forces soldiers in Vietnam to border surveillance and control, operations against infiltration routes, and operations against Viet Cong war zones and base areas.[70] Even the official U.S. Army History of the Special Forces describes the process as the "conventionalization" of the CIDG.[71] Looking back, General William DePuy thought that CIDG "had worked rather well and the history of Vietnam is that anything that worked well with ten good men, we tried to expand to 10,000 men right away. We thought Special Forces had a role to use its own troops, but we didn't want them to play it under the Agency. The Army wanted to play its own game."[72]

It is difficult to fault Colby's assessment that such CIA innovations as the CIDG "were essentially marginal in scope and in impact, especially in comparison with the major thrust of the U.S. programs at the time."[73] The most flexible of all U.S. government organizations was unable to alter U.S. Army counterinsurgency policy with a program that achieved demonstrable results in a comparatively short time and with relatively few resources expended; the organizational culture of the army was too formidable a barrier to permit learning from the CIA's success.

ROBERT THOMPSON AND THE BRITISH ADVISORY MISSION

"I fear that in this as in other respects the Americans are too apt to
think that quantity is a substitute for quality and method."[74]
—Gordon Etherington-Smith, UK Commissioner-General for South-
East Asia, 3 July 1961

With the U.S. Army and its leaders entrenched in an organizational culture that accepted military victory through annihilation as the only way to
win a war, it is not surprising that the five British colonial civil servants
and senior policemen comprising the British Advisory Mission (BRIAM)
from 16 September 1961 through 31 March 1965 were in their turn ignored.[75] BRIAM was Britain's answer to repeated American requests for
its assistance in the fight against the Viet Cong;[76] Sir Robert Thompson,
who led the mission, had played a large role in the Malayan Emergency,
serving as minister of defense in Malaya after independence. Thompson
was unable to prevail with his view that the American focus on firepower
and military solutions to political problems was counterproductive and that
population control strategies such as those that had worked in Malaya
would be more effective. His efforts to recreate Malayan New Villages in
Vietnam in the form of "Strategic Hamlets" failed, largely because of an
overly enthusiastic implementation effort that created new hamlets before
the old ones had been pacified.[77] The intent was to create expanding rings
of security in the countryside. In a message to U.S. Ambassdor Lodge,
Thompson noted:

Pacification requires drive, concentration of effort and control of direction. . . .
There will need to be the strictest control to ensure strategic direction of the advance. Another requirement, equally essential, is consolidation of the secure areas
so that the armed threat to them is completely removed, thereby releasing resources.
It is in these areas that political and economic measures have their main part to
play.[78]

Thompson advocated a focus on small critical areas rather than indiscriminate operations unconnected with a political and strategic plan. He
noted in a memorandum to Secretary of Defense McNamara on 9 March
1964 that

prospects of winning the war in South Vietnam are now gloomy . . . [but] there is
no valid reason why, during the next year, the position should not be partially
retrieved and the security situation improved. Our immediate objective should be
limited to making certain key areas of the country reasonably secure so that the
Government of Vietnam can maintain its existence and so that we can, at a later
date, decide whether further progress can be made into the insecure areas, or

whether we must accept an indefinite holding operation, with or without greater United States involvement.[79]

In a letter to the Foreign Office dated 27 April 1965, Thompson suggested that the best course of action available to the Americans was "to undertake a holding operation of the key areas vital to the government, including the main air bases, and, as it were, challenge the Viet Cong to take them." He thought that a more offensive use of American forces than this enclave strategy would be counterproductive: "If the American force went above two divisions then I would regard the involvement as unprofitable. It would mean that major American ground forces were committed in Asia and we would end up with a Korean-type war with the fighting being done by the Americans and not the Vietnamese."[80] The most serious problem he foresaw with this long-haul strategy was the issue of "whether the American people are prepared to support a long-drawn-out struggle which will cost much blood and treasure and earn them little or no applause."[81]

BRIAM was almost completely ineffective in influencing U.S. counterinsurgency theory or practice in Vietnam, largely because the American military was not interested in learning from it. This fact was apparent to the highest levels of the Johnson administration:

There is ample indication that our own mission, *specifically the military element*, looks upon third country assistance with very little zeal. This is partly because of their experience in allied commands, such as Korea, in which the care and feeding of these third country elements has always proved far more trouble than it is worth. It is also been [*sic*] reflected in the fact that such an organization as the British Advisory Mission, which is composed of skilled counterinsurgency and police officers, *has sat for nearly three years in Viet Nam with only limited relationships with the United States command.*[82]

Finally despairing of the effort, Thompson dissolved the mission at about the same time U.S. ground forces began to be deployed in strength to South Vietnam.

VOICES NOT HEARD

Harkins and MACV

The Joint Chiefs of Staff proposed that the MAAG be upgraded to the status of an army command on 23 November 1961, and President Kennedy reluctantly concurred. Military Assistance Command—Vietnam (MACV) became operational on 8 February 1962, its first commander a protégé of Maxwell Taylor's, Lieutenant General Paul D. Harkins. Hilsman argues that "the ideal choice" would have been a Special Forces or OSS officer "who shared the conviction that guerrilla warfare was as much a political as a military problem" and notes that two candidates with that trait, Brigadier General William P. Yarborough and Colonel William R. Peers, were in fact suggested to Kennedy. But as Hilsman notes, "Reaching down so far for the top man in Vietnam would arouse antagonism in the top brass of the Pentagon, and so would the appointment of an officer from among the ranks of the somewhat unorthodox Special Forces."[83] Kennedy accepted Taylor's recommendation rather than upset the army.

Harkins was a purely conventional warrior who had fought under Patton in World War II. When later asked about the selection of a conventionally schooled warrior for an unconventional war, Taylor remarked, "A general is a generalist who knows [how to do] everything." Krepinevich notes that Harkins, who owed his progress through the ranks and his appointment as MACV commander to Taylor, was therefore unlikely to "engage in any revolt from below against . . . the Army Staffs' notions of how to handle the war."[84]

Harkins quickly demonstrated that he was unlikely to modify American army doctrine in Vietnam substantially from its firepower-intensive ARVN focus. He showed neither the intellectual curiosity nor the healthy skepticism that are essential factors in changing patterns of organizational behavior from the top; even a fellow army general, Bruce Palmer, later noted that Harkins "was not regarded within the Army as an intellectual giant."[85] Harkins exemplified the traditional army "can-do" spirit of professional optimism, even at the expense of reality, in an early 1962 statement quoted by Stanley Karnow: "I am optimistic, and I am not going to allow my staff to be pessimistic."[86]

Demonstrating a similar sensitivity to the need for winning the hearts and minds of the local populace (tellingly reduced to the acronym WHAM during his command), Harkins replied to a question about the political consequences of the use of napalm on villages with the words "It really puts the fear of God into the Viet Cong. And that is what counts."[87]

Army Chief of Staff Harold K. Johnson describes the optimism of Harkins and of the entire generation of senior officers who led the U.S. Army in Vietnam:

Thirty years ago would be the end of World War II and at that time you were measured, in many respects, on your "can do" attitude . . . People with essentially the same qualifications and same background and the same experience were differentiated because of the manner of presentation of ideas and solutions to problems. Somebody would be totally negative and would never see any way to get around the obstacles and someone would lay out the obstacles and then have half a dozen ways of overcoming them. It was the fellow that could overcome them that got ahead.[88]

Neil Sheehan describes the culture from which Harkins grew and that he represented:

Twenty years after the debacle at the Kasserine Pass, it was hard to find a general in the U.S. Army who worried that he or his colleagues might squander resources and waste the lives of soldiers. The junior officers of World War II, now the generals of the 1960s, had become so accustomed to winning from the later years of that war that they could no longer imagine they could lose. (The failure in Korea they rationalized away as the fault of a weak civilian leadership which had refused to "turn loose" the full potential of American military power against China.) They assumed that they would prevail in Vietnam simply because of who they were.[89]

Sheehan believes that "time and the bureaucratization of the officer corps had distorted the memory of how World War II had been won. Harkins' strategy was a fantasy of the past, but the fantasy was real because it had been institutionalized and he and most of his fellow generals had faith in it."[90] The dominance of such an attitude at the head of MACV exerted a chilling effect throughout the organization, creating a demand for positive reports on the performance of the ARVN from the advisers in the field and preventing any recognition of the substantial problems that were showing themselves in the countryside.

The number of American advisers in South Vietnam tripled to over three thousand by the end of 1962. With the advisers entered American aircraft, including nearly three hundred helicopters. Although these at first terrified them, the Viet Cong quickly adapted their tactics to take advantage of the ARVN's growing reliance on American-provided airpower and artillery, as they demonstrated at the Battle of Ap Bac.

The Battle of Ap Bac

On 2 January 1963, the ARVN acted on rare intelligence to swoop down upon a battalion of Viet Cong in the village of Ap Bac. An ARVN battalion accompanied by two Civil Guard battalions and a company of M-113 armored personnel carriers supported by artillery and close air support made the attack. Despite being heavily outnumbered, the Viet Cong downed five helicopters and inflicted nearly two hundred casualties on the government forces, killing three American advisers. Lieutenant Colonel John Paul Vann, senior adviser to the ARVN Seventh Division, later described the ARVN's effort as "a miserable damn performance, just like it always is." Brigadier General Robert York, walking through a now VC-deserted Ap Bac the next day, responded to the reporter Neil Sheehan's question "What happened?" with the answer, "What the hell's it look like happened, boy. They got away, that's what happened." Moments later, York and Sheehan were nearly killed by ARVN artillery targeted on Ap Bac some eighteen hours too late. Five ARVN soldiers were killed and fourteen wounded by their own artillery.[91] York was the only one of the twelve army generals physically present in Vietnam in January 1963 who personally visited the site of the battle.[92]

Harkins, who had not visited the battlefield, was at this time being briefed on the battle. He told Halberstam, who had just returned from Ap Bac and knew that there were no longer any VC in the village, "We've got them in a trap and we're going to spring it in half an hour." Halberstam notes, "As on so many other occasions in Vietnam, we never knew whether Harkins believed what he was saying, or whether he felt that it should be said."[93]

Harkins's optimism was shared by his boss, Admiral Harry Felt, CINC-PAC, who called Ap Bac a success because the Viet Cong had abandoned their positions. "His assessment, shared by other senior U.S. officers and civilians, again underlined their concept of the conflict: a conventional contest for territory, like World War II or the Korean War, the experiences that had marked them." The spirit of perpetual optimism was so strong that when Peter Arnett asked a question that was critcial of the performance of the ARVN in the battle Admiral Felt snapped, "Get on the team."[94]

Vann tried desperately to burst the bubble with a ninety-one-page after-action review of the battle, which he submitted through Colonel Daniel B. Porter, his immediate supervisor, to Harkins. Porter wrote a glowing endorsement of Vann's report, recommending "a series of joint US/GVN conferences or seminars at the national level for all Vietnamese general officers, the key members of the corps and higher staffs, and division and brigade commanders" and their advisers to "openly and frankly discuss" the changes that the debacle at Ap Bac clearly demonstrated were needed.[95] Brigadier General York's own report on the battle, which echoed Vann's and which he personally delivered to General Harkins, was not favorably received by COMUSMACV, who continued to state: "I consider it a victory. We took the objective."[96] The damage done by Harkins's attitude was substantial; Halberstam remarks: "Consciously or unconsciously, the Army staff system tends to reflect the thinking of the senior officer. If the commander wants to see an aspect of the war a certain way, the staff will find facts to support their superior's thesis."[97]

Revolt of the Advisers

The unshakable optimism of Harkins reflected an inability to seek out the causes of poor performance of ARVN and RF/PF forces as a result of a refusal to acknowledge that shortcomings existed. The problems, however, were not so easy to ignore for the army captains, majors, and colonels assigned as advisers to ARVN companies, battalions, and divisions. Failures in ARVN leadership, aggressiveness, and initiative confronted the advisers on a daily basis, and, at substantial risk to their own careers, many of them initiated the institutional learning process by forwarding accurate reports of ARVN performance to MACV Headquarters.

Thus even as General Harkins was stating, "Barring greatly increased resupply and reinforcement of the Viet Cong by infiltration, the military phase of the war can be virtually won in 1963,"[98] some of the officers in daily contact with the VC were sounding a different note. In his Final Report to COMUSMACV on 13 February 1963 Colonel Daniel B. Porter, senior adviser to III and IV Corps, noted the counterproductive nature of ARVN methods: "In many operations against areas and hamlets which are considered to be hard-corps [sic] VC strongholds all possibility of surprise is lost by prolonged air strikes and artillery bombardments prior to the landing or movement of troops into the area. The innocent women, children and old people bear the brunt of such bombardments."[99] Porter also told COMUSMACV: "Commanders of regular ARVN units rarely if ever conduct night operations. In fact, only on rare occasions will commanders attempt to contain VC which may have been 'bottled up' after nightfall."[100] Far from evaluating the performance of the ARVN in the light of this information in order to develop changes in American advisory and assistance procedures, Harkins ordered the report destroyed. In the words of Halberstam, "The Americans in Saigon were, in fact, to do everything [with the information they had gained about VC tactics and ARVN failures from Ap Bac] but learn from it."[101]

Harkins's eternal optimism not only prevented learning in Vietnam by the army officers whose careers he controlled,[102] but also had a decisive impact on perceptions of army performance at higher levels of government, precluding learning forced on the Army from above. Harkins briefed McNamara and Taylor during their September 1963 visit to Saigon. "Misled by the unsubstantiated assertions of progress on the military front made by Harkins, McNamara and Taylor upon their return to Washington gave a monumental misreading of the Vietnamese situation to the National Security Council on 2 October 1963."[103]

Taylor had already ensured that the Joint Chiefs would not hear one particularly well-informed dissenting view. In a continuing effort to force the army to face the fact that the advisory mission in South Vietnam was failing, Lieutenant Colonel John Paul Vann told his side of the Battle of Ap Bac to anyone who would listen. By 8 July 1963 he was scheduled to brief the Joint Chiefs of Staff. JCS Chairman General Taylor canceled the brief literally hours before Vann was to walk into the Tank, the Joint Chiefs' Briefing Office. Marine General Victor Krulak, Kennedy's special assistant for counterinsurgency, had obtained a copy of Vann's briefing packet and did not want Vann's dissent on record.[104]

While Vann continued to attempt to teach the highest levels of the U.S. Army that its policies in Vietnam were counterproductive, his efforts met

Figure 6-1
Viet Cong Terrorism Against Civilians, 1957–1965

	Assassinated	Kidnapped	Total
1957–1959	432	580	1,012
1960	1,400	700	2,100
1961	1,000	2,000	3,000
1962	1,719	9,688	11,407
1963	2,073	7,262	9,335
1964	1,795	9,554	11,349
1965	1,895	12,778	14,673

with at best a polite brush-off. On 14 January 1964 Major General Bruce Palmer, then serving as the highly influential assistant deputy chief of staff for military operations in the Pentagon, sent Vann a letter thanking the junior officer for a letter and supporting documents detailing lessons Vann believed that the army needed to learn. Palmer states, "It was an education to read them and, as a result, I believe that I have a much better idea of what the basic problems are in the RVN. There are, no doubt, many others who think as you do and, consequently, I feel that eventually our efforts in Vietnam will be directed in a more promising way."[105]

Vann's revolt did have some effect: professional optimism was institutionalized. In May 1963, advisers en route to Vietnam were instructed: "Avoid gratuitous criticism. Emphasize the feeling of achievement, the hopes for the future, and instances of outstanding individual or personal achievement by gilding the lily."[106]

COUPS, ASSASSINATIONS, AND CHANGES AT THE TOP

A high-level fact-finding mission, dispatched to Vietnam to determine progress in the war effort on 18 January 1963, decided that "we are winning slowly on the present thrust and . . . there is no compelling reason to change."[107] Sheehan notes, "The mission of inquiry the Joint Chiefs sent to South Vietnam in January 1963 demonstrated that the military institutions of the United States were so overcome by their malady of victory that they could not respond to events and adjust themselves to reality even when reality took them by the shoulders and shook them."[108] The Viet Cong had obtained 200,000 U.S. weapons by mid-1964. Meanwhile, Viet Cong terrorism grew steadily (see Figure 6-1[109]).

As the Viet Cong activity increased, so did the repressive nature of Diem's regime. Public discontent with Diem burst into flames in the summer of 1963 after Diem and his brother, Nhu, brutally quelled protests led by Buddhist monks. Diem and Nhu were killed during a coup carried out with U.S. approval on 2 November 1963. Kennedy himself was assassinated in Dallas three weeks later, unsuccessful in his attempts to change the army to make it an effective instrument for counterinsurgency. Hilsman states, "The Kennedy administration had developed a strategic concept for fighting guerrilla warfare, an idea for a political program into which military measures were meshed, but we had failed so far to convince the Diem regime or even the top levels of the Pentagon to give it a fair trial."[110] A scholar of the Kennedy administration agrees: "The loss of the most avid promoter of COIN doctrine signaled a traditional military solution of mass and firepower would be given dominance. In South Vietnam, COIN doctrine was never fully applied or tested."[111]

Lyndon Johnson assumed the U.S. presidency as military juntas rose and fell in South Vietnam with alarming speed. As the truth about Diem's repression and the poor performance of the ARVN under his command came to light in the wake of the coup, General Harkins, who had been one of Diem's strongest supporters, was seen as a liability. Scheduled to retire in September 1964, he left Saigon three months early, turning over command to General William Westmoreland. A fellow general said of his departure, "It wasn't a retirement, it was a relief."[112] McNamara once said Harkins "wasn't worth a damn so he was removed."[113] Henry Cabot Lodge departed as ambassador less than a month after Harkins, replaced by another army general, Maxwell Taylor. As the insurgency reached crisis proportions the top civilian and military jobs in Vietnam would be filled by U.S. Army generals. But how much had the U.S. Army learned about defeating insurgency during its already fifteen-year-long involvement with the insurgency in Vietnam?

ORGANIZATIONAL LEARNING IN VIETNAM, 1950–1965

Did the U.S. Army Develop a Successful Counterinsurgency Doctrine in Vietnam, 1950–1964?

An assessment of the U.S. Army's success in developing doctrine and techniques to assist the GVN to defeat the insurgency it faced through 1964 shows very poor results. The steady rise in assassinations and kidnappings of South Vietnamese civilian officials reveals that *victory* is far from being achieved and that the American goal of a non-Communist South Vietnam free to choose its own form of government is still a long way off. The *objective* of creating an ARVN and RF/PF militia capable of defending against an insurgency has not been achieved; the Army had not yet recognized that an insurgency was the immediate threat confronting the fledgling government of South Vietnam. In an orientation briefing delivered to newly arrived MAAG personnel on 31 May 1957, the MAAG chief, Samuel T. Williams, proclaimed:

> It is believed that any attack by the Viet Minh against South Vietnam would be part of an overall Communist attempt against a greater part of Southeast Asia. . . . It is estimated that the Viet Minh have the equivalent of 18 Infantry Divisions supported by two artillery divisions. . . . The best invasion routes into South Vietnam would be the Mekong River Valley approach into the Saigon area. Also the route from the North using Highway Number 1 as the axis.[114]

The U.S. Army's MAAG focused on the creation of an ARVN mechanized, reliant on air support and artillery, and oriented toward defense in the event of a conventional invasion—in direct insubordination to the instructions of President Eisenhower's Secretary of State Dulles and of President Kennedy. The ARVN, as did the U.S. Army, sent a bullet (or a shell, or a bomb) rather than a man wherever possible; indiscriminate use of airpower and artillery made many peasants more inclined to favor the Viet Cong than the GVN. The ARVN, formed in divisions and corps at the expense of pacification efforts and at the cost of neglect of the RF/PF and militia, was not structured appropriately for the threat it faced. The ARVN had been created to withstand the projected threat of a conventional war rather than the unconventional war it actually confronted.

There was a notable lack of *unity of command* and direction of effort among the disparate U.S. agencies attempting to advise the young nation. Army Chief of Staff Harold K. Johnson complained that the nation-building efforts were flawed by the lack of dedication of civilians, which left the hard jobs to the military:

> USAID, the Agency for International Development, which is a State Department subsidiary, had an interest but they weren't really interested in being a resident in the subsector, in the district level. They would prefer to spend some time out there, but retreat to the major population centers to spend the majority of their time. This I think again reflected differences in attitude and that's why in the end a great number of sector and subsector advisers came from military sources.[115]

Unfortunately, the officers sent by the army to do the job were not always capable of performing their assigned missions. During his first visit to Vietnam in March 1964, General Johnson visited an ARVN battalion at Long Vae that had been led by the same commander for five years. His U.S. Army adviser was a lieutenant with less than one year of service; Johnson later reflected, "I just don't think the concept of our advisors at the subordinate levels was all that sound with the level of experience we could provide."[116] There were both advantages and disadvantages connected with putting military officers in positions of civil responsibility for which they had little training or experience: "At least the fellow in the military is an activist. This doesn't necessarily mean that it's good because he does get things done. It may be the wrong things."[117]

A letter to the editor of *ARMY* magazine, printed in the special counterinsurgency issue of March 1962, helps explain why the army paid so little attention to the advisory effort:

You raise the question as to why we have done little in this field and I can answer specifically. The whole field of guerrilla operations was the burial place for the future of any officer who was sincerely interested in the development and application of guerrilla warfare. The conventionally trained officer appears to feel that guerrilla operations are beneath his dignity and are something that possibly might happen but the chance is so remote that it is not worth considering.[118]

The same issue of *ARMY* editorializes in a manner that not only supports the argument of the letter writer but goes a long way to explaining the army's failure to adopt successful counterinsurgency doctrine in Vietnam over this period: "The 'general purpose' soldier need not be able to speak the language of the country in which he is fighting . . . nor [understand] the subtleties involved in training the soldiers of a land without a military tradition and whose cultural background is far removed from the machine-age culture of mid-century America."[119]

The army's best hope for a successful, minimum-force counterinsurgency organization had been co-opted by the system. U.S. Army Special Forces entered the war in Vietnam with the mission of serving as guerrillas in conjunction with conventional military efforts in Europe; a contemporary observer stated, "The primary mission of a Special Forces detachment is to direct local guerrilla units in offensive actions such as ambushes, demolitions, raids, and limited attacks."[120] The appropriate structure existed, but it had a guerrilla focus of its own, rather than a population-control strategy designed to help defeat guerrillas.

The army itself recognized its failure to develop the correct counterinsurgency doctrine and even explained why, in the revealing special issue of *ARMY* magazine:

The President is an innovator; old methods haven't worked and he wants to find ones that will; therefore, he is receptive to the unconventional idea and is impatient for action if not results. The Army is more inhibited. Its memory is long and its problem-solving techniques emphasize caution, thoroughness, and a highly developed, ingrained degree of skepticism. The Army can change, sometimes with startling rapidity, but this is abnormal to it. The "crash" that is normal to the Army's Pentagon staff is rarely the crash of new ideas toppling old ones in a ten-strike; usually it is the crash of endless concurrences, sought or rejected, of the gloss of new gobbledegook hurriedly spread over old programs.[121]

Figure 6-2
Did the U.S. Army Develop a Successful Counterinsurgency Doctrine in
South Vietnam, 1950–1964?

Victory: the achievement of national goals	No
Objective: the setting of realistic national goals	No
Unity of command: military subordination to political objectives	No
Minimum force: minimum necessary force	No
Mass: appropriate structure for threat	No

In a final word from the *ARMY* magazine of March 1962, "In summary it can be said that if the Army has been slow in meeting the challenge of communist sublimited warfare, it was in a significant degree because the Army's battle for survival required it to concentrate on other things."[122] The U.S. Army's progress in developing a successful counterinsurgency doctrine is summarized in Figure 6-2.

Was the American Army in Vietnam a Learning Institution from 1950 Through 1964?

The performance of the American army as a learning institution from 1950 through 1964 is similarly mixed. Although there was a great deal of input from the advisers in the field, and even from Brigadier General York in his capacity as a troubleshooter and institutional innovator, the American generals who ran the MAAG and General Harkins as MACV commander were not open to *theoretical thinking*; they were often openly hostile to suggestions for change from below. In retrospect, William Westmoreland recognized the extent of the learning required:

When we committed troops to Vietnam or even went over as advisers, it was a new ball game for us, we were dealing in an situation where the US Army had little experience. I guess one could say that, after the Civil War, when we were expanding our frontiers to the west and fighting the Indians, there was some similarity. That was a war of a different character but with some similarities. In Vietnam, we were on the learning curve for several years. We learned from experience and we learned from trial and error.[123]

Yet learning had already occured at the field level and been revealed in semiofficial Army publications; Major Boyd T. Bashore, formerly an adviser to an infantry regiment in Vietnam, wrote about the "Soldier of the Future" in September 1961, reminding the U.S. Army that little "unsoldierly" guerrillas like Quang have patiently padded along their trails, fighting hard and almost constantly since 1946 in the swamp of the Mekong. Quang, his methods of fighting, and the ideology which impels him are formidable adversaries. Right now he and his comrades are in the process of attempting to take over two more countries of Asia. Our black combat boots are spit-shined, our fatigues starched and pressed, our spring-up field caps well blocked. But we must never disdain Private Quang. He could very well be the soldier of the future.[124]

General Harold K. Johnson later described army attempts to learn from other nations with counterinsurgency experience:

We solicited the advice of the British experts and Australian experts in the same field. I think we sought all the information we could find, but didn't really define counter-insurgency in a way that you could confront it directly. . . . The real lesson is that you try to understand, not only the military and political factors, but the sociological factors as well, which we did not do in Vietnam, and then try to cope with those factors. But destruction is not the answer to a situation like that, and you've got to find ways of coping with the preservation of providing security for people, and providing security for physical installations without contributing to their destruction in the course of the protection.[125]

General Westmoreland also later described an inherent flaw in the process. Although this quotation is directly related to the development of the Airmobile Division, the "can-do" attitude it describes played an important role thoughout the American advisory and combat involvement in Vietnam: "The people who manned the newly activated 101st Airborne Division were especially picked people, and they were sent there with a mission, which they interpreted as 'make the new concept work.' And then there was an evaluation group that was established, and they interpreted their mission 'to make it work,' and they did their best."[126]

Learning was handicapped by the fact that those who truly understood the problems of counterinsurgency, such as Vann and Lansdale, were ignored or worse by their conventionally minded supervisors:

Americans attuned to this kind of war have not been very well treated by the services. These are not the sorts who rise to the top, for their specialties . . . are not recognized or appreciated. These officers . . . will have to continue to work regularly in some other military field. For it will be in the second field—one probably less crucial to the national interests—that promotion and recognition will come. In terms of promotion, advising remains a road to nowhere.[127]

Learning was further crippled by the fact that Americans sent as advisers had next to no knowledge of the Vietnamese nation or its people. The language barrier further exacerbated learning difficulties; a senior Vietnamese general later recalled, "I know of no single instance in which a U.S.

Figure 6-3
Learning in Vietnam, 1950–1964

Bottom-up input: Suggestions from the field	Yes
Superiors questioned	Yes
available	No
Theoretical thinking	Low Level Only
Local doctrine development	No
Local training centers	No
Small, responsive staff	No

adviser effectively discussed professional matters with his counterpart in Vietnamese."[128] General DePuy later admitted, "I guess I should have studied human nature and the history of Vietnam and of revolutions and should have known it, but I didn't."[129]

The vast size of the organization also made it resistant to change. By 1964, the MACV staff was already too large to fit in one building; the 1964 MACV Command History cites coordination problems from the physical separation between J4 (Supply and Logistics Headquarters) in the MACV-2 compound and the rest of the staff in the MACV-1 compound.[130] Colonel Hutton sums up the learning difficulties: "The organizational culture of the US Army is very big and hard to change. Our Tables of Organization and Equipment and our doctrine require standardization because of the U.S. Army's personnel rotation system. An officer doesn't grow up in one regiment, learning 'how we do it here.' It's much easier to change one regiment [in the British Army] than the U.S. Army; once one regiment changes, it's easier to change other regiments."[131]

Doctrine did not begin to be developed until the 1960s, and then in the United States rather than in-theater. The American high command preferred to stay in Saigon rather than visit the field to gain firsthand knowledge of the effectiveness of U.S. training for counterinsurgency. MACV Commander Harkins and his superiors in the Pentagon were even resistant to innovation personally sponsored by their commander in chief, convinced that "the essence of the problem is military" and that they could solve military problems in Vietnam as they had during World War II and in Korea. The learning process of the U.S. Army through 1964 is shown in Figure 6-3.

NOTES

1. Andrew F. Krepinevich, Jr., *The Army and Vietnam* (Baltimore: Johns Hopkins University Press, 1985), 5–6; Krepinevich interview, 17 September 1996.

2. Stanley Karnow, *Vietnam: A History* (New York: Viking, 1991), 119.

3. Ibid., 134.

4. Ibid., 147.

5. Ibid., 169. For U.S. policy toward Indochina from 1941 to 1945, see *The Pentagon Papers: The Senator Gravel Edition*, Vol. I (Boston: Beacon Press, 1971), 1–3.

6. Memorandum from John Carter Vincent, director of the Office of Far Eastern Affairs, to Under-Secretary Acheson, 23 December 1948, in *Pentagon Papers*, Volume I, 29.

7. NSC Staff Study, December 1949, quoted in *Pentagon Papers*, Volume I, 37–38.

8. See Andrew J. Rotter, *The Path to Vietnam: Origins of the American Commitment to Southeast Asia* (London: Cornell, 1987).

9. *Pentagon Papers*, Volume II, 56.

10. The best source on the French war in Indochina is Bernard Fall, *Street Without Joy: Insurgency in Indochina, 1946–63* (London: Pall Mall Press, 1963). French counterinsurgency learning in Indochina and Algeria begs to be studied by a scholar with an understanding of the organizational culture of the French army. For an examination of why the American government did not learn from the French experience in Indochina, see Yuen Foong Khong, *Analogies at War: Korea, Munich, Dien Bien Phu, and the Vietnam Decisions of 1965* (Princeton, NJ: Princeton University Press, 1992), esp. 148–173.

11. *Pentagon Papers*, Vol. I, 471–472. "It is my belief that the analysis which the Army made and presented to higher authority played a considerable, perhaps a decisive, part in persuading our government not to embark on that tragic adventure." Matthew B. Ridgway with Harold H. Martin, *Soldier: The Memoirs of Matthew B. Ridgway* (New York: Harper & Brothers, 1956), 277. General Ridgway, then serving as Army Chief of Staff, states his pride in preventing U.S. involvement in Indochina in 1954: "When the day comes for me to face my Maker and account for my actions, the thing I would be most humbly proud of was the fact that I fought against, and perhaps contributed to preventing, the carrying out of some hare-brained tactical schemes which would have cost the lives of thousands of men. To that list of tragic accidents that fortunately never happened I would add the Indo-China intervention." *Soldier*, 278. See also William C. Westmoreland, *Senior Officer Oral History Project* (hereafter *SOOHP*), U.S. Army Military History Institute Archives, Vol. I, 220. Westmoreland was a brigadier general on the Army Staff at this time; he sat in on some of the deliberations concerning possible U.S. involvement in 1954.

12. *Pentagon Papers*, Vol. I, 31.

13. General Cao Van Vien et al., *Indochina Monographs: The U.S. Adviser* (Washington, DC: U.S. Army Center for Military History, 1980), 24.

14. Ibid., 3; internal quotation is from Memorandum No 1891/TTM/MG, dated 10 April 1955 and signed by Major General Le Van Tye, chief of the Vietnamese General Staff.

15. Edward G. Lansdale, *In the Midst of Wars: An American's Mission to Southeast Asia* (New York: Harper & Row, 1982), 111; see also *Pentagon Papers*, I, 256.

16. Col. Hoang Ngoc Lung, *Indochina Monographs: Strategy and Tactics* (Washington, DC: CMH, 1980), 64, in Krepinevich, *The Army and Vietnam*, 22.

17. Ronald H. Spector, *The United States Army in Vietnam: Advice and Support, the Early Years, 1941–1960* (Washington, DC: GPO, 1983), 169.

18. Ibid., 221.

19. *Pentagon Papers*, II, 432.

20. William C. Westmoreland, *A Soldier Reports* (New York: Da Capo, 1989), 57.

21. Major General (Retired) John Tillson interview, Washington, D.C., 9 September 1996. In addition, "We really had very little respect for any ARVN forces. We didn't think they could do the job."

22. Then–USMC captain John Grinalds, who served as a Vietnamese marine battalion adviser in 1966–1967, telephone interview, 12 September 1996. He adds, "ARVN units didn't stay in one place long enough to get to know the people and the area." On the subject of the relative merits of U.S. Marines and the U.S. Army, the Canadian chief military adviser in Saigon "thought the Americans could manage to produce a large number of good calibre instructors if they drew on their Marines, whose standards of course are higher than those of the American Army." FO 371/160157, Mr. Stewart of the British Advisory Mission, to the Foreign Office, Saigon telegram #349, 16 June 1961.

23. *Pentagon Papers*, II, 433.

24. Ibid., 408.

25. William Colby, *Lost Victory* (Chicago: Contemporary Books, 1989), 28.

26. *Pentagon Papers*, I, 314.

27. *Pentagon Papers*, II, 434–435.

28. *Pentagon Papers*, II, 436.

29. Roger Hilsman, *To Move a Nation: The Politics of Foreign Policy in the Administration of John F. Kennedy* (Garden City, NY: Doubleday, 1967), 525.

30. *Pentagon Papers*, I, 257. Diem would in fact call upon the Civil Guard to go to his rescue during the coup of November 1963. See David Halberstam, *The Making of a Quagmire* (New York: Ballantine, 1965), 309–310.

31. *Pentagon Papers*, II, 435.

32. *Pentagon Papers*, II, 409.

33. Gen. Cao Van Vien et al., *Indochina Monographs: The U.S. Adviser*, 73.

34. Ibid., 73–74.

35. Hilsman, *To Move a Nation*, 419. Hilsman was a West Point graduate who had fought a guerrilla campaign in Burma against the Japanese in World War II; he served as director of the State Department's Bureau of Intelligence and Research and as assistant secretary of state for Far Eastern affairs during the Kennedy administration.

36. Colby, *Lost Victory*, 69.

37. *Pentagon Papers*, II, 433.

38. *Pentagon Papers*, I, 256. An example is the Field Exercise of the ARVN First Field Division, conducted during the period 9–16 July 1957. This was a four-phased operation in which the ARVN First Field Division was involved: "Fighting

the enemy side by side with friendly divisions, the maneuvering division is responsible for screening the withdrawal of another division and developing a delaying action according to a fixed plan in order to retreat to a defensive position and to keep it." The First Field Division fought three ARVN divisions in an "umpired" battle arranged according to U.S. Army training methods of the day. File Folder 141, *The Samuel T. Williams Papers*, Military History Institute (MHI) Box 1, A3, B2.

39. "Miscellaneous Papers of General Williams, Folder 134," *The Samuel T. Williams Papers*, MHI, Box 1, 1.

40. Neil Sheehan, *A Bright Shining Lie: John Paul Vann and America in Vietnam* (New York: Vintage, 1989), 195.

41. Hilsman, *To Move a Nation*, 413.

42. Ibid., 53.

43. Douglas Kinnard, *The Certain Trumpet: Maxwell Taylor and the American Experience in Vietnam* (London: Brassey's, 1991), 54–56. Taylor, who had served as Chief of Staff of the U.S. Army under President Eisenhower and chafed at the neglect of the army's ability to fight conventional wars under the doctrine of massive retaliation, wrote *The Uncertain Trumpet* (New York: Harper, 1959) to call attention to the neglect of the U.S. Army's conventional warfighting ability. However, Taylor was as enamored of conventional warfighting as were most army officers who, like him, had led the U.S. Army to victory in World War II and Korea; he was as incapable of understanding the new political-military demands of counterinsurgency as were his peers. In thinking him "unconventional" the Kennedy administration in fact propagated the army's focus on conventional firepower-and-maneuver warfare.

44. Kinnard, *The Certain Trumpet*, 102.

45. Westmoreland, *A Soldier Reports*, 38.

46. The speech is reprinted in Franklin Mark Osanka, ed., *Modern Guerrilla Warfare: Fighting Communist Guerrilla Movements, 1941–1961* (New York: The Free Press of Glencoe, 1962), 452–463.

47. Ibid., 458.

48. JCSM 717–61 (9 October 1961), *Pentagon Papers*, II, 12.

49. Douglas S. Blaufarb, *The Counterinsurgency Era: U.S. Doctrine and Performance 1950 to the Present* (New York: The Free Press, 1977), 71. In refuting the charge that he was a "by the book" general, William Westmoreland notes that in his military career he graduated from just two army schools: Parachute School and Cooks' and Bakers' School. Westmoreland, *A Soldier Reports*, 17. Unfortunately, he attended the latter before the block on counterinsurgency was added to the curriculum.

50. Interview with Elvis J. Stahr by Robert H. Farrell, Center for Military History (CMH) (18 August 1964), 33, in Krepinevich, *The Army and Vietnam*, 31.

51. Robert A. Doughty, *The Evolution of U.S. Army Tactical Doctrine, 1946–1976* (Leavenworth, KS: Combat Studies Institute, 1979), 28, quoting 1957 Estimate of the Situation, Department of Combat Aviation, U.S. Army Aviation School, Fort Rucker, Alabama, 11.

52. Doughty, *The Evolution of U.S. Army Tactical Doctrine, 1946–1976*, 26.

53. Romie L. Brownlee and William J. Mullen, III, *Changing an Army: An Oral*

History of General William E. DePuy, USA Retired (Washington, DC: USGPO, 1988), 117.

54. Doughty, *The Evolution of U.S. Army Tactical Doctrine, 1946–1976*, 26.

55. Ibid., 25. See also Office, Director of Strategic Plans and Policy, Special Warfare Division (O/DCSOPS), *Counter Insurgency Operations: A Handbook for the Supression of Communist Guerrilla/Terrorist Operations* (1 March 1962), 43.

56. Doughty, *The Evolution of U.S. Army Tactical Doctrine, 1946–1976*, 26.

57. Lieutenant General Hamilton H. Howze, *Special Warfare Board, Final Report* (Fort Monroe, VA: Headquarters USCONARC, 28 January 1962), 12.

58. Hilsman, *To Move a Nation*, 419. Hilsman notes in on p. 439, footnote 1, that the State Department subsequently tried three times to get Lansdale to Vietnam, but the Pentagon vetoed the assignment until U.S. Ambassador Henry Cabot Lodge finally succeeded in overcoming its objections in 1965.

59. Ibid., 426.

60. Denis Warner, "Fighting the Viet Cong," *ARMY* 12, 2 (September 1961), 20.

61. Colby, *Lost Victory*, 85.

62. Ibid., 90–91; Krepinevich, *The Army and Vietnam*, 70–71. See also CIA Report, "The Civilian Irregular Defense Groups (CIDG) Political Action Program" (3 March 1965), CMH, and ODCSOPS, Memo for DCSOPS, "CIA Operations in Vietnam (S)," (13 July 1962), CMH.

63. Rosson and Yarborough to Decker, *Special Warfare Activities Field Inspection Visit* (2 May 1962), 6, in Krepinevich, *The Army and Vietnam*, 71.

64. Johnson *SOOHP*, Vol. III, Section XII (23 April 1973), 8–9.

65. Twenty-fifth Infantry Division Command Historian Robert K. Wright, Jr., interview 11 September 1996.

66. ODCSOPS, Cable, Lieutenant General Barksdale Hamlett to General Collins (15 August 1962), CMH, in Krepinevich, *The Army and Vietnam*, 72. See also Colby, *Lost Victory*, 164, who argues that the CIA's loss of credibility that followed the Bay of Pigs invasion made possible Taylor's transfer of CIDG to MACV control.

67. Sheehan, *A Bright Shining Lie*, 272–275.

68. Hilsman, *To Move a Nation*, 455. Hilsman notes that because of York's position outside the chain of command, "he was free of any commitment to any particular policy line or interpretation" and was thus ideally suited to learn from operations. Organizational learning theory points out that his lack of command authority also meant that he could not create an institutional consensus that change was required on the basis of his observations.

69. Colonel Wilbur Wilson to COMUSMACV, *Integration of Montagnard Village Defenders and Strike Forces into GVN Forces* (12 March 1963), CMH, in Krepinevich, *The Army and Vietnam*, 73.

70. HQ, USASF, V, Letter of Instructions Number 1, *The Special Forces Counterinsurgency Program* (1 January 1965), CMH, in Krepinevich, *The Army and Vietnam*, 75.

71. Francis J. Kelly, *U.S. Army Special Forces 1961–1971* (Washington, DC: GPO, 1973), 48.

72. General William E. DePuy, in Brownlee and Mullen, *Changing an Army*, 118.

73. Colby, *Lost Victory*, 95.

74. FO 371/160157, Letter from Etherington-Smith to J.I. McGhie of the Foreign Office, sent from Phoenix Park, Singapore, commenting on USMAAG's intent to provide more direct training to the ARVN.

75. Dennis J. Duncanson, *Government and Revolution in Vietnam* (Oxford: Oxford University Press, 1968), 408.

76. LBJ once asked for "a platoon of bagpipers, so long as they bring the Union Jack with them." Harold K. Wilson, *The Labour Government 1964–1970: A Personal Record* (London: Weidenfeld and Nicolson, 1971), 264.

77. FO 371/170102/DV1017/41, Letter from Thompson to Fred Warner (Foreign Office) dated 18 September 1963, 3. The size of the problem in Vietnam was far greater than it had been in Malaya; the situation was not helped by the fact that the head of the program was a Viet Cong agent. William Prochnau, *Once Upon a Distant War* (New York: Times Books, 1995), 76. For an analysis of the reasons behind the failures of the Strategic Hamlet program, see J.P.D. Dunbabin, *The Post-Imperial Age: The Great Powers and the Wider World* (London: Longman, 1994), 118.

78. FO 371/175482 (7161/64), 9 April 1964, Letter from Thompson to Lodge, 1–2.

79. FO 371/175482 (115), 9 March 1964, Memorandum from Thompson to the United States Secretary of Defense, 1.

80. FO 371/180595/PV1093/81, 27 April 1965, Letter from Thompson to E.H. Peck, 2.

81. "What is even worse from our point of view, such a defeat may give rise to such pressures within America that it will cause the American Administration in the future to fumble the ball during the difficult years ahead." Ibid., 4.

82. Memorandum from the Secretary of State's Special Assistant for Vietnam (William H. Sullivan) to the President's Special Assistant for National Security Affairs (McGeorge Bundy), Washington, 24 June 1964. Reprinted in *Foreign Relations of the United States, 1964–1968*, Vol. I, #223, 526–527, emphasis in original.

83. Hilsman, *To Move a Nation*, 426.

84. Krepinevich, *The Army and Vietnam*, 64–65. Taylor quotation is from Krepinevich's 17 June 1982 interview.

85. General Bruce Palmer, Jr., *The 25-Year War: America's Military Role in Vietnam* (New York: Da Capo, 1984), 11.

86. Karnow, *Vietnam: A History*, 274–275.

87. Hilsman, *To Move a Nation*, 442. The army's attitude toward counterinsurgency is also evident in the crude but telling catch phrase, "When you've got 'em by the balls, their hearts and minds will follow."

88. Johnson, *SOOHP*, Vol III, Section XVI, 17.

89. Sheehan, *A Bright Shining Lie*, 287.

90. Ibid., 288.

91. Halberstam, *Quagmire*, 163–164. The battle is exhaustively described in Neil Sheehan's biography of Vann, *A Bright Shining Lie*, 203–265. See also David Toczek, *The Battle of Ap Bac, Vietnam: They Did Everything but Learn from It* (Westport, CT: Greenwood Press, 2001).

92. Sheehan, *A Bright Shining Lie*, 272–275.

93. Halberstam, *Quagmire*, 164.

94. Karnow, *Vietnam: A History*, 279.

95. Sheehan, *A Bright Shining Lie*, 277–282; quotation from Porter's memorandum is on p. 282.

96. Ibid., 283. Harkins refused to tour the countryside to gain a firsthand perspective of the war. When Horst Faas of the Associated Press asked when he could take a picture of Harkins in the field with ARVN troops Harkins told him, "I'm not that kind of a general." Ibid., 285.

97. Halberstam, *Quagmire*, 181.

98. MACV, "Summary of Highlights," *Pentagon Papers*, II, 180.

99. HQ IV Advisory Group, *Final Report* (13 February 1963), 11–12, CMH in Krepinevich, *The Army and Vietnam*, 81.

100. Ibid., 13, in Krepinevich, *The Army and Vietnam*, 82.

101. Halberstam, *Quagmire*, 155.

102. Krepinevich observes that whereas both Vann and Porter left the army after their outspoken advisory tours without being promoted, Colonel Hal D. McCown, who on 10 October 1963 reported, "We are winning clearly, steadily, and as far as I can see, inexorably," retired as a major general (82–84).

103. Bruce Palmer, *The 25 Year War: America's Military Role in Vietnam* (New York: Da Capo, 1984), 12.

104. Sheehan, *A Bright Shining Lie*, 336–342.

105. Letter from Assistant Deputy Chief of Staff for Military Operations to John Paul Vann (14 January 1964), in the John Paul Vann Papers, 1964 Folder, USA MHI.

106. ODCSOPS, DCSOPS to USCONARC, *Special Orientation of U.S. Army Personnel Being Assigned to Vietnam* (16 May 1963), 3, CMH in Krepinevich, *The Army and Vietnam*, 81.

107. Sheehan, *A Bright Shining Lie*, 303.

108. Ibid., 305.

109. Hilsman, *To Move a Nation*, 525.

110. Ibid., 572.

111. Fred Berry, Jr., *Kennedy's War in Vietnam, 1961–1963* (University Microfilms International: Unpublished M.A. Thesis, University of Houston—Clear Lake, 1990), 117.

112. General Hamlett, interview with Krepinevich (11 March 1976), in Krepinevich, *The Army and Vietnam*, 94.

113. Lewis Sorley, *Thunderbolt: General Creighton Abrams and the Army of His Times* (New York: Simon & Schuster, 1992), 178.

114. Samuel T. Williams, *MAAG Orientation Briefing* (31 May 1957) Folder #154, Box 3, 9, *The Samuel T. Williams Papers*, MHI. He does note on p. 10, "It is recognized here that any attack from the North would certainly be accompanied by flaming guerrilla activity from guerrillas already in place." Folder #154 also makes direct comparisons between SVN and U.S. Army divisions in such areas as units and armaments, pp. 12–13.

115. Johnson *SOOHP*, Vol. III, Section XII, 22–23.

116. Ibid., Vol. II, Section VIII, 16.

117. Ibid., 18.

118. "Big Push in Guerrilla Warfare: The Army Beefs Up Its Counter-Insurgency Doctrine," *ARMY* 12, 8 (March 1962), 36.

119. Ibid., 35.

120. USMC Capt. Robert B. Asprey, "Special Forces: Europe," *ARMY* 12, 6 (January 1962), 56.

121. "Big Push in Guerrilla Warfare," *ARMY* (March 1962), 35.

122. Ibid., 36.

123. Westmoreland, *SOOHP*, II, 196–197.

124. Major Boyd T. Bashore, "Soldier of the Future," *ARMY* 12, 1 (September 1961), 27–28.

125. Johnson *SOOHP*, III, Section XIII, 26.

126. Westmoreland *SOOHP*, II, 33.

127. George Ashworth, "Who'll Volunteer to Advise on Brush-Fire Wars?" *Christian Science Monitor* (3 March 1970), 3, in Peter Dawkins, "The U.S. Army and the 'Other' War in Vietnam" (Unpublished Ph.D. Dissertation, Princeton University, 1979), 64.

128. General Cao Van Vien et al., *Indochina Monographs: The U.S. Adviser*, 31–32.

129. General William E. DePuy in Brownlee and Mullen, *Changing an Army*, 160.

130. *MACV Command History 1964*, U.S. Army MHI, 135.

131. Colonel (Retired) Powell Hutton interview, 17 September 1996.

7

The U.S. Army in Vietnam: Organizational Culture and Learning During the Fighting Years, 1965–1972

"A STRONG TEMPTATION TO HIT SOMEONE"

During General Westmoreland's first year as MACV commander, the performance of the ARVN continued to decline while Viet Cong terrorism increased in both frequency and effectiveness. The Viet Cong occupied the village of Binh Gia on the night of 28 December 1964; the village was only forty miles southeast of Saigon. Five days later seven battalions of ARVN troops responding to a Viet Cong ambush of two ARVN ranger companies were soundly thrashed. After the defeat, in which over two hundred ARVN soldiers were killed in action (KIA) and five American advisers died, one U.S. officer in Saigon ventured the opinion "The Vietcong fought magnificently, as well as any infantry anywhere. But the big question for me is how its troops, a thousand or more of them, could wander around the countryside so close to Saigon without being discovered. That tells something about this war. You can only beat the other guy if you isolate him from the population."[1]

The Viet Cong exploded a bomb in the Brinks Hotel, killing two Americans, injuring fifty-eight, and rousing fears that Saigon might fall to the Communists. General Westmoreland sent CINCPAC a message requesting the deployment of a U.S. Army division, stating, "I am convinced that U.S. troops with their energy, mobility and firepower can successfully take the fight to the VC. The main purpose of the additional deployments recommended below is to give us a substantial and hard hitting [offen]sive capability on the ground to convince the VC that they cannot win."[2]

Optimism was high that U.S. forces, with their mobility and firepower, would quickly defeat the VC. A senior U.S. military spokesman in Saigon said in October 1964: "Our fervent hope is that they'll stick their neck out with about six battalions around here some day and try to hold something, because as of that time, they've had it. The VC are excellent at ambushes, but that's kind of a coward's way of fighting the war."[3]

The "cowardly" technique was remarkably effective. A Pentagon analyst looking at the situation later concluded:

The enemy in this war was spreading his control and influence slowly and inexorably but without drama. The political infrastructure from which he derived his strength took years to create, and in most areas the expansion of control was hardly felt until it was a *fait accompli*. Only when he organized into units of battalion and regiment size, did the enemy voluntarily lend some dramatic elements to the war. Whenever these units appeared and engaged the RVNAF [Republic of Vietnam Armed Forces], the government and its U.S. helpers had something they could handle.[4]

The U.S. military, meanwhile, was deciding whether to adopt a defensive "enclave" concept, in which U.S. troops were committed to the security of populated areas, or whether troops should be committed to active "search and destroy" missions. Views diverged along service lines: "The Chief of Staff of the Air Force and the Commandant of the Marine Corps were known proponents of the enclave concept, but the Chairman of the JCS and the Chief of Staff of the Army were equally determined to see the deployment of several divisions of troops for unlimited combat operations."[5] Even the army, however, was not unanimous in its support for the search and destroy method. An important dissenter was Maxwell Taylor, now serving as U.S. Ambassador to Vietnam, who cabled his support for the enclave strategy to the State Department on 22 February 1965:

The use of Marines in mobile counter-VC operations had the attraction of giving them an offensive mission and one of far greater appeal than that of mere static defense. However, it would raise many serious problems which in [the] past have appeared sufficiently formidable to lead to rejection of [the] use of US ground troops in a counter-Guerrilla role. [An American] White-faced soldier armed, equipped, and trained as he [is, is] not [a] suitable guerrilla fighter for Asian forests and jungles . . . There would be [the] ever present question of how [the] foreign soldier would distinguish between a VC and friendly Vietnamese farmer.[6]

Another influential army officer agreed: "Lieutenant General Jim Galvin thought instead of going out on big operations we should secure selected areas—enclaves. I guess it never happened because our commanders never thought about it very much. General Westmoreland just kept flying around in his helicopter, fighting big operations with fancy names, and never thought about doing it any other way."[7]

President Johnson shared many of Taylor's concerns; after the Brinks Hotel bombing, he had cabled Taylor in response to army and air force requests for bombing reprisals against North Vietnam:

I have never felt that this war will be won from the air, and it seems to me that what is much more needed and would be more effective is a larger and stronger use of rangers and special forces and marines, or other appropriate military strength on the ground and on the scene . . . I know that it might involve the acceptance of larger American sacrifices [but] I myself am ready to substantially increase the number of Americans in Vietnam if it is necessary to provide this kind of fighting force against the Vietcong.[8]

As U.S. military enthusiasm for a deployment of American ground forces continued to grow, President Johnson maintained his interest in finding a way to prevent "our committing a good many American boys to fighting a war that I think ought to be fought by the boys of Asia to help protect their own land."[9] McGeorge Bundy reminded Ambassador Taylor on 15 April 1965, "The President had repeatedly emphasized his personal desire for a strong experiment in the encadrement of U.S. troops with the Vietnamese."[10] General Westmoreland turned the idea over to his deputy, Lieutenant General Throckmorton, who noted that there would be both language difficulties and increased support requirements for American personnel under such a plan. He recommended that the experiment not be tried: American soldiers simply did not lead native forces. Westmoreland agreed and the idea was put to rest at the 18 April 1965 Honolulu Conference.[11] In a similar vein, Secretary of Defense McNamara authorized the creation of a unified command such as the one that had coordinated U.S., Korean, and third-country forces during the Korean War, but the concept was vetoed by Taylor, Westmoreland, and the CINCPAC Admiral Sharp.[12]

The first American ground combat forces in Vietnam were two battalions of marines sent to protect logistical installations at Danang.[13] They splashed ashore on 8 March 1965, "committed to provide initial security of U.S. installations and facilities, to be expanded to include engagement in counterinsurgency operations."[14] The U.S. military's blood was up; it was about to fight a war that it had no doubt it would win, and win quickly.[15] A press release trumpeted, "The United States has enormous military power—greater than any nation in the history of the world. It will use whatever portion of that power is needed to help defend the freedom of the Vietnamese people and to help defeat the ambitions of the Communist aggressors."[16] A Joint Chiefs of Staff Study Group Report dated 14 July 1965 relegated GVN forces to what the Americans considered to be a secondary role:

Presently organized and planned GVN forces, except for reserve battalions . . . would retain control over areas now held, extend pacification operations and area control where permitted by the progress of major offensive operations, defend critical areas and installations against VC attack and seek out and eliminate VC militia units. U.S., SVN, and Third-Country forces, by offensive land and air action would locate and destroy VC/DRV forces, bases and major war-supporting organizations in SVN. The cumulative effect of sustained, aggressive conduct of offensive operations, coupled with the interdiction of DRV efforts to provide the higher level of support required in such a combat environment, should lead to progressive destruction of the VC/DRV main force battalions.[17]

Westmoreland's strategy similarly postponed the "Phase II task" of "Resume and/or expand pacification operations," to follow the Phase I task of "Conduct offensive operations against major VC base areas in order to divert and destroy VC main forces."[18] The offensive orientation gained strength, as Wheeler led Westmoreland to ask for more troops: "We are also considering what additional U.S. Combat Support units you might be able to employ in key locations. In this regard, we are thinking in terms of artillery, tanks and APCs [Armored Personnel Carriers]."[19] The same attitude showed when Wheeler argued for more troops at a meeting of the National Security Council on 21 July 1965: "The more men we have, the greater the likelihood of smaller losses. . . . This means greater bodies of men—which will allow us to cream them."[20] The Joint Chiefs of Staff agreed, stating on 27 August: "By aggressive and sustained exploitation of superior military force, the United States/Government of Vietnam would seize and hold the initiative in both the DRV and RVN, keeping the DRV, the Viet Cong, and the PL/VM [Pathet Lao/Viet Minh] at a disadvantage, progressively destroying the DRV war-supporting power and defeating the Viet Cong."[21]

Westmoreland later explained his strategy.

Even those troops assigned security missions participated in offensive operations. Only minimum numbers remained in static defense, while the bulk of the units pushed into the countryside, patrolling to find the enemy, attacking him, and preventing him from massing to hit the installations. Without a vast expenditure of manpower, providing leakproof defensive lines around installations or cities in the manner of Confederate trenches before Richmond was impossible.[22]

Instead, "Base camps established, all units were constantly on the offensive, seeking any enemy that might be encountered: guerrillas, local force, or main force. This is not to say that the men were constantly under fire, as they might have been in a prolonged conventional campaign. As often as not, the enemy was not to be found."[23]

When the enemy was found, Westmoreland's tactics was to "pile on" as many troops as were available, supported by close air support, artillery, and even B-52 strikes, to kill as many of the Viet Cong and North Vietnamese

Army (NVA) soldiers as possible. USMC Major General John Grinalds recalls: "Everyone was very excited about counterinsurgency operations, but when we got into it and started doing it, we forgot everything we'd learned from studying the textbooks. The way we used US forces wasn't after the right objective; we should have unhinged the VC from their infrastructure."[24]

An important early battle was fought by the army's First Cavalry Division in the Ia Drang Valley in November 1965; the most intense fighting took place between 14 and 18 November. Immediately after the battle Lieutenant Colonel Moore, the battalion commander, informed his higher command that U.S. tactics and strategy were incorrect and requested a study group be formed; he was overruled.[25] On 28 January 1966 the Third Brigade of the First Cavalry Division attacked Bong Son, a densely populated region on the coast of central Vietnam. The heavy firepower caused civilian casualties; however, "Within one week after we pulled out, the North Vietnamese and Viet Cong Main Force units had returned." Moore states:

The American Mission and the Military Assistance Command—Vietnam had not succeeded in coordinating American and South Vietnamese military operations with follow-on Vietnamese government programs to reestablish control in the newly cleared regions. If they couldn't make it work in Bong Son—where the most powerful American division available had cleared enemy forces from the countryside—how could they possibly hope to reestablish South Vietnamese control in other regions where the American military presence was much weaker?[26]

Once the Viet Cong experienced American firepower they quickly changed their tactics, "hugging" American units to preclude the use of close air support and artillery strikes. The Viet Cong thus demonstrated tactical flexibility and willingness to admit and learn from their mistakes, quite unlike U.S. forces. Stanley Karnow records that criticism and self-criticism forums were held in VC units after operations: officers and men admitted mistakes and denounced each other for errors in battle. The sessions not only contributed to group cohesion but also encouraged the learning of tactical and operational lessons.[27]

The army's focus on firepower and attrition increased for the next several years. In Operation MASHER (later renamed WHITE WING because of President Johnson's public relations concerns), the First Cavalry Division fired 140,000 artillery rounds, killed 1,342 Viet Cong, and captured 633 Viet Cong soldiers and 1,087 suspected VC in Binh Dinh province during January, February, and early March 1966. As a result, the enemy had been driven from the coastal plain, according to the division's after action report, and "So far as is now known, the GVN intends to reestablish a government in this area."[28]

The results were short-lived. As Major General Tillson recalled, "There was no main line of resistance in Vietnam. It was a completely different war. A unit would pacify an area in Vietnam and wouldn't hold it after a large operation and a year later would have to clear it again because the VC had reinfiltrated."[29] Almost exactly a year after MASHER, the First Cavalry Division fought again for control of Binh Dinh in Operation THAYER II. After thousands more artillery shells and 171 B-52 strikes, the division's official report stated that 80 percent of the population of Binh Dinh were "free from organized Vietcong control, at least temporarily. This is not to mean that they have been brought under government control . . . As far as political control is concerned, the AO [Area of Operations] is still a power vacuum."[30] The creation of refugees in such operations was actually part of the American strategy, as General Westmoreland admitted. "I tried to explain . . . why refugees were created and used the 'fish in the water' concept, whereby we can pacify an area by catching the fish (the communist political and military officials) or drain off the water (the people) in order to strangle the fish. We therefore found it necessary in some cases to displace the population as a means of getting at the communist infra-structure."[31]

During Operation CEDAR FALLS from 8 to 27 January 1967 in the "Iron Triangle" northwest of Saigon, two U.S. infantry divisions with ARVN support faced little organized VC resistance, though a great deal of rice, ammunition, uniforms, and documents were captured. Less than two weeks after the conclusion of CEDAR FALLS, an Assistant Division Commander reported, "The Iron Triangle was again literally crawling with what appeared to be Viet Cong."[32]

In Operation JUNCTION CITY, from 22 February through 15 April 1967, twenty-two U.S. and four ARVN battalions "confirmed . . . that such multi-division operations have a place in modern counterinsurgency warfare,"[33] but that "it was a sheer physical impossibility to keep the enemy from slipping away whenever he wished if he were in terrain with which he was familiar—generally the case."[34]

The U.S. Army focused its efforts on destroying the enemy through the use of the American advantages of artillery, close air support, and mechanized forces despite evidence that the tactics were less than effective in accomplishing strategic objectives. Yet in the northernmost part of South Vietnam—ironically, where the threat of a conventional invasion was greatest—the U.S. Marine Corps (USMC) was taking a very different tack.

USMC AND THE COMBINED ACTION PLATOON

"You cannot win militarily. You have to win totally, or you are not winning at all."
—USMC Lieutenant General "Brute" Krulak, July 1966

In contrast to Westmoreland, who advocated a "search and destroy" strategy, Major General Lew Walt, commander of the III Marine Amphibious Force (MAF) in I Corps, in the northernmost part of South Vietnam, took advantage of the USMC's organizational history of pacification in small wars. Walt created a coordinating council of the regional civilian agency heads in sector, ARVN and U.S. military commanders, and a Vietnamese government representative. He also integrated marine rifle squads into Vietnamese Regional Forces platoons. These "Combined Action Platoons" lived in the villages of I Corps and focused on pacification while regular marine battalions divided their time between platoon-sized patrols and civic programs. Lieutenant General Krulak, Commanding General Marine Force Pacific, appealed to Secretary of Defense McNamara that the safer roads and more secure hamlets in I Corps, although "harder to quantify," were a better measure of success than MACV Commander Westmoreland's body count: "The raw figure of VC killed . . . can be a dubious index of success since, if their killing is accompanied by devastation of friendly areas, we may end up having done more harm than good."[35] General Westmoreland disagreed: "Rigidity in doctrine is not a virtue and problems exist to be overcome. I believed the Marines should have been trying to find the enemy's main forces and bring them to battle, thereby putting them on the run and reducing the threat they posed to the population."[36] On 8 December 1965 Westmoreland wrote:

The Marines have become so infatuated with securing real estate and in civic action that their forces have become dispersed and they have been hesitant to conduct offensive operations except along the coastline where amphibious maneuvers could be used with Naval gunfire support which is available. Over the last several months, this matter has been discussed with General Walt and I have written two letters to him emphasizing the importance of having adequate reserves to take the fight to the enemy.[37]

Despite the encouraging results of the combined action platoon (CAP) experiment, Westmoreland did not widen the concept to include army units. "Although I disseminated information on the platoons and their success to other commands, which were free to adopt the idea as local conditions might dictate, I simply had not enough numbers to put a squad of Americans in every hamlet; that would have been fragmenting resources and exposing them to defeat in detail."[38]

William Lederer noted that in 1967 the number of villages under Communist control increased except in one small area where the United States Marine Corps CAPs were operating. Lederer judged CAPs to be "the only successful American project of any kind whatsoever in Vietnam."[39] Brigadier Kenneth Hunt of the International Institute of Strategic Studies (IISS) was also impressed with the CAP concept, but "When I went down to MACV and referred to this, they said that I had been fixed by the Marines, been brain-washed! They did not agree and said that in any case it would be too expensive."[40]

The CAP strategy originated in the village of Phu Bai, an outgrowth of Walt's memories of a similar technique in Nicaragua.[41] It worked almost immediately:

As a result of these joint patrols, the Vietcong network in four villages around Phu Bai has been measurably damaged, though the Communists still slip in eight or ten armed agents at a time to collect food and taxes from the population and nothing as advanced as a Census/Grievance and Aspiration unit can yet function safely. Road traffic in the area has picked up noticeably, and hamlet markets now attract buyers and sellers from as far off as two kilometers, which may not sound like much but is a lot compared with what the safe-travel radius was six months ago.[42]

The CAP experiment was begun by Marine Captain Jim Cooper, commander of a marine company near Chlai. Cooper decided to deploy his marines inside the hamlet of Thanh My Trung and leave them there. Increasing both night and combined operations with the Popular Forces unit in the hamlet, Cooper's tactics resulted in the Viet Cong, abandoning Thanh My Trung.[43] A marine observer credited the Regional Forces and Popular Forces (RF/PF) with rising to the challenge: "The Vietnamese like being part of an organization which cares, and they respond well and bravely. . . . There are sufficient men who will fight if they know the system is competent and cares."[44]

General Taylor reported that Westmoreland was encouraging the experiment: "He endorses the expansion of US/Free World forces of control over terrain and population around base areas in application of the 'oil spot' concept as the Marines have been doing in the I Corps area (and other US forces elsewhere to a lesser degree)."[45] As did Westmoreland, however, Taylor hesitated to expand the program: "Perhaps it should be approved, but only after a careful analysis and in full knowledge of its implications."[46] U.S. Marine Corps Major General John Grinalds has a more positive assessment. "CAP utilized the oil spot concept, promulgated by Krulak and supported by Abrams. If we had devoted the time early on to building links in the urban areas in order to get to know the population and begin to find the VCI, it would have made a real difference. There was too little CAP, too late."[47]

PROGRAM FOR THE PACIFICATION AND LONG-TERM DEVELOPMENT OF SOUTH VIETNAM

Perhaps the best chance for the army to learn that its counterinsurgency procedures were flawed, to accept that fact at a high level within the organization, and to implement organizational and doctrinal change as a result was Army Chief of Staff Harold K. Johnson's decision to commission a high-level study in mid-1965. The Program for the Pacification and Long-Term Development of South Vietnam (PROVN) group, under the leadership of General Creighton Abrams, was tasked with "developing new courses of action to be taken in South Vietnam by the United States and its allies, which will, in conjunction with current actions, modified as necessary, lead in due time to successful accomplishment of U.S. aims and objectives."[48] The conclusions of the study were striking; it repudiated the army's current emphasis on search-and-destroy operations and urged a move toward pacification through winning over the population to the government's cause. Most notable is the lack of enthusiasm for false optimism as practiced by MACV. The final report of the PROVN study, submitted to the Chief of Staff of the Army in March 1966, simply stated:

The situation in South Vietnam has seriously deteriorated. 1966 may well be the last chance to ensure eventual success. 'Victory' can only be achieved through bringing the individual Vietnamese, typically a rural peasant, to support willingly the GVN. The critical actions are those that occur at the village, district, and provincial levels. This is where the war must be fought; this is where that war and the object which lies beyond it must be won.[49]

The PROVN study, after turning on its head the army priority of killing Viet Cong, next enumerated a number of specific changes in U.S. Army policy necessary to accomplish the true goal of winning support for the government. Many struck directly at COMUSMACV's authority as well as his strategy; U.S. military operations should be scaled down and decentralized "on the provincial level to include the delegation of command authority over U.S. operations to the Senior U.S. Representative at the provincial level."[50] Further, COMUSMACV would work for the ambassador if the group's recommendations were followed; the ambassador would be granted "unequivocal authority as the sole manager of all U.S. activities, resources, and personnel in country" and would be responsible for developing "a single integrated plan for achieving U.S. objectives in South Vietnam [which were] . . . a free and independent noncommunist South Vietnam."[51]

This would require the unification of all security forces into a single entity dedicated to ensuring the security of the people under the command of the province chief. "These integrated national security forces must be associated and intermingled with the people on a long-term basis. Their capacity to establish and maintain public order and stability must be physically and continuously credible. The key to achieving such security lies in the conduct of effective area saturation tactics, in and around populated areas, which deny VC encroachment opportunities."[52]

In short, the entire American policy since the development of the

MAAG—creating an ARVN in the image of the U.S. army, equipping it with heavy weapons and helicopter support, using American troops on firepower-based search and destroy missions—was repudiated by the PROVN study. The key to success in Vietnam was the creation of security forces "associated and intermingled with the people on a long-term basis" such as the CIDG under CIA control, or the USMC's combined action platoons. PROVN was described in the *Pentagon Papers* as "a major step forward in thinking"; the *Pentagon Papers* hypothesized that "the candor with which it addressed matters was probably possible only because it originated within a single service, and thus did not require the concurrences of an inter-agency study."[53]

Although an internal army study, PROVN failed to gain immediate concurrence from its parent service. Army Chief of Staff General Johnson, initially permitted no discussion of PROVN outside the Army Staff in the Pentagon.[54] Eventually the Joint Chiefs of Staff and Secretary of Defense McNamara were briefed on the study, and only then was a copy forwarded to COMUSMACV for his comments. General Westmoreland was predictably cool to the proposals, cautioning, "It must be realized that there are substantial difficulties and dangers inherent in implementing this or any similar program. . . . [A]ny major reorganization such as envisioned by PROVN must be phased and deliberate to avoid confusion and slow-down in ongoing programs."[55]

In a final attempt to preclude any tampering with his authority or strategy, Westmoreland recommended that the PROVN study be downgraded to a "conceptual document, carrying forward the main thrusts and goals of the study" to "be presented to National Security Council for use in developing concepts, policies, and actions to improve the effectiveness of the American effort in Vietnam."[56]

Thus, the army's best chance of reforming itself was pushed upstairs to the level of the National Security Council (NSC). The PROVN study is a remarkable document, demonstrating the spirit of dispassionate appraisal of organizational effectiveness that is the first step of the organizational learning cycle—the same step taken by John Paul Vann and a number of his fellow advisers a few years previously. The authors of PROVN demonstrated integrity and moral courage in presenting what were certain to be unpopular conclusions to the highest levels of the army, men who had previously written and approved the very policies their juniors were now questioning. The learning cycle stopped at the level of COMUSMACV and the chief of staff of the army, both of whom were unwilling or unable to change policies and viewpoints rooted deep in the organizational culture of the U.S. army. Even if the army failed to adapt itself as a result of PROVN, however, its masters would force adaptation on the organization as a result of the study and of the increasingly inescapable reality of failed American policy in South Vietnam.[57]

CHANGE FROM ABOVE?

Whereas the MACV commander's downgrading of the PROVN study to a "conceptual document" and referral of those concepts to the NSC for study precluded the army as a whole from changing its focus away from search and destroy to pacification, the army's political masters were about to change Westmoreland's strategy for him. That strategy is well summed up by General Westmoreland's statement on the relative importance of the two missions in August 1966, just after the PROVN study was released:

The essential tasks of Revolutionary Development and nation building cannot be accomplished if enemy main forces can gain access to the population centers and destroy our efforts. US/Free World Forces, with their mobility and in coordination with RVNAF, must take the fight to the enemy by attacking his main force units and invading his base areas. Our ability to do this is improving steadily.... Sustained ground combat operations will maintain pressure on the enemy.[58]

MACV's conceptualization of the military and revolutionary development tasks as separate and separable was of long standing; early on in the commitment of U.S. ground forces, in successive paragraphs of the January 1965 MACV Monthly Evaluation Report, COMUSMACV reports that "the military experienced the most successful single month of the counterinsurgency effort," although "pacification made little progress this month."[59] The importance of pacification to MACV is clearly shown in the designation of the effort to win the support and security of the population as "the other war."[60] Major General Tillson, MACV operations officer in 1966, remembers: "We never did pay any attention to the COIN area. My predecessor, Major General Bill DePuy, never hesitated about heavy artillery preparation. He never thought about COIN—he was fighting nothing but a conventional war."[61]

The American Mission in South Vietnam under the leadership of Ambassador Lodge established a Priorities Task Force in April 1966 to examine all American efforts in South Vietnam from an interagency perspective. It noted the high cost to the nation inflicted by the army's emphasis on preventing a repeat of a Korean-style invasion: "After some 15 months of rapidly growing U.S. military and political commitment to offset a major enemy military effort, the RVN had been made secure against the danger of military conquest, but at the same time it has been subjected to a series of stresses which threaten to thwart U.S. policy objectives."[62]

A number of those stresses, including rising inflation and the pervasive American presence, were the results of American policies; others, including endemic corruption in the Government of South Vietnam, were influenced by that presence. Consequently, "GVN control of the countryside is not now being extended through pacification to any significant degree and pacification in the rural areas cannot be expected to proceed at a rapid rate."[63]

Even MACV was beginning to acknowledge, under firm prodding from Washington and Deputy U.S. Ambassador Porter in Vietnam, that its own policies had been counterproductive in the pacification effort. MACV Operations Officer Major General Tillson briefed the Mission Council on 8 August 1966, acknowledging: "Since its inception, ARVN has been oriented, trained, and led towards the task of offensive operations. . . . It is difficult, in a short period of time, to redirect the motivation and training of years, and to offset the long indoctrination that offensive action against the VC is the reason for the existence of the Army."[64]

Westmoreland was beginning to feel the pressure; on 24 August 1966 he sent CINCPAC and the Joint Chiefs of Staff (JCS) a statement of the strategy he planned to follow for the coming year. Although the aggressive orientation on drawing the enemy into battle in a "general offensive" by U.S. forces remained, COMUSMACV emphasized the role of ARVN in rural development (RD). "The growing strength of US/FW Forces will provide the shield and will permit ARVN to shift its weight of effort to an extent not heretofore feasible to direct support of RD. . . . The priority effort of ARVN forces will be in direct support of the RD program; in many instances the province chief will exercise operational control over these units."[65]

In another bow to traditional population security counterinsurgency methods, Westmoreland promised that a "significant number" of allied combat troops would be committed to the pacification of tactical areas of responsibility (TAORs): "These missions encompass base security and at the same time support RD by spreading security radially from the bases to protect more of the population."[66] Helping to explain the shift in strategy was Ambassador Lodge's endorsement at the conclusion of the message, stressing his "agreement with the attention paid in this message to the importance of military support for RD. After all, the main purpose of defeating the enemy through offensive operations against the main forces and bases must be to provide the opportunity through RD to get at the heart of the matter, which is the population of SVN."[67]

Westmoreland's strategy statement found receptive ears in Washington. After another trip to Saigon, Secretary of Defense McNamara sent President Johnson a memorandum highlighting the value of pacification and the need for dramatic changes in military operations to encourage it. Dated 14 October 1966, the statement is one of the most important indicators of McNamara's emerging doubts about military solutions in Vietnam:

The large-unit operations war, which we know best how to fight and where we have had our successes, is largely irrelevant to pacification as long as we do not lose it. . . . Success in pacification depends on the interrelated functions of providing physical security, destroying the VC apparatus, motivating the people to cooperate, and establishing responsive local government. An obviously necessary but not sufficient requirement for success of the RD cadre and police is vigorously conducted and adequately prolonged clearing operations by military troops who will "stay" in the area, who behave themselves decently and who show respect for the people.[68]

The Joint Chiefs of Staff, after reviewing McNamara's statement, profoundly disagreed, making a case for increases in the bombing of North Vietnam and in the commitment of U.S. troops to the conflict. They also expressed their belief that COMUSMACV should be placed in charge of pacification rather than Deputy Ambassador William Porter, who was currently running the program.[69]

Continuing the conflict between the military and their civilian masters over the proper balance between offensive operations and population security, Ambassador Lodge cabled Washington on 6 November that in order to increase security in the villages, which he believed to be the crux of the problem, "We must make more U.S. troops available to help out in pacification operations as we move to concentrate ARVN effort" toward pacification. Lodge argued for a cadre system in which a force composed of 10 percent U.S. soldiers leading ARVN troops would be the "catalyst" for their Vietnamese "buddy system" partners; U.S. troops would "lead by example" to "get the whole thing moving faster." Noting that the procedure had already been tried by the U.S. Marines, the First and Twenty-fifth Infantry Divisions, and the Korean Army, Lodge contended, "It can be made to work" and "would eventually get at Viet Cong recruiting—surely an achievement which would fundamentally affect the course of the war." Sensitive to the army's emphasis on "seizing and maintaining the offensive," Lodge wondered "whether the above result could not be achieved if the phrase 'offensive operations' were to be redefined so that instead of defining it as meaning 'seek out and destroy,' which I understand is now the case, it would be defined as 'split up the Viet Cong and keep him off balance.'" Lodge claimed that several advantages would result from the change, noting that redefining "the phrase 'offensive operations' would mean fewer men for the purely 'military' war, fewer U.S. casualties and more pacification. It would also hasten the revamping of the ARVN . . . by 'on-the-job-training.'"[70]

Here Lodge had gone too far, awakening fears in Washington that the South Vietnamese would become as dependent on U.S. forces in pacification as they had in conventional military operations. On 12 November Secretary of State Rusk, Secretary of Defense McNamara, and Robert Komer replied to Lodge in a cable: "General Westmoreland plans use of limited number U.S. forces in buddy system principle to guide and motivate ARVN in RD/P [Revolutionary Development Program]." The cable also expressed serious doubts about any further involvement of U.S. troops beyond that in straight pacification operations. We fear this would tempt Vietnamese to leave this work more and more to us and we believe pacification, with its intimate contact with population, more appropriate for Vietnamese forces, who must after all as arm of GVN establish constructive relations with population. Hence we believe there should be no thought of U.S. taking substantial share of pacification.[71]

This ended Lodge's attempt, against the wishes of MACV and the Joint Chiefs, to force direct U.S. army participation in the provision of local security to the populace. His vision of changing the army's orientation on offensive operations collided with the army's concept of how it wanted to fight the war and was defeated by its organizational consensus on warfighting at the expense of pacification.

CIVIL OPERATIONS AND REVOLUTIONARY DEVELOPMENT SUPPORT, 1967–1971

Whereas both political and military leader of the United States paid lip service to the importance of combined political military efforts to defeat the rural insurgency in Vietnam, little effort was actually expended in this arena before 1967. Robert Komer notes "delayed and inadequate execution in practice owing mostly to the bureaucratic obstacles to generating such an atypical effort through existing institutions."[72] There was no organization in the United States government trained and equipped to perform this mission, and little incentive for existing institutions to adapt to meet the need for such an organization even if that need had been widely recognized. "It's the great difficulty of getting things done by the bureaucracy, especially when you're confronted with an exceedingly atypical situation which requires exceedingly atypical responses. . . . We were very unsatisfied with the military performance in support of pacification."[73]

Komer's personal and very vigorous intervention (he was nicknamed "the Blowtorch" for his manner of getting accomplished what he wanted) was instrumental in creating perhaps the most remarkable example of American institutional innovation during the Vietnam War: Civil Operations and Revolutionary Development Support, or CORDS.

The CIA was the driving force behind the creation of the Revolutionary Development (RD) program in 1965, which was spearheaded by armed fifty-nine-member RD teams. At about the same time there were early efforts to create a Vietnamese paramilitary structure for local security: the Police Field Force (PFF), sponsored by the American Agency for International Development (AID). Komer believes that they were ineffective because of their "insufficient scale in relation to the needs of the countryside, and lack of a territorial security environment within which they could thrive."[74] Nonetheless, RD teams and the PFF troops were an important step in the right direction. Major General Lansdale was initially assigned to be the chief adviser to the RD program, but he created more enemies than friends and was replaced by Deputy Ambassador Porter after the Honolulu Conference of February 1966. At this conference, Komer was also appointed to serve as special assistant to the president to manage the Washington end of what was then still called "the other war." Komer pushed for the creation of the Office of Civil Operations (OCO) in Saigon in December 1966 to coordinate the pacification activities of all U.S. civilian agencies. "I discovered very early on that the key to the Other War was local security, and that the guts of local security was pacification. And in order to do the civilian things that needed to be done you had to get local security that the big American battalions, or ARVN, were not handling."[75]

He knew that progress would be slow without active military involvement: "If you are ever going to get a program going, you are only going to be able to do it by stealing from the military. They have all the trucks, they have all the planes, they have all the people, they have all the money—and what they did not have locked up, they had a lien on."[76]

Komer was able to pull together all of the American civilian and military pacification programs into Civil Operations and Revolutionary Development Support (CORDS) under MACV control on 1 May 1967. The cause of this dramatic change, in which civilians and the military worked together in support of pacification, was "cumulative Washington frustration with the reluctance, even inability, of the fragmented U.S. Mission in Saigon to get a major pacification effort going."[77] Komer's desire for the job and his creative bureaucratic infighting did a great deal to overcome institutional resistance. He became the first deputy for CORDS, with the rank of ambassador.

CORDS was a dramatic change from business as usual, incorporating personnel from CIA, USIA, AID, the State Department, the White House, and all the military services. In addition to Komer, who worked directly for COMUSMACV, each of the four American corps commanders had a deputy for pacification; the "cutting edge" of CORDS, however, was unified civil-military advisory teams in all 250 districts and forty-four provinces.[78] In addition to being purpose-built for the demands of counterinsurgency warfare in Vietnam and integrating civilian and military personnel at all levels to promote a combined political-military approach to problem recognition and solution, CORDS had the dramatic advantage of not being constrained by an institutional culture with preconceived ideas of how missions should be accomplished: "CORDS in effect wrote the field manual as it went along."[79] The organization, a revolutionary development in its own right, encouraged innovation from its personnel as a primary facet of its developing organizational culture, creating or improving:

(a) a series of new measurement systems designed primarily for management purposes

(b) the "Chieu Hoi" defector program

(c) 59-man RD teams and associated village self-development programs

(d) the GVN National Training Center at Vung Tau

(e) a new Vietnam Training Center in Washington to train CORDS advisers

(f) the GVN Phung Hoang program, an ambitious effort to destroy Viet Cong infrastructure by any means necessary, known as "Phoenix" to Americans

(g) the CORDS Evaluation Branch to provide accurate reports of conditions in the field to top management

(h) the People's Self-Defense forces, created after the 1968 Tet Offensive[80]

CORDS spurred changes in the GVN as well. William Colby, the director of the Phoenix Program, notes:

President Thieu quickly understood that a major strategy of pacification required the kind of unified management structure the Americans had finally produced in the CORDS machinery. In response, he set up a Central Pacification and Development Council to direct the campaign and the work of all the Ministries and agencies of the government involved in it. . . . All of the government ministries, including Defense plus the Joint General Staff, were represented in the council, so that its directives were specific and binding on all the local organs involved in the pacification campaign.[81]

Komer notes, "In strong contrast to the sheer conventionality of most aspects of the GVN/U.S. response, it did eventually prove possible to set up and carry out a major US/GVN wartime program specifically designed to meet many of the atypical problems of people's war in South Vietnam."[82]

That CORDS was able to do so, and in so doing to win the grudging acceptance of the army for its efforts, speaks more of Komer's personal characteristics and ability to gain the ear of the president than of the army's willingness to adapt to the demands of counterinsurgency warfare in Vietnam. Komer and CORDS well deserve Colby's assessment: "For the first time there was an American with responsibility for and interest in these essential units [RF/PF], so long neglected in the American military's enthusiasm for building up the regular Army, Navy, and Air Force—on those occasions, that is, when American attention turned from the disposition and operations of American forces themselves."[83] But in the end, as Komer himself puts it, "The greatest problem with pacification was that it wasn't tried seriously until too late, or if not too late certainly very late in the day."[84]

TET AND AFTER

Amid the optimism that the Army's search and destroy strategy was winning the war in South Vietnam, the Tet Offensive of February 1968 had a huge impact on American public opinion and led to substantial changes in American support for the war. Westmoreland, steeped in the U.S. Army's organizational culture, which saw the battlefield as the place where wars were won and lost, was convinced that Tet had been an American victory. The uprising resulted in the destruction of much of the Viet Cong infrastructure in South Vietnam, and in purely military terms could be viewed a victory; Westmoreland, who saw all events in SVN through a military prism, was thus strictly correct.[85] Those with a broader perspective thought differently.

General Earle Wheeler, Chairman of the JCS, took advantage of the post-Tet air of panic in Washington to urge Westmoreland to ask for more troops for South Vietnam. The Joint Chiefs were concerned that the vast deployment of 525,000 men to Vietnam was stripping the United States of its strategic reserve and continued to press President Johnson to call the Reserves to active duty to reconstitute America's military power. Westmoreland, at Wheeler's urging, therefore requested reinforcements "not only to contain [the enemy's] I Corps offensive but also to capitalize on his losses by seizing the initiative in other areas. Exploiting this opportunity could materially shorten the war."[86]

President Johnson sent Westmoreland another 10,000 men without calling up the Reserves over the Joint Chiefs' protests that doing so would further weaken the strategic reserve; JCS Chairman Wheeler returned from a visit to Saigon to brief Johnson that Westmoreland urgently needed another 200,000 troops. The president balked at his request, which would have necessitated the call-up of a quarter of a million reservists, and requested Clark Clifford, who was due to take over as secretary of defense from Robert McNamara the next day, to reassess U.S. strategy in Vietnam completely.

Of the resulting analyses, that of the Secretary of Defense's Department of International Security Affairs (ISA) was the most pessimistic. Noting that although Tet had resulted in heavy VC casualties, it had also damaged the ARVN substantially, an ISA memo dated 22 February 1968 questioned the ability of the ARVN to recover:

In the new, more dangerous environment to come about in the countryside, and as currently led, motivated, and influenced at the top, ARVN is even *less* likely than before to buckle down to the crucial offensive job of chasing district companies and (with U.S. help) provincial battalions. In that environment, informers will clam up, or be killed; the VC will get more information and cooperation, the GVN less; officials and the police will be much less willing to act on information on VC suspects and activities.[87]

The study concluded that U.S. forces, at *any* level, could not win the war; only fundamental improvement in the military and political leadership of South Vietnam could defeat the insurgents. To assist the GVN in accomplishing this objective, the U.S. should adopt a strategy of population security along the demographic frontier, abandoning search and destroy missions in the sparsely inhabited parts of Vietnam and concentrating on separating the enemy from his sources of support in the population. The study gives very specific corps-by-corps instructions to COMUSMACV on how to implement the strategy; unimpressed by MACV's ability to perceive and understand failure and implement better policies, ISA analysts do that work.[88]

It is hardly surprising that this complete repudiation of MACV's strategy was not popular in the military high command. The author of the *Pentagon Papers* describes the reaction: "The Chairman of the Joint Chiefs of Staff found 'fatal flaws' in this strategy, could not accept the implied criticism of past strategy in the ISA proposal, did not think that the Defense Department civilians should be involved in issuing specific guidance to the military field commander, and supported this field commander in his request for the forces required to allow him to 'regain the initiative.' "[89] The chairman's objections led to a watering down of the analysis of the search and destroy strategy and of the proposed changes in U.S. strategy toward population control. American strategy in Vietnam should instead be reappraised in another interagency study, said the approved version; no changes to the strategy had yet been proved to be necessary.

President Johnson, confronted by disagreement between the civilian and military leaders of his Department of Defense and struggling with the issue of providing another 200,000 men to COMUSMACV, convened a panel of "Wise Men" for advice. On 22 March 1968 Johnson announced that General Westmoreland would be the army's next chief of staff; on 31 March, the president announced restrictions on the bombing of North Vietnam and on the number of soldiers he was sending to Vietnam (13,500 support troops); further, Johnson announced that he would not be a candidate for reelection.

ABE

Westmoreland was replaced as COMUSMACV by General Creighton Abrams on 1 July 1968. Abrams had worked on the 1966 PROVN study that had recommended that pacification become the top priority of the US effort in South Vietnam and had been quashed by Westmoreland.[90] Abrams's approach had been formed during 1967 when he had responsibility for the advisory relationship of the U.S. Army with the ARVN. According to William Colby, "This exposed him directly to the Vietnamese commanders and caused him to concentrate on the war from their point of view rather than from only the Americans."[91] Abrams's viewpoint is clear in a 4 June 1967 cable: "It is quite clear to me that US Army military here and at home have thought largely in terms of US operations and support of US forces. Political pressures and prestige items have forced us spasmodically to give attention to Free World Forces. ARVN and RF/PF are left to the advisors. . . . The ground work must begin here. I am working at it."[92]

Though Abrams attempted to steer the army away from search and destroy—his "one war" plan stated that "the key strategic thrust is to provide meaningful, continuing security for the Vietnamese people in expanding areas of increasingly effective civil authority"—the army culture was too strong even for him. The die had already been cast. Shortly after Abrams was assigned as Westmoreland's deputy, Bruce Palmer, then serving as III Corps commander, listened to Abrams voice his uncertainties about U.S. strategy in Vietnam. Already in 1967, however, Abrams felt that "it was really too late to change U.S. strategy. As for any major changes within MACV, the pattern was set in concrete. He felt that Westmoreland, with far more continuity of experience in Vietnam, had made up his mind, and that his job as Westmoreland's deputy was to support him in every possible way. . . . Abrams did say that he too was dismayed by the U.S.-Vietnamese organizational and operational setup that had evolved." Abrams did not further communicate his doubts: "Loyalty to his chief was his first commandment."[93]

Though some army officers maintained their habitual emphasis on search and destroy operations, in other areas there was finally substantial progress. Tet had served as "a kind of Pearl Harbor," awakening the people and government of South Vietnam to the fact that the insurgency was truly a threat and that American willingness to shoulder the burden of fighting the war was diminishing.[94] Under CORDS sponsorship a People's Self Defense Force (PSDF) was created and the U.S. Army turned to wider use of small-unit patrols conducted with ARVN units. These benefited from the comparative weakness of the VC infrastructure, much of which had been destroyed or exposed during the Tet uprising.

The pacification of the Quang Dien district of Thua Thien province in I Corps northwest of Hue by 1–502 Infantry of the U.S. 101st Airborne Division is an example of the new strategy at work. Beginning in April 1968, this operation defeated the enemy main force units and then rooted out the VC infrastructure in the villages. Relying on information provided by RF/PF forces rather than indiscriminate use of airpower and artillery, the combined US/GVN forces soon destroyed enough of the VC infrastructure to convince many VC to surrender. Performance of RF/PF forces improved under U.S. tutelage, and the RF/PF was soon conducting independent operations with U.S. helicopter support. By November the district had been pacified.[95]

Figure 7-1
General Goodpaster's Capabilities Matrix

	South Vietnam / United States	Viet Cong / North Vietnam
Infrastructure	RF/PF	VCI
Guerrilla Forces	CORDS/ARVN	Viet Cong
Main Forces	U.S. Military/ARVN	NVA

The new strategy again reflected learning at the top of the organization. General Andrew J. Goodpaster, Abrams's deputy, developed in conjunction with Abrams a matrix showing differing enemy capabilities and U.S. abilities to counter them (Figure 7-1[96]).

Goodpaster recalls: "One of my responsibilities was to put more emphasis on CORDS and RF/PF. We had a lot of differing capabilities to meet their capabilities at differing levels. Our main forces had little to do with engaging the VCI except in destroying supply caches. The third dimension of the matrix was geography, including terrain and weather as well as the human geography, how people lived in the terrain."[97]

As a result of this more sophisticated understanding of the political and military threats to the government and people of South Vietnam, and because of the exposure of much of the Viet Cong Infrastructure (VCI) during the Tet uprising, Goodpaster argued:

In Fall 1968 and Spring 1969 we could finally launch an accelerated pacification program in which ARVN and RF/PF secured areas we had cleared. Our job was to keep the NVA Main Force away from secured areas; inside them, ARVN, RF/PF, and CORDS was essential but not sufficient; it had to be part of a coordinated whole. The fact is that it was a war for the hearts and minds of the people *and* a war against the Main Force units.[98]

It is important to note that even Goodpaster, who understood the war far better than most senior army officers, persisted in positing military solutions—Regional and Popular Force militia units—to the political problems of building local support for the government, the army definition of infrastructure. More appropriate learning was occurring at even higher levels. Henry Kissinger, soon to become President Nixon's national security adviser, had criticized Westmoreland's attrition strategy in a *Foreign Affairs* article in January 1969:

We fought a military war; our opponents fought a political one. We sought physical attrition; our opponents aimed for our psychological exhaustion. In the process, we lost sight of one of the cardinal maxims of guerrilla war: the guerrilla wins if he does not lose; the conventional army loses if it does not win. The North Vietnamese used their main forces the way a bullfighter uses his cape—to keep us lunging into areas of marginal political importance.[99]

The American people were no longer willing to accept the casualties and endless commitment of U.S. forces required by this strategy, argued Kissinger; instead, it was time for the army "to adopt a strategy which is plausible because it reduces casualties. It should concentrate on the protection of the population, thereby undermining Communist political assets. We should continue to strengthen the Vietnamese army to permit a gradual withdrawal of some American forces."[100]

Abrams's campaign plan, approved early in 1969, accepted that public support for the war had diminished: "The realities of the American political situation indicate a need to consider time limitations in developing a strategy to 'win.' "[101] Abrams completely changed the emphasis of MACV strategy in his appropriately named "One War: MACV Command Overview, 1968–72," which stated:

The key strategic thrust is to provide meaningful, continuing security for the Vietnamese people in expanding areas of increasingly effective civil authority. . . . It is important that the command move away from the over-emphasized and often irrelevant "body count" preoccupation. . . . In order to provide security for the population our operations must succeed in neutralizing the VCI and separating the enemy from the population. The enemy Main Forces and NVA are blind without the VCI. They cannot obtain intelligence, cannot obtain food, cannot prepare the battlefield, and cannot move "unseen."[102]

Abrams's new strategy ran head-on into the organizational culture of the army. Although Chief of Staff of the Army Johnson was interested in raising the stature of each U.S. adviser to the ARVN to "help him escape his nagging feeling that he is a second class citizen," Johnson later stated: "We still must maintain the basic position that the Army is a *fighting* force and that our success is measured in terms of the leaders' or commanders' ability to command US troops effectively. I had to start from that basic position and I could not erode it in any way."[103]

Douglas Blaufarb's description of the reasons for halfhearted ARVN support of the pacification fight echoes the American generals' complaints:

In fact, the pacification support mission was not popular with ARVN commanders who, naturally, derived their values from their American mentors. It seemed demeaning compared with the main-force war. It also called for tedious, very basic, small-unit operations with little opportunity for dramatic battles using the full panoply of weapons at their command. Success in pacification did not bring glory and promotions. It brought hard, tedious work, nighttime operations, and casualties.[104]

Or, to quote an anonymous senior U.S. Army officer, "I'll be damned if I permit the United States Army, its institutions, its doctrine, and its traditions to be destroyed just to win this lousy war."[105] Abrams faced a tough fight in which he was only partially successful. As a low-ranking Army officer noted at the time, "Our military institution seems to be prevented by its own doctrinal rigidity from understanding the nature of this war and from making the necessary modifications to apply its power more intelligently, more economically, and above all, more relevantly."[106] Abrams's position, an analyst notes, "illustrated the powerlessness of the powerful" because, although aware of his subordinates' failure to change their operations in accordance with his directives, he was unwilling to ruin their careers for neglecting his orders and unsure that their replacements would be any more willing to fight the war in a manner antithetical to everything they had been taught was how wars should be fought.[107]

One of Abrams's subordinates, Lieutenant General Julian J. Ewell, first as Ninth Infantry Division commander and later as II Field Force commander, continued to demonstrate a preoccupation with body counts rather than pacification.[108] In his debriefing report of September 1969 Ewell wrote: "I guess I basically feel that the 'hearts and minds' approach can be overdone. In the Delta the only way to overcome VC control and terror is by brute force applied against the VC."[109] The Twenty-fifth Infantry Division combat historian Jim Wright, who served as part of Ewell's II Field Force Vietnam, remembers that "division policy was to bring in all available firepower—airstrikes and all the artillery in II FFV—and then go in and sweep after the firepower had done the killing."[110] In one such "brute force" operation under General Ewell's command, Operation SPEEDY EXPRESS, conducted from 1 December 1968 through 1 June 1969 in the densely populated Upper Delta, American forces reported killing 10,883 of the enemy at a cost of 267 Americans killed. CORDS observers on the scene, however, reported that "The high body counts achieved by the 9th were not composed exclusively of active VC. The normal ratio of three or four enemy KIA for every weapon captured was raised at times to fifty to one; this leads to the suspicion that many VC supporters, willing or unwilling, and innocent bystanders were also eliminated."[111]

The same offensive orientation was displayed by Major General Melvin Zais's 101st Airborne Division in Operation APACHE SNOW in the A Shau Valley 11–20 May 1969 in an assault on Hill 937, soon to become

Figure 7-2
Decline of U.S. Combat Role, 1968–1972

	U.S. Troop Strength	Ground Operations (BTN or Larger)	KIA	KIA per 1,000
January 1968	498,000	NA	1202	2.4
July 1968	537,000	71	813	1.5
January 1969	542,000	56	795	1.5
July 1969	537,000	89	638	1.9
January 1970	473,000	58	343	0.7
July 1970	404,000	64	332	0.8
January 1971	336,000	64	140	0.4
July 1971	225,000	40	65	0.3
January 1972	133,200	9	16	0.1
July 1972	45,600	0	36	0.8

famous as "Hamburger Hill." Fifty-six Americans were killed and 420 wounded during the ten-day fight for a hill that was abandoned as soon as it was captured; the objective had been to engage the enemy where he was found.[112] The Battle of Hamburger Hill captured the attention of the nation, leading President Nixon to visit Vietnam on 30 July. During that visit, Nixon "changed General Abrams' orders so that they were consistent with the objectives of our new policies. Under the new orders, the primary mission of our troops is to enable the South Vietnamese forces to assume the full responsibility for the security of South Vietnam."[113] If Abrams was unable to change the strategy of the U.S. Army, the president was able to bring the army home; the number of U.S. forces declined steadily for the next three years, as did the number of large search and destroy operations and American casualties (see Figure 7-2[114]).

The Nixon administration's policy of turning over fighting responsibilities to the South Vietnamese while the United States continued to supply material and financial assistance, including air support for the ARVN, was announced in Guam in July 1969 and dubbed *Vietnamization* by Secretary of Defense Melvin Laird.

As American combat forces were being withdrawn, the North Vietnamese Army and Khmer Rouge insurgents in neighboring Cambodia increased their preparations for decisive attacks against South Vietnam. President Nixon ordered that their base areas be raided in early 1970. A coordinated

U.S.-ARVN attack began on 1 May 1970; it ended within two months without capturing the elusive Central Office of South Vietnam (COSVN) Headquarters. The offensive also revealed serious shortcomings in ARVN organization and performance and led to widespread protests against the widening of the war in the United States.[115] The aftermath of tragedies such as the deaths of four student protesters at Kent State University on 4 May included congressional action to force an acceleration of the U.S. withdrawal and prohibitions on operations outside SVN involving U.S. ground forces. Thus, the February 1971 invasion of Laos ordered by President Nixon was conducted entirely by ARVN forces without U.S. advisers, who had played a key role in controlling American fire support for all ARVN operations for the preceding ten years. The attack was repulsed by the NVA, displaying further weaknesses in ARVN and GVN leadership.

As Vietnamization intensified, Saigon rapidly increased the size of its regular and paramilitary forces. The U.S. advisory effort in Vietnam, however, was being scaled down concurrently, as U.S. advisers were assigned only down to ARVN corps, division, and province levels by mid-1972.[116] The ARVN struggled to create its own artillery, armor, logistical, and helicopter capabilities; taught by the U.S. Army to fight with these resources, it had grown dependent on them. The ARVN still had American airpower to call upon for support when the NVA launched a conventional invasion of the South on 31 March 1972; with that support the attack was defeated, albeit at great cost.[117] The last American ground troops were withdrawn from SVN in August 1972. The loss of American public support for the government's Vietnam policy in the wake of the Watergate scandal meant that when the North Vietnamese attacked again in April 1975, the GVN received no American air support. On 30 April 1975 Saigon fell to the North Vietnamese Army, twenty-five years to the day after President Truman had first authorized U.S. military assistance to Indochina.

ORGANIZATIONAL LEARNING IN VIETNAM, 1965–1972

Did the U.S. Army Develop a Successful Counterinsurgency Doctrine in Vietnam, 1965–1972?

An assessment of the U.S. Army's success in developing doctrine and techniques to accomplish its twin objectives in South Vietnam from 1965 through 1972—creating an ARVN capable of defeating insurgency in SVN and assisting in the defeat of the insurgency and of the NVA units in SVN through the directed application of U.S. combat power—reveals very limited success, little of which could be described as a result of the U.S. Army's own initiatives. The overall American goal remained the creation of a non-Communist SVN free to choose its own form of government.

Yet until the departure of General Westmoreland from MACV command, the means the U.S. Army used to achieve this objective were actually counterproductive in many ways. During the creation of the combined campaign plan for fiscal year 1969, the briefer stated that the mission was to "seek out and destroy the enemy"—the mission of MACV under General Westmoreland for the previous four years. Abrams stopped the briefing and wrote out on an easel, "The mission is not to seek out and destroy the enemy. The mission is to provide protection for the people of Vietnam."[118] Even when General Abrams had changed the objective at the top of the American command structure, the organizational culture remained resistant to change below him—and a great deal of damage had, of course, already been done to the social fabric of South Vietnam. In the words of Robert Franks, a lieutenant with the U.S. First Cavalry Division from July 1966 through July 1967: "We did everything we could to alienate the people. We depopulated whole provinces and moved the people to refugee centers—the perfect place for the VC to create fifth-column insurgents. The ARVN would go through and burn the villages."[119]

As a result of the confusion over the army's objectives in South Vietnam, desired results were not achieved. In the words of an official 1968 study done for the army by the Advanced Research Projects Agency: "At present there is no effective hamlet security in most of South Vietnam. Current strategy is directed toward protecting the autonomous cities, province and district capitals, and the lines of communication which connect them."[120]

One of the reasons for the failure to develop a comprehensive plan for the achievement of national objectives was the inability or unwillingness of the many organizations involved in the counterinsurgency effort to coordinate their programs, at least until the creation of CORDS in 1968. Until that time, "The 'other war'—it was all one war, as Abrams used to say, but it was being run by all sorts of different agencies. There was no unified management of the whole war . . . and that made it very difficult. The only guy fully in charge was the President, and that is not the optimum way to do things."[121] There had been an earlier effort to unify command in Vietnam, as Bob Komer recalls: "Now McNamara had considered this [Unified Command]; Westmoreland had indeed at one time proposed it back before Westmoreland became a U.S. Army commander, when he was still just the MAAG Chief, in effect. As soon as Westmoreland got an American army, he lost interest."[122]

The army that General Westmoreland commanded was a firepower-based army, one broadly inappropriate to the demands of counterinsurgency warfare in South Vietnam. Chief of Staff of the Army Harold K. Johnson described how that army implemented counterinsurgency policies during the war: "We were indiscriminate in our application of firepower, in the true sense of being discriminating, because too much of it went out on a relatively random basis. If we were really oriented after people we should have been discriminating against those people that we were after and not against all people. I think we sort of devastated the countryside. Now I don't know what the alternative to that is."[123]

The truth of General Johnson's assertions is borne out by General West-moreland's instructions to his staff on 10 December 1965. "I emphasized the importance of troops being poised for reaction against VC initiatives, for fire support to be ready [sic] available to include an airborne alert when troops are on the move, and reconnaissance by fire should be a normal procedure when moving over rough terrain using artillery and fighter bomber either dropping bombs or strafing."[124]

In restrospect, the Army Chief of Staff at the time, General Johnson, presented an alternative to the army's inappropriate use of force. "The alternative is that you control closely all of your supporting fires, direct and indirect, and that your indirect fire particularly, would be used very sparingly. Now this will cause an awful outcry from people who are prone to use that old cliche 'let's send a bullet and not a man,' but I think that it basically is a cliche, because sending the bullet didn't forestall having to send the man; as a matter of fact, it hardly ever did."[125]

It was not just the U.S. Army's employment of excessive firepower, but also the reliance on large unit operations that made it ineffective in a counterinsurgency role. To cite Johnson again: "So the large unit, I think was something like the elephant tromping down, and a lot of stuff sprayed away. People there just never did come to grips with it. Our forces employed an enormous amount of firepower which caused people just to take cover."[126]

Despite the fact that the combat environment had changed dramatically—to what the Mechanized/Armor Combat Operations in Vietnam (MACOV) study called "Area Type Warfare," in which "the elusive nature of the enemy and insufficient friendly intelligence regarding the location and activities of the enemy require that units must expect contact with the enemy at any time and from any direction"[127]—the army remained oriented in relation to its past rather than to the realities of the situation it now faced: "Current U.S. doctrine concerning combat tactics and techniques employed by armor and mechanized infantry units is based principally on experience gained during World War II and the Korean War."[128]

The ARVN remained dependent on large infusions of American artillery and close air support, logistics, and helicopters; the Regional Forces and Popular Forces were a poor stepchild until the aftermath of the Tet Offensive made "Vietnamization" a priority. Both the U.S. combat forces in SVN and their ARVN emulators used air power and artillery indiscriminately to destroy enemy forces—and, too often, the population of SVN. The U.S. Army remained organized in corps and divisions despite the success of such experiments as CIDG and CAP, which incorporated small numbers of American soldiers into local fighting units to provide population security. In short, the U.S. Army's concept of how to fight and win precluded the development of a successful counterinsurgency doctrine in South Vietnam (see Figure 7-3).

Figure 7-3
Did the U.S. Army Develop a Successful Counterinsurgency Doctrine in South Vietnam, 1965–1972?

	1950–1964	1965–1972
Victory: the achievement of national goals	No	No
Objective: the setting of realistic national goals	No	No
Unity of command: military subordination to political objectives	No	No
Minimum: minimum necessary force	No	No
Mass: appropriate structure for threat	No	No

Was the American Army in Vietnam a Learning Institution from 1965 Through 1972?

The performance of the American army as a learning institution from 1965 through 1972 is similarly mixed. Suggestions continued to percolate upward from the field, most notably from the United States Marine Corps in its Combined Action Platoons. Innovative thinking also was shown in the PROVN study, which questioned the basic assumptions of the U.S. combat role in Vietnam. Nevertheless, the learning cycle stopped at the level of the Chief of Staff of the Army in Washington and COMUSMACV in Vietnam; innovative thinking from above as well as below foundered on the army's idea of how wars should be fought. Isolated from the war by their staffs and seeing only what they wanted to see, these generals precluded organizational learning on counterinsurgency (although they did encourage innovation more in keeping with the organizational culture of the army, of which more later).

That suggestions for change continued to filter up from below, is clear in Chief of Staff of the Army Harold K. Johnson's memories of spending Christmas Day 1965 discussing tactics with a group of U.S. Army lieutenants and captains in South Vietnam:

These young fellows were saying that they were not going to be able to get the enemy out to engage in battle, as long as they were moving around in big outfits, and that they preferred to sort of set up bait situations with themselves as the bait, I think it was a platoon or a company. And I said well, I agreed with their philosophy that this was the way to get the enemy out, but I disagreed that this was the tactic that we were going to be able to adopt because there were two factors that entered in. One is that we were not going to be able to respond to public outcry in the United States about casualties by acknowledging the fact that one unit could not come to the assistance of another unit within about 10 or 15 minutes. Secondly, we could not respond to the charges of callousness toward casualties that would inevitably result from an occasional fight in that kind of an environment.[129]

Johnson's reasons for not adopting the suggestions of the junior officers in the field are echoed in Lieutenant General William Rossons's memories of institutionalized optimism at MACV Headquarters and the U.S. Embassy in Saigon when the decision was first made to deploy U.S. combat forces to South Vietnam: "The idea that the increase of U.S. effort and the seeming increase in effectiveness of the South Vietnamese units would achieve an early victory was not supported fully at the lower field levels, whereas in Saigon itself at the Military Assistance Command and embassy level it seemed to be almost the party line. We had found the secret to success; we could expect an earlier end to the conflict than many would have thought."[130]

More official analysis was also taking place that similarly was constrained by the Army's organizational culture. Colonel (Retired) Powell Hutton described the Army Combat Operations in Vietnam (ARCOV) study, conducted in early 1966 to learn lessons from the early months of direct American involvement in ground combat:

George Mabry, the Assistant Division Commander of the 1st Armored Division, ran the study. It tried to determine the best size and structure of the Army to fight in Vietnam, since the Army was still configured to fight a mechanized war in Germany. Seventy observers, Sergeants to Lieutenant Colonels, went out into the field with clipboards and asked operations research and systems anlaysis questions. Statistical analysis of many engagements over a 3-month period of time in early 1966 led to a clear picture of small, fleeting engagements. One night, at the Brink Hotel in Saigon two of us drew up the table of organization and equipment (TO&E) for an infantry battalion: four line companies per battalion, broke the Headquarters Company into two (headquarters and service), added Light Antitank Weapons (LAWs), took out recoilless rifles, added machine guns. We were trying to devise a light, mobile organization that could fight these small, scattered engagements all over the country. Combat elements of a company had to be movable by Huey; those of a battalion, by medium helicopter (the UH-21 at the time), and of a brigade, by heavy lift helicopter.[131]

Hutton describes the results of the study: "Virtually all of the changes that we recommended to the TO & E of the maneuver battalion were adopted eventually." The changes were all in line with a conventional combat orientation; "We were not into pacification at all."[132]

There were common institutional blocks to presenting a true picture of the situation on the ground and to admitting that programs are ineffective and that change is necessary. As Komer stated:

I too never heard of an establishmentarian who is supposed to be building up operating programs, who is supposed to be strengthening the morale of the troops, who is supposed to be bidding for a bigger share of the pie to get the other war going—I never heard of a guy who in the middle of a war, in particular, is going to be going out and from his position as a staff officer to the President saying:

"Jesus, this is a mess. This war stinks. These programs are no good. Everybody is incompetent, etc."[133]

Whereas the military command in Vietnam shared this requirement to report progress in the war, thus ignoring bad news that might have served to initiate change, civilians in the Department of Defense in Washington were not so hobbled by their institutional culture and by desires to protect their careers and institutions that they had failed to learn by 1967 that the army's strategy in Vietnam was ineffective. Stanley Karnow notes: "In contrast to their military colleagues, the civilians were not fettered with a rigorous belief that firepower yielded results. Nor did they fear that their careers hinged on proving that bullets and bombs would succeed. So they could assess the situation more dispassionately—or at least express their misgivings more candidly."[134]

The "can-do" attitude of the professional American military stifled prospective dissent and precluded more theoretical thinking, as General William Rosson admits in retrospect:

To move ahead, I will say that once it became apparent that we were going to send in massive forces, I was of the opinion that that was a major strategic mistake. It entailed risks we need not have taken. There were others who shared that view, but the course of action selected by the administration was clear; as I had come to learn in my military career, once decisions are made by the civilian authorities of our government or by military superiors, it is not the business of subordinates to criticize and complain about them, but to put all shoulders to the wheel and carry them out effectively. I did that.[135]

When the military did attempt to evaluate its strategies for achieving its goals in Vietnam, the institutional culture prevented truly original thinking. Thus, on 21 January 1966 General Westmoreland received a briefing from his own staff "on alternate strategies for pursuing the war, a study that I had asked him [the J-5, a staff officer] to make several weeks earlier. Nothing significant came out of the study."[136] Conducted by the same officers who had developed the strategy then in effect, it was highly unlikely to cast aspersions on its authors' previous work or reflect the intellectual acumen to break free of (or even to recognize) the assumptions on which the army's strategy was based. The same unrecognized pitfalls doomed a later study conducted just before the Tet attacks of 1968:

On 6 February J-5 briefed me on alternate courses of action. This study, which was initiated several weeks before, had as its purpose an independent appraisal of the intelligence and operational concepts and plans with the view of coming up with alternate courses of action. In other words, I wanted to have an independent look at the way we were approaching the war, disposing our forces, projecting our plans, and devising our tactics. This independent appraisal served to validate the approach we were pursuing, to include tactics, deployments, and plans.[137]

General Abrams recognized the intellectual trap into which MACV had fallen after receiving an eight-month progress report from the MACV operational analysis section: "Some of the effort going into analysis is wasteful because the data is bad. A review of the MACV operational reporting system is under way in an effort to improve the situation locally."[138] General Johnson casts doubt not just on the quality of analysis emanating from MACV, but on the entire process that was intended to capture, analyze, and disseminate lessons learned in Vietnam: "I don't really know whether the lessons we purported to have learned, were necessarily the right lessons, or conversely like every sort of a directed activity—people had reports to make, and they very faithfully made the reports, but perhaps without a full idea of what those reports ought to contain."[139]

The huge size and unwieldy structure of the Military Assistance Command—Vietnam made not only change but also learning extremely difficult. General Westmoreland refused to permit the creation of an intermediate Army Component Headquarters between the four Field Force Headquarters and him, prompting Rosson to ask, "Still, I have wondered on occasion [whether] freedom from direct responsibility for field operations would have enabled the U.S. commander to devote more of his time and thought to the larger aspects of the war, including non-military aspects."[140]

One army officer who did understand the war and had attempted to implement organizational learning in South Vietnam understood that the culture and ethos of the organization buffered General Westmoreland from bad news and thus helped put a stop to learning at the top. John Paul Vann wrote: "I feel sorry for him [Westmoreland] because even his best subordinates (and I consider General Weyand his best) continually screen him from the realities of the situation in Vietnam. As an honorable man, he has no choice but to accept what they say and report it all to his superiors."[141]

Robert Komer offers the final word on the army's inability to learn from 1965 through 1972: "Everything ran its own compartment. I think that far more than people realize, Viet Nam was a tragedy of bureaucratic inability to adapt to unconventional situations."[142]

Only when the Tet Offensive made the reality of American failure too obvious to ignore did the army respond to firm direction from its political masters to change its policies through the innovations of CORDS and the replacement of General Westmoreland with General Abrams. Abrams, who had recognized the failures of the army's policies during his leadership of the PROVN study and attempted to change the army's focus with his "One War" policy, confronted a culture that by then was so entrenched in its attitude that even the MACV commander could not change it. The organizational culture of the United States Army precluded organizational learning on counterinsurgency during the Vietnam War (See Figure 7-4).

Figure 7-4
Learning in Vietnam

	1950–1964	1965–1972
Bottom-up input: Suggestions from the field	Yes	Yes
Superiors questioned:	Yes	Yes
available:	No	Yes
Theoretical thinking;	Low Level Only	CORDS, CAP Only
Local doctrine development:	No	No
Local training centers:	No	No
Small, responsive staff:	No	No

NOTES

1. Stanley Karnow, *Vietnam: A History* (New York: Viking, 1983), 423.

2. *The Pentagon Papers: The Senator Gravel Edition*, Volume III (Boston: Beacon Press, 1971), 440.

3. Roger Hilsman, *To Move a Nation: The Politics of Foreign Policy in the Administration of John F. Kennedy* (Garden City, NY: Doubleday, 1967), 447–448.

4. *Pentagon Papers* Vol. III, 437.

5. *Pentagon Papers* Vol. III, 397.

6. Ibid., 419.

7. Major General (Retired) John Tillson interview, Washington, D.C., 9 September 1996. Tillson, MACV operations officer in 1966, admits: "I was guilty of that, too. I just never thought of any other way of doing it."

8. Karnow, *Vietnam: A History*, 425.

9. President Johnson, quoted in Neil Sheehan, ed., *The Pentagon Papers* (New York Times Editon) (New York: Bantam, 1971), 311.

10. *Pentagon Papers*, II, 475

11. Ibid.

12. *Pentagon Papers* Vol II, 477.

13. For an examination of U.S. Air Force learning from the strategic bombing and interdiction campaigns it conducted in Laos and Vietnam, see Earl Tilford, *Crosswinds: The Air Force's Setup in Vietnam* (College Station: Texas A & M University Press, 1993).

14. COMUSMACV to CG, 9th MEB, Da Nang, *Mission of the 9th MEB* (161400Z April 1965), CMH, in Andrew F. Krepinevich, Jr., *The Army and Vietnam* (Baltimore: Johns Hopkins University Press, 1985), 149.

15. "I think you can assume that the United States will be stubborn and will go blundering ahead with a strong temptation to hit someone." Robert Thompson, quoting Governor Harriman of New York in FO 371/175482 (76911/64) letter to E.H. Peck from BRIAM, Saigon (12 June 1964).

16. Memo from Barry Zorthian (director JUSPAO), regarding leaflets explaining the Presence of US Troops in Vietnam, Tab 43 to WCW, #16 History Backup, 10 May–30 June 1965 (30 June 1965), CMH.

17. *Pentagon Papers*, Vol. IV, 294.

18. Ibid., 296–297.

19. Message from General Wheeler, JCS 2360–65, regarding U.S. Military Actions in Vietnam. Tab 36 to WCW, #16 History Backup, 10 May–30 June 1965 (242123Z June 1965), CMH.

20. Larry Cable, *Unholy Grail: The U.S. and the Wars in Vietnam* (London: Routledge, 1991), 3.

21. JCSM 652–65, in *Pentagon Papers*, Vol IV, 299–300.

22. William C. Westmoreland, *A Soldier Reports* (New York: Da Capo, 1989), 162.

23. Ibid., 164.

24. Major General John Grinalds interview, Washington, D.C., 12 September 1996.

25. Harold Moore and Joseph Galloway, *We Were Soldiers Once . . . And Young* (New York: Random House, 1992). The movie, released in 2002, ignores this issue, but is a ripping good yarn and a fairly accurate tactical portrayal of the battle.

26. Ibid., 342–343.

27. Karnow, *Vietnam: A History*, 477. A similar technique was adapted by the U.S. Army at its training centers in the 1980s; called the After Action Review (AAR), it is recognized as the most important part of the training exercise. Through embarrassment in front of peers, lessons—and determination to perform better next time—are pounded into officers. For good descriptions of the AAR process and its impact on learning conventional tactics in today's U.S. Army, see James R. McDonough, *The Defense of Hill 781* (Novato, CA: Presidio Press, 1988), 52–55, and Daniel Bolger, *Dragons at War: 2–34 Infantry in the Mohave* (Novato, CA: Presidio, 1988).

28. First Cavalry Division, *AAR, MASHER/WHITE WING, 25 January–6 March 1966* (28 April 1966), 23; in Guenter Lewy, *America in Vietnam* (Oxford: Oxford University Press, 1978), 58. The author is grateful to Major Paul Yingling, USA, for so freely sharing his personal experience of the usefulness of artillery in peacekeeping and combat operations.

29. Tillson interview, 9 September 1996.

30. First Cavalry Division (Airmobile), *AAR, THAYER II, 25 October 1966–12 February 1967* (25 June 1967), Inclosure. 6–5; in Lewy, *America in Vietnam*, 56–60.

31. William C. Westmoreland, *History Notes, 28 December 1967–31 January 1968; Thursday, 4 January 1968*, 2, CMH.

32. Lewy, *America in Vietnam*, 64–65. quotation from Lieutenant General Bernard W. Rogers, *Cedar Falls–Junction City: A Turning Point* (Washington, DC: GPO, 1974), 158.

33. HQ, First Infantry Division, "After Action Report: Operation Junction City, 22 February 1967–15 April 1967," MHI, I, in Krepinevich, *The Army and Vietnam*, 191.

34. Rogers, *Cedar Falls–Junction City: A Turning Point*, 74.

35. Neil Sheehan, *A Bright Shining Lie: John Paul Vann and America in Vietnam* (New York: Vintage, 1989), 636.

36. Westmoreland, *A Soldier Reports*, 165.

37. Westmoreland, *History Notes*, Volume I. *29 August 1965–1 January 1966. Wednesday, 8 December 1965*, 160, CMH.

38. Westmoreland, *A Soldier Reports*, 166.

39. William Lederer, *Our Own Worst Enemy* (New York: W.W. Norton, 1968), 158, 186, in Robert B. Asprey, *War in the Shadows: The Guerrilla in History* (New York: William Morrow, 1994), 954. See also *Pentagon Papers*, vol. II, 476, 517, 533–536, 531.

40. Royal United Services Institute Seminar, *Lessons from the Vietnam War* (London: RUSI, 1969); in Asprey, *War in the Shadows*, 955.

41. See T. R. Fehrenbach, *U.S. Marines in Action* (Derby, CT: Monarch, 1962), 73–88, for a description of the Nicaraguan counterinsurgency efforts of the marines. See also *The Marines in Vietnam 1954–1973: An Anthology and Annotated Bibliography* (Washington, DC: Headquarters, U.S. Marine Corps/GPO, 1985).

42. Robert Shaplen, *The Road from War* (New York: Harper & Row, 1970), in Asprey, *War in the Shadows*, 820. Shaplen's description is of Phu Bai in early 1966. For a description of the United States Marine Corps guardia nacional operations in Nicaragua from 1929 to 1933, in which marine officers and noncommissioned officers led Nicaraguan troops in counterinsurgency tactics, see Asprey, *War in the Shadows*, 287–289. See also Larry Cable, *Conflict of Myths* (New York: New York University Press, 1988), 158–173, "Tribal Memories."

43. F.J. West, *The Enclave: Some Military Efforts in Ly Tin District, Quang Tin Province, 1966–1968*, TM-5941-ARPA (Santa Monica, CA: RAND, December 1969), 3. See also West, *The Village* (New York: Harper & Row, 1972).

44. Lewy, *America in Vietnam*, 117.

45. Memo 30 August 1966 to LBJ from Taylor, "Concept of Military Operations in South Vietnam," in Larry Cable, *Unholy Grail: The U.S. and the Wars in Vietnam* (London: Routledge, 1991), 134.

46. Ibid., 135.

47. Grinalds interview, 12 September 1996.

48. *Pentagon Papers*, Vol. II, 501.

49. Ibid., 576.

50. Ibid.

51. Ibid., 577.

52. Ibid.

53. Ibid.

54. The *Pentagon Papers* author notes, "Its value was reduced for a long time by the restrictions placed on its dissemination," ibid.

55. Ibid., 579.

56. Ibid., 580.

57. In 1967 Paul Nitze, secretary of the navy, formed a group of ten admirals and one marine general to assess the situation in Vietnam and recommend possible U.S. military options under the direction of Rear Admiral Gene R. La Rocque. "The appraisal my group provided demonstrated that a military victory was highly unlikely and it was our intent to report this formally to the Secretary of the Navy, the Secretary of Defense and senior officials in the Pentagon. . . . The Vice Chief of

Naval Operations, Admiral Horacio Rivero, personally and forcefully made it clear to me that distribution of the report would be detrimental to the U.S. prosecution of the war and my future in the Navy. His adamant opposition blocked subsequent distribution of the report." Eugene J. Carroll, Jr., Rear Admiral, USN (Ret.), to Jeanne Moore, September 24, 1993, and Attachment, RSMP, in Robert S. McNamara, *In Retrospect: The Tragedy and Lessons of Vietnam* (New York: Times Books, 1995), 276.

58. Westmoreland, August 1966, in *Pentagon Papers*, Vol. II, 491–493.

59. *Pentagon Papers*, Vol. II, 545–546.

60. See Peter Dawkins, *The U.S. Army and the "Other" War in Vietnam* (Unpublished Ph.D. Dissertation, Princeton University, 1979).

61. Tillson interview.

62. *Pentagon Papers II*, 580.

63. Ibid., 582.

64. Ibid., 587.

65. Ibid., 588.

66. Ibid.

67. Ibid.

68. Ibid., 599.

69. Ibid.

70. Ibid., 602–603.

71. Ibid., 604.

72. Robert Komer, *Bureaucracy Does Its Thing: Institutional Constraints on U.S.–GVN Performance in Vietnam* (Santa Monica, CA: RAND, 1973), 111.

73. Robert Komer, LBJ AC 94–2, 38.

74. Komer, *Bureaucracy Does Its Thing*, 112.

75. Paige E. Mulhollan interview with Komer (15 November 1971), LBJ AC 94–3, 32–3.

76. W. Scott Thompson and Donald D. Frizzell, eds., *The Lessons of Vietnam* (New York: Crane, Russak, 1977), 191.

77. Komer, *Bureaucracy Does Its Thing*, 114.

78. Ibid., 115.

79. Ibid.

80. Ibid., 116–117.

81. William Colby, *Lost Victory* (New York: Contemporary Books, 1989), 260.

82. Komer, *Bureaucracy Does Its Thing*, 117.

83. Colby, *Lost Victory*, 211.

84. R.W. Komer, "Organization and Management of the New Model Pacification Program, 1966–1969." Charles B. MacDonald interview (7 May 1970), 2. RAND D(L)-20104-ARPA; released by Komer 19 January 1995, CMH.

85. Westmoreland's lack of appreciation for political considerations is evident in his study of the use of tactical nuclear weapons to assist in the defense of Khe Sanh, an isolated—and surrounded—marine outpost near the Demilitarized Zone (DMZ). In his memoirs, Westmoreland argues, "Surely small tactical nuclear weapons would be a way to tell Hanoi something, just as two atomic bombs had spoken convincingly to Japanese officials during World War II." Westmoreland, *A Soldier Reports*, 338.

86. Ibid., 352.

87. *Pentagon Papers*, Vol. II, 562.

88. Ibid, 566–569.

89. *Pentagon Papers*, Vol. IV, 583.

90. Krepinevich, *The Army and Vietnam*, 182.

91. Colby, *Lost Victory*, 213.

92. General Abrams, Deputy COMUSMACV, Saigon, to General Johnson, CSA (4 June 1967), Abrams Messages, Box 1 (1–856), #06, CMH.

93. Bruce Palmer, *The 25-Year War: America's Military Role in Vietnam* (New York: Da Capo, 1984), 63–64.

94. Lewy, *America in Vietnam*, 134.

95. Leslie D. Carter, *Pacification of Quang Dien District: An Integrated Campaign* (1 March 1969), US Forces and Pacification 1969–72 file, CMH; Lewy, *America in Vietnam*, 135–136.

96. General (Retired) Andrew J. Goodpaster interview, 1 October 1996.

97. Ibid.

98. Ibid.

99. Henry Kissinger, "The Vietnam Negotiations," *Foreign Affairs* 47/2 (January 1969), 214.

100. Ibid., 233.

101. MACV, "Commander's Summary of the MACV Objectives Plan," 28–29, CMH; in Lewy, *America in Vietnam*, 137.

102. MACV, "One War: MACV Command Overview 1968–72," 15, CMH, in Lewy, *America in Vietnam*, 137.

103. Johnson CSA Washington to Abrams DEP COMUSMACV (15 July 1967), Abrams Messages, Box 1 (1–856), #27. CMH.

104. Douglas S. Blaufarb, *The Counterinsurgency Era: U.S. Doctrine and Performance 1950 to the Present* (New York: The Free Press, 1977), 253.

105. Brian M. Jenkins, *The Unchangeable War*, RM-6278-1-ARPA (Santa Monica, CA: RAND, 1972), 3, in Lewy, *America in Vietnam*, 138.

106. Jenkins, Unchangeable War, 2, in Blaufarb, *The Counterinsurgency Era*, 269.

107. Lewy, *America in Vietnam*, 138–139. There was an unwritten rule that officers would not fire incompetent subordinates, said Major General John Tillson in an interview on 9 September 1996. See Romie L. Brownlee and William J. Mullen, *Changing an Army: An Oral History of General William E. DePuy, USA Retired* (Washington, DC: GPO, 1988), 152–154, for a discussion with General DePuy about the army's culture and dismissal of subordinates.

108. Krepinevich, *The Army and Vietnam*, 53–54. Major Josiah Bunting satirized Julian Ewell in *The Lionheads: A Novel* (New York: George Braziller, 1972), his thinly disguised memoir of his own service with the Ninth Infantry Division in 1968. Focused on generating high body counts and on impressing his supervisors, Major General George Simpson Lemming reminds his staff, "We are an *infantry* division. We are not configured, either as to attitude or TO & E, to do anything but locate VC and kill them off." (43).

109. *Senior Officer Debriefing Report: LTG Julian J. Ewell, CG, 9th Infantry Division, Period 25th February to 5th April 1969* (17 September 1969), 12, CMH, in Lewy, *America in Vietnam*, 143.

110. Robert K. Wright interview, 13 September 1996.

111. MACCORDS-PSG, *Redeployment Effects of the 9th U.S. Division from Kinh Tuang and Kien Hoa Province* (3 August 1969), 2, CMH, in Lewy, *America in Vietnam*, 142.

112. Melvin Zais, *Battle at Dong Ap Bia (Hamburger Hill)* (5 January 1971), CMH.

113. Address to the Nation, 3 November 1969, U.S. President, *Public Papers of the Presidents of the United States: Richard Nixon 1969* (Washington, DC: GPO, 1971), 906, in Lewy, *America in Vietnam*, 146.

114. OASD (Comptroller), SEA Statistical Summary, Table 6 (18 August 1973), Table 9, 7 November 1973, in Lewy, *America in Vietnam*, 147.

115. See William Shawcross, *Sideshow: Kissinger, Nixon, and the Destruction of Cambodia* (New York: Simon & Schuster, 1979).

116. Now that the direct U.S. combat role was winding down, "The advisory effort enjoyed the highest priority for quality personnel, a status it had not always enjoyed in the past," when the best American officers fought for jobs leading U.S. forces in combat. Palmer, *The 25-Year War*, 118.

117. John Paul Vann, then serving as the senior American adviser to II Corps, died in a helicopter crash on 1 June 1972 after assisting in the defeat of what became known as "the Easter Offensive." The author deeply appreciates the assistance of Lieutenant Colonel (Ret.) James H. Willbanks, Ph.D., in understanding the Easter Offensive and the latter stages of the war; see his *Thiet Giap! The Battle of An Loc, April 1972* (Leavenworth, KS: U.S. Army Command and Staff College Combat Studies Institute, 1993) for a firsthand account of one of the bloodiest of the Easter Offensive battles.

118. Lewis Sorley, *Thunderbolt: General Creighton Abrams and the Army of His Times* (New York: Simon & Schuster, 1992), 237.

119. 27 September 1996 interview with Robert Franks, platoon leader 1/A/1–8 Cav/1CD July 1966–67, CMH.

120. Advanced Research Projects Agency (ARPA 1108–68), *Village Defense Study—Vietnam*, Volume I (Santa Barbara, CA: General Research Corporation, November 1968), 6, MHI.

121. Komer interview, Lyndon Baines Johnson Presidential Library, Ac 94–2, 27.

122. Ibid., 60.

123. Johnson, *SOOHP*, Vol. II, Section X, 31. Interview conducted 22 January 1973, MHI

124. *William C. Westmoreland Histories Notes, 29 August 1965–1 January 1966*, Volume I (Friday, 10 December 1965), 164–165. CMH.

125. Johnson, *Senior Officer Oral History Project*, Volume II, Section X, 32, MHI.

126. Johnson, *SOOHP*, Volume III, Section XII, 55, MHI.

127. U.S. Army, Vietnam, *Mechanized and Armor Combat Operations in Vietnam (MACOV)* (Saigon: GPO, 1967), 51.

128. Ibid., 49.

129. Johnson, *SOOHP*, Volume III, Section XII, 54–55. MHI.

130. Rosson, *SOOHP*, 296–297, MHI.

131. Colonel (Retired) Powell Hutton interview in Washington, 17 September 1996.

132. Colonel (Retired) Powell Hutton interview in Washington, 18 Spetember 1996.

133. Komer, LBJ, Ac 94–3, 46.

134. Karnow, *Vietnam: A History*, 579.

135. Rosson, *SOOHP*, 323–324, MHI.

136. *General Westmoreland's History Notes, 2 January–28 January 1966* (Volume 2) (21 January 1966), 30, CMH.

137. *Westmoreland History Notes, 28 December 1967–31 January 1968*, 35–36, CMH.

138. Abrams to Westmoreland, CSA, *MACV Operations Analysis* (17 July 1968), General Abrams Messages, July 1968–January 1969, Message # 911, CMH.

139. Johnson, *SOOHP*, Vol. III, Section XIII, 27, MHI.

140. Rosson, *SOOHP*, 347, MHI.

141. John Paul Vann letter to Leroy Wehrle, deputy director, Vietnam Bureau, Agency for International Development, Department of State (7 March 1968), 2. Catalogued in John Paul Vann Papers, 1968 file, MHI.

142. Komer, LBJ Ac 94–2, 49.

IV

LESSONS FROM MALAYA AND VIETNAM

8

Hard Lessons: The British and American Armies Learn Counterinsurgency

INTRODUCTION

The British and American armies ended World War II with doctrine, equipment, organizations, and thought patterns well suited to winning conventional wars through a strategy of attrition. Within five years both armies were engaged in another conventional war on the mainland of Asia that further reinforced their mind-set toward conventional war. The British army, however, was simultaneously involved in a very different kind of war, a rural Communist insurgency in Malaya. After initially attempting to defeat the insurgents through the use of conventional attrition-based strategies, the British army slowly evolved a combined civil-military-political strategy that defeated the insurgency with small unit military tactics based on intelligence derived from a supportive local population.

Even as the British were painfully learning how to defeat the Communist Terrorists, the American army became involved in a struggle against another rural Communist insurgency. Despite the efforts of the large number of officers on the ground who knew that the army's conventional approach was ineffective—and was in fact counterproductive in many ways—the U.S. Army continued to rely on a conventional approach to defeating the insurgents through an attrition-based search and destroy strategy.

Why did one army encourage its junior officers to seek out organizational performance gaps and alternative organizational paths of action, hammer out a consensus on the effectiveness of the new doctrines, publish the changes in doctrine, train the organization in the new doctrine and enforce its application to ensure change in organizational behavior, and observe the effectiveness of the new doctrine out in the field—in short, why did one army actively learn how to conduct a successful counterinsurgency campaign—whereas the other did not?

This chapter will compare the organizational learning process of the British army in Malaya with that of the American army in Vietnam. It will focus on the differences in the training, history, organization, and personnel of the two armies—their organizational cultures—that resulted in such dramatically different learning performances. This comparison is not based on the contention that the two conflicts were of similar intensity or scope, but only that both Malaya and Vietnam presented a challenge in which traditional attrition-based maneuver warfare strategies would be ineffective. Organizational effectiveness in the two conflicts required organizational change. The British army was far better at making those changes than was the U.S. Army; this chapter will attempt to understand why by tracing the way the two armies progressed through the organizational learning process, using Richard Downie's Institutional Learning Cycle (Figure 8-1) as a road map.

BRITISH ARMY COUNTERINSURGENCY LEARNING IN MALAYA, 1948–1960

The successful efforts of the British army to adapt a conventional doctrine to the demands of rural Communist insurgency in Malaya demonstrate several complete iterations of the organizational learning cycle. The process also reveals the flexibility of thought and action that has long been a tradition of the British army. The flexibility is enhanced by a number of factors unique to that army and to its organizational culture, including the class basis of order in British society and the consequent relaxation of rank structure; the unwritten doctrine governing British military operations, like the unwritten British constitution ultimately flexible because unwritten; the British appreciation of every foreign country as its own unique entity; and finally, the impact of military experience gained by guerrilla fighting against the Japanese in the jungles of Burma and Malaya during World War II.

Tactical Innovation

The crucial first step in organizational learning is identifying a need to learn by recognizing that the institution is not accomplishing its objectives in the situation it faces. Identifying organizational performance gaps in counterinsurgency is a task most often performed by relatively junior officers who are physically and intellectually in close proximity to both the people threatened by the insurgency and the small military units most often engaged in pursuing the insurgents.

Figure 8-1
The Institutional Learning Cycle: The Process of Doctrinal Change

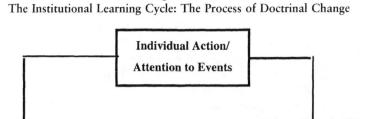

One individual who recognized the need for changes in British army organization and training in response to the Emergency was Lieutenant Colonel Walter Walker. Walker's creation of Ferret Force, an organization designed to out-guerrilla the guerrilla, sprang directly from his own guerrilla warfare experience in the jungles of Burma during World War II. It was too unconventional for General Sir Neil Ritchie, who ordered Ferret Force disbanded but saw the value in Walker's innovative tactics. Ritchie's instructions to Walker to establish the Far East Land Force Training Centre (FTC) had a much greater impact on the British army as a whole than Ferret Force ever could have had. Every battalion that was deployed to fight in the Malayan Emergency sent its noncommissioned officers (NCOs) and senior officers to be trained at the FTC and to take the tactics, techniques, and procedures they learned there back to their units. Crucially, Ritchie not only was willing to visit Walker in the field, but he also examined the merit of his subordinate's ideas free of a preconceived notion of how war ought to be fought. Ritchie's varied experiences during his own service in the British army created a receptive attitude to the idea that different wars fought in different locations might well require completely different methods of training and organization.

Doctrine was not prescribed from a central point in the British army, to be learned by rote by young officers as they progressed through Staff Colleges and similar schools; in fact, it was not written at all. The decision not to impose a single doctrine on all of the far-flung regiments across the empire left young officers not just the freedom, but also the necessity, to create their own answers. As David Charters notes,

The tactical or organisational problems [the British army officer] confronts in an overseas conflict will probably be handled locally with the resources—material, human, and intellectual—he has at hand. Historical experience has taught him not to expect a flood of assistance from Britain—there is usually little to be spared— nor to look to some sacrosanct body of "doctrine" for advice; there was none. Instead he must make do. . . . In short, he must adapt.[1]

The same spirit of the slightly eccentric individual experimenting to meet the demands of the specific theater of war in which they were stationed led Brigadier Michael Calvert, formerly one of Wingate's Chindit irregular warriors, to form and lead the Twenty-second Malayan Scouts SAS. Just as important as the creation of the Malayan Scouts was the willingness of the British army to accept this innovation that sprang from the field rather than from Whitehall.[2] The spirit of innovation was contagious, not just because it was effective but because Calvert's methods promised relief from the standard shoulder-to-shoulder sweeps through the jungle that were then the accepted way of taking on the insurgents. Calvert remembers: "It produced a sense of rivalry and everybody else wanted to emulate what we were doing and people realised that if they came in the jungle for prolonged times and [did] this and that [then] they could forget about parade ground soldiering. [General Poett] said that it had an almost immediate effect throughout the whole operation there. It was the beginning of our defeat of the Chinese guerrillas."[3]

Not all members of the British army were so open to innovation. While in the process of establishing the Twenty-second Malayan Scouts SAS, Calvert went on an inspection tour of forces operating in the jungle; there he found a battalion of the Scots Guards operating in traditional fashion and having remarkably little success.

I suggested that they should patrol in small parties because, I said (and this is a teaching of mine) that the smaller the number in a patrol the more frightened you are therefore the more cautious you are therefore the more silent you are and therefore the more likely you are to meet the enemy. So I had recommended that the patrols, having formed a patrol base you should patrol out in fours or something like that. [The Commanding Officer replied] "Look, my battalion shouldn't be here. We were raised and trained and organized to fight in Europe. I'm not going to upset the whole organisation and training of my battalion just to chase a lot of [Communist Terrorists] around the jungle."[4]

General Harding relieved that colonel on the day he heard the story, giving him only an hour to depart from his battalion. It is not hard to imagine the impact of that relief on colonels commanding other battalions in theater, nor on the receptiveness Brigadier Calvert found for his ideas and suggestions on his next inspection tour.

The most critical aspect of the learning process is not the innovator, even if the British army does seem to produce more than its share. The key to organizational learning is getting the decision-making authority to allow such innovation, monitor its effectiveness, and then transmit new doctrine with strict requirements that it be followed throughout the organization.

The British High Command in Malaya appears to have been remarkably open to suggestions from below. Thomas Mockaitis suggests that the social structure of the United Kingdom has a great deal to do with producing this flexibility in senior officers. Because most officers are from public schools and rank is "a matter of ability reinforced by birth . . . interactions between all ranks could become much more comfortable."[5] Many regiments do not wear rank on their Mess uniforms;[6] officers are often on a first-name basis with their superiors as well as their subordinates. The informality is a reflection of confidence about the structure and about each individual's position in it. Subordinates are given their head, and everyone knows how far rights and privileges are allowed to go; there is no risk to the social standing of a superior officer who accepts suggestions from a junior. A social theorist explains: "Members of socially homogeneous elites are quite capable, under certain circumstance, of taking unorthodox radical decisions. Indeed, it is often the newcomers who are reluctant to stick their necks out and who therefore conform more than necessary. The more confident people are of belonging, the less need do they have to be purely defensive, and the more open they can be."[7]

Strategic Vision

More important than the tactical innovations of Calvert and Walker— use of small unit actions, ambush weapons and procedures, communications techniques, and the like—is the strategic vision required to put the military component of a counterinsurgency campaign in proper perspective vis-à-vis the economic and political actions necessary to defeat insurgents. This vision was present at an early stage in the Malayan Emergency in the person of Harold Briggs, the architect of the plan that ultimately defeated the insurgents. Briggs was an army officer schooled in the unique political and military demands of the empire; Robert Thompson recalls, "Briggs would have had a fair amount of what you might call Indian history behind him."[8]

The men who wrote the Briggs Plan had a common understanding of the demands of empire and a common appreciation for the role of good administration and good police officers in minimizing the role of the army in colonies across the empire. This understanding was a part not only of the development of any army officer who had served in India but also of that of their counterparts who worked in the Colonial Office in London. The bonds go deeper than similar postings in the outposts of Empire as junior officers in the army or Colonial Service; most top officers in both services had attended the same public schools and were members of families who knew each other and thus had common personal as well as cultural and intellectual ties.[9] This shared perspective, again derived from the British strategic and colonial culture, is one of the primary causes for the shared vision in Whitehall and in Kuala Lumpur on the political and military steps required to defeat the insurgency.

The Man

David Lloyd Owen believes, "You need a man with a lot of imagination to run this kind of war, and one with an understanding of the political nature of the war."[10] Revolutionary wars are fought with ideas as much as they are contested with weapons; a man with a compelling vision who persuades others to believe in his ideas is the most potent force in any revolutionary army. Chin Peng and Ho Chi Minh were warriors whose ideas took root in a small but very committed group of their compatriots, fertilized by nascent nationalism, anticolonialism, and political and economic grievances.

Counterrevolutionary forces also fight with ideas, their battleground the hearts and minds of the population and of those who fight to defend it. Creating a political-military-economic strategy to defeat an insurgency is every bit as revolutionary as planning to overthrow a government, and a great deal more difficult. As important as were the tactical innovations and the strategic vision to tie them together, there can be little doubt that Templer created a revolution of his own in Malaya. He encouraged innovation from below and demanded a new approach to solving the problems of Malayan society. He not only refused to focus exclusively on the insurgency as a military problem, but did not even see it *primarily* as such—and he insisted that all of his subordinates share that worldview. Templer played an essential role in creating an institutional climate in Malaya predisposed toward a wider view of the conflict and a spirit of innovation throughout the command. He was a man of drive and of imagination; "easily the best man for the job," as Montgomery told Churchill in a note dated 7 January 1952.[11]

But Templer, for all his outstanding personal qualities and admitting the decisive role he played in adapting the British army to the challenge it faced in Malaya, was a product of an army and of a culture. From service pacifying Iraq in 1920 after a tour in the trenches in France through service as the military governor of the British Zone in occupied Germany, Templer had learned how to combine political and military leadership to achieve political and military goals. Already in Palestine in 1936 Templer was establishing joint headquarters with the district commissioner and the district superintendent of police in Nazareth to coordinate a solution to Palestinian unrest there. He also demonstrated tactical flexibility by putting soldiers in gym shoes, armed with fixed bayonets, in a convoy that was ambushed from usually impassable high ground; they charged, capturing the snipers.[12] Even during World War II, when Templer's Fifty-Sixth Infantry Division was sent to Egypt from Italy for retraining and reequipping, the assistant commandant of the Cairo City Police complimented Templer on the bearing of his troops, noting that "on all possible occasions they have assisted the Civil Police when it has been necessary to do so . . . an unsolicited testimonial from the Civil Police!"[13]

Throughout his career, Templer had been steeped in a culture that combined political and military responsibility in service across the empire. Both Templer and his army knew that there were no easy answers to the problems of developing nations. In his initial address to the people of Malaya on 7 February 1952, Templer demonstrated the result of the years of experience—his own and his nation's: "I have not come here with any ready-made, clear-cut solution to Malaya's present problems. That is not possible. The solution lies not in the hands of any one man, nor alone in the hands of the government here or in the hands of the United Kingdom. It is in the hands of all of us, the peoples of Malaya and the governments which serve them."[14]

A remarkable statement from a remarkable man—but also a testimonial to an institution that had taught him to appreciate and value the traditions and culture of different nations. As Morris Janowitz noted in his study of the American army, "It has been those men whose unconventional careers have involved them in politico-military assignments who display the most sustained political consciousness."[15] Critical as was Templer's role in encouraging and driving political-military innovation during the British counterinsurgency effort in Malaya, the culture of the British army played just as important a part. There were many British officers who appreciated the primacy of politics in unconventional warfare; Lloyd Owen notes, "John Harding, who was CIGS before Templer, had been in charge of Cyprus beforehand. There were a whole series of great thinkers with this kind of experience."[16] It is a mark of the British government's trust in the capability of her army that a single army general was given political *and* military authority—and responsibility—over Malaya at the height of the Emergency. The organization had previously demonstrated its ability to perform both tasks, and the British government understood that the two missions were inseparable.

U.S. ARMY COUNTERINSURGENCY LEARNING IN VIETNAM, 1950– 1972

The idea that drove U.S. Army policy in Vietnam was in marked contrast to the spirit of innovative solutions to combined political-military-economic problems that allowed the British army to defeat the Communist Terrorists in Malaya. Advisers in the MAAG, authors of several internal army studies, U.S. Marines, the CIA, and even MACV commander Creighton Abrams all identified organizational performance gaps and sought alternative organizational actions, often risking their own career in so doing, but to little avail. Even President Kennedy's attempts to change the army's reliance on conventional attrition-based strategies were rejected. A Jominian emphasis on defeating the enemy army in the field prevented the army from reaching a sustained consensus on innovations suggested from below. General Westmoreland later described his philosophy on how to end the war in Vietnam as "To hurt the enemy across the spectrum of his efforts until he concluded that he could not win and thus seek and agree to a political settlement."[17]

The institutional culture was too strong. An army that saw its raison d'être as winning wars through the application of firepower and maneuver to annihilate enemy forces simply could not conceive of another kind of war in which its weapons, technology, and organization not only could not destroy the enemy, but usually could not even find or identify him. The learning cycle began well, identifying shortcomings in army counterinsurgency doctrine on the ground and then seeking and suggesting solutions, but these were rejected because they failed to conform to the army's concept of how wars were to be fought and won.

That it was the army concept of victory through the application of firepower that prevented organizational learning, rather than merely the impact of personalities, can be seen through two examples. First, the innovations that the U.S. Army *did* adapt in Vietnam were all in keeping with the army's ideas of how wars ought to be fought. Second, when an army general who did not accept the conventional wisdom that wars were won through firepower and attrition became MACV commander, General Abrams was unable to create a consensus that attrition was not the answer. Even the U.S. Army's interpretation of British success in Malaya betrays the military lens through which all revolutionary warfare was viewed; a 1959 army study argued, vehemently but absolutely incorrectly, "Complete annihilation of the Communist Terrorists has been the governing consideration for the organization and utilization of Security Forces in Malaya."[18]

Tactical Innovation

The United States Army developed a large number of tactical and technological innovations during the war in Vietnam, all designed to assist in bringing conventional firepower to bear. Money was no object: Robert Komer notes, "In the best American tradition, we spent heavily on advanced technology for coping with an elusive enemy."[19] The single most important example is undoubtedly the helicopter, used as a gunship, for casualty evacuation, and as a troop carrier, making the "search and destroy" attrition strategy possible.[20] The army published *Tactical and Material Innovations* in 1974; that volume not only touted "the widespread use of the helicopter" as "the most significant advance of the Vietnam war," but also stated, "It is difficult to exaggerate the capabilities of the airmobile team in Vietnam; the team represented *the most revolutionary change in warfare since the blitzkrieg.*"[21]

General Westmoreland concurs: "Every unit became proficient in air assaults by helicopter. With Department of the Army approval, I changed the structure of the American infantry battalion from three companies to four, which, among other purposes, provided a company for base defense while still maintaining the triangular structure for operation outside the base."[22] This was a dramatic change in army organization and manning that reverberated throughout the entire army, demanding huge modifications in recruiting and training to provide the additional thousands of combat infantrymen to fill the fourth rifle company in the many infantry battalions that fought in Vietnam; it was, however, a change in keeping with the army's concept of fighting wars with infantry battalions bringing firepower to bear on the enemy. Breaking battalions down into small teams of soldiers who would live with villagers, as did the U.S. Marines in their combined action platoons, would have required far fewer resources, but a much greater change in the institutional mind-set of the U.S. Army.

The same is true for the bewildering array of tactical innovations developed by the army for use in Vietnam. Imaginative in the best tradition of American technological solutions to all problems, they ranged from useful to ridiculous. Westmoreland notes the gunship-mounted Riverine Force in the Delta; C-47 gunships nicknamed "Spooky" and "Puff the Magic Dragon" by ground forces; "Road Runner" operations in which spotter aircraft in contact with artillery and fighter-bombers hovered over truck convoys to pick out enemy ambushes and in which "the convoys in wooded regions made rapid dashes through likely ambush sites, guns blazing to keep the enemy down."[23] Unrestrained and uncontrolled firepower was substituted for patient work developing intelligence sources in the local population, who, given real security and belief in the government, might have provided information on which locals were setting the ambushes, and where.

Infiltration along the Ho Chi Minh Trail provoked a variety of technological "fixes" ranging from Starlight Scopes mounted on rifles to make target acquisition easier in the dark through "People Sniffers" that detected human urine and body heat in free-fire zones. Scientists contributed a "chemical solvent that when mixed with water and soil turned the soil to slush, which as long as it was wet would not stabilize. At the start of the rainy season they dumped tons of the solvent from C-130s on a constricted road in the A Shau Valley, but no substantial evidence was ever found that it proved effective in deterring movement."[24] The air force also made its contribution: "In the hope of slowing traffic on the Ho Chi Minh Trail by mud, Air Force planes seeded the clouds above the Laotian panhandle, but there was no appreciable increase in rain."[25]

Many of these innovations were, if useless, at least not harmful to the achievement of American goals; the same can hardly be said for the use of strategic B-52 bombers in a tactical close air support role, which produced a vast number of civilian causalities and provided duds (5 percent of the bombs failed to explode) for booby traps that killed more than one thousand U.S. soldiers in 1966 alone.[26] The U.S. Air Force's RANCH HAND defoliation operations (Motto, "Only you can prevent forests") to destroy Viet Cong rice supplies did not discriminate whose rice and rubber they killed, caused birth defects in Vietnamese children, and created a number of long-term health problems in U.S. servicemen exposed to the "Agent Orange" used in the spraying.[27]

The army, for all the technological and organizational innovations it promulgated in Vietnam, in the final analysis had just one solution to the problem of countering insurgency, a single word that General Westmoreland used in response to a reporter's question at a press conference on the answer to insurgency: "Firepower."[28] Chief of Staff Gen. Harold K. Johnson says of Westmoreland:

But we got caught up in one of his clichés—"send a bullet instead of a man." Whether he manufactured it or whether somebody else did, I don't know, and it is something that was very difficult to overcome. As a matter of fact, we simply didn't overcome it and we got into a firepower war out there, where firepower was not really effective. Ammunition costs were simply astronomical, and when we first began to examine where our artillery ammunition went, we found something in the neighborhood of 85% of it was unobserved fire, which was a rather staggering volume. I don't know what good it was doing. That got changed in time, but, nonetheless, I think it reflected the following of generality and cliché in contrast to a real examination of what the requirements of the situation demanded out there.[29]

The Man

> "In war, it is extraordinary how it all comes down to the character of one man."[30]
>
> —General Creighton Abrams

The U.S. Army generals who commanded MAAG-V and MACV repeatedly rejected innovative suggestions for changes in American counterinsurgency doctrine in Vietnam. It is tempting to dismiss officers such as MAAG Commander Lieutenant General Lionel McGarr, who often stayed out of his headquarters for days at a time, sending his staff tape-recorded messages telling them what to do, as incompetents who had no business being entrusted with so much responsibility, but that answer is insufficient.[31] The U.S. Army of the time exercised a demanding system of performance reviews, promotion boards, and educational requirements. Although some less able individuals may have slipped through, most officers who achieved senior rank were capable men who were dedicated to the welfare of their soldiers and the winning of their nation's wars. As Westmoreland notes in his memoirs, "If an officer progresses through the United States Army's demanding promotion system to reach the rank of general, he is, except under most unusual circumstances, clearly competent, even if he may not be the best man for every assignment, and bad assignments inevitably occur."[32] Vietnam presented Westmoreland and his fellow senior officers with just such "most unusual circumstances"—conditions their training and experience left them completely unprepared to handle.

Westmoreland and his fellow leaders were, if anything, *too* dedicated to winning their nations' wars. American army officers had little of the political-military experience in their early careers that so decisively shaped the development of a British officer such as Gerald Templer. They spent their noncombat time in garrison tours in the continental United States, isolated not only from the experience of solving political problems in foreign countries but even from the political life of their own people. The "Code of the Army Officer" includes the "Tradition of Avoiding Matters of Politics."[33] Westmoreland himself asks: "When does a professional military man put his fingers into the political mud and try to influence the political mechanisms by his actions, either direct or indirect actions? . . . I am personally disposed to say he doesn't."[34] This is a longstanding principle of the American army: "Strategy begins where politics ends," instructed a 1936 Command and General Staff College Manual.[35] The 1985 edition of *The Army Officer's Guide* notes: "A change has occurred in the traditional concept of the keeping of peace and the waging of war. It needs the spotlight. *In this era*, the soldier fights alongside the statesman to *maintain* the peace."[36]

The officers who led MAAG-V and MACV had not developed in an institutional culture that recognized that change; "in the spotlight" as late as 1985, it was certainly not featured in the editions of *The Army Officer's Guide* they received at graduation from West Point, nor were political-military assignments a feature of their career. They served in an institution that saw World War II and the application of superior firepower as the essence of a military career; mentored and selected for promotion by those who had fought in such a way, the culture was reinforced and passed on. "Higher rank means longer organizational experience, greater commitment to the organization, and more selecting out of deviant perspectives," says the military theorist Morris Janowitz.[37]

The primary rule of military command holds "commanders responsible for everything their command does, or fails to do."[38] The commanders of MAAG-V and MACV are, therefore, ultimately responsible for the failures of their organizations to adapt to the demands of counterinsurgency warfare in Vietnam. As a more junior officer recently observed: "Nurturing ideas and mentoring those willing to adopt and advance them are the responsibilities of operational commanders. The leaders who set the command climate can determine the success or failure of innovation."[39]

Innovative suggestions from John Paul Vann and Hal Porter and from the CIA's CIDG program, as well as the advice of Robert Thompson and the British Advisory Mission, all got no further than General Harkins,[40] and General Westmoreland failed to implement the suggestions of the authors of the PROVN study, the United States Marine Corps and its combined action platoon experiment, Ambassador Lodge, and President Johnson. These two MACV commanders' failures to create a consensus on alternative counterinsurgency techniques were a direct cause of the U.S. Army's failure to learn and implement successful counterinsurgency doctrine in Vietnam. General Johnson recalls:

Now these lessons, I don't think that we learned very early, and the kind of analysis that would develop this very clear picture really was not made in a way that it laid it out clearly. The analyses that were presented periodically by MACV, to support increased levels of troops, did deal with enemy concentration, enemy capabilities, projections of enemy efforts to seize key areas, and in turn the allied effort to deny those areas. But the total picture I don't think emerged as clearly as it should have, and I must say that I do not know why. Now I should also say that in retrospect, I probably devoted so much attention to detail that perhaps some of the larger picture tended to escape me.[41]

Generals Harkins, Johnson, and Westmoreland must be seen in the context of their time and of their organizational culture, both of which compelled them to see Vietnam as an conventional war to be won by conventional methods. As Ronald H. Spector points out, "McGarr and

Harkins had not appointed themselves."[42] The culture that selected them was so strong that it has persisted ever since, continuing to prevent any organizational consensus on the "lessons" of Vietnam. It is this mind-set, the idea that the U.S. Army could defeat any enemy on any battlefield given enough firepower and the freedom to apply it indiscriminately, that precluded organizational learning on counterinsurgency during the Vietnam War.

Despite the opprobrium that hangs on Westmoreland as a result of Vietnam, he is widely regarded as a good conventional warrior who deeply cared for his soldiers, his army, and his nation. Both his memoirs and those of the people who served under him recall innumerable instances of General Westmoreland's visiting wounded soldiers in hospitals, visiting units to decorate soldiers on the completion of search and destroy operations, and addressing units prior to operations.[43] Unlike his predecessor, Westmoreland was a concerned and capable (if very conventional) commander; unfortunately, he was directly responsible for conducting uniquely unconventional war, and neither he nor his institution had the conceptual flexibility to adapt to the change. As Robert Thompson notes: "This [Vietnam] war had been fought entirely by a professional army (except for draftees in the ranks). It has been undiluted by civilian brains not bound by the rigid orthodoxy of the book. While there have been plenty of younger Americans both military and civil, who have had a good understanding of the war, they have made no impression at all on the system."[44]

General Westmoreland himself admitted:

Like most Americans who served in South Vietnam, I had at first only vicarious experience in counterinsurgency warfare. Although I had dealt closely with the local population during my service in post–World War II Germany, no earlier assignment had involved such an intricate relationship between the military and the political. . . . My colleagues and I in Vietnam were for a long time on what I called a learning curve. There was no book to tell us how to do the job.[45]

A former Vietnam search and rescue pilot noted: "U.S. civilian and military leaders did not fail for lack of conceptualization. In the final analysis, these leaders, intelligent, dedicated, hard working men that they were, failed, not because they did not conceptualize, but because the concepts they developed were fatally flawed."[46]

Or, to use a piece of folk wisdom, if the only tool you have in your toolbox is a hammer, all problems begin to resemble nails. The United States Army in Vietnam relied on the tools that it had used with such success for the past century: firepower and maneuver, battalions and divisions. Completely conditioned to seeing all wars as purely military problems, it repeatedly rejected innovators who suggested that perhaps a political-military-economic screwdriver was necessary. Robert McNamara remembers *In Retrospect*: "Like many people, the U.S. Commanders . . . misunderstood the nature of the conflict. They viewed it primarily as a military operation when in fact it was a highly complex nationalistic and internecine struggle."[47]

BRITISH ARMY COUNTERINSURGENCY LEARNING AFTER MALAYA

The British army that adapted so well to the political-military demands of countering Communist rural insurgency in Malaya faced many more "Brushfire Wars" in the aftermath of the Emergency. Even after the failures of the British Advisory Mission in changing U.S. thinking in Vietnam, British veterans of the Malayan Emergency continued to give advice to the American army. Field Marshal Templer said in 1968:

I don't believe the way the Vietnam problem—which is basically not a military problem—was handled in the early days was the right one. I didn't carry out my tactics in Malaya by raising masses of local troops and putting them all in British uniforms and giving them enormous loads to carry so that they became completely immobile. We did it by equipping them and training them as near as possible to the enemy they had to compete with in a particular terrain. This applied not only to the local forces, but also to all the British units. Their street fighting and jungle techniques were worked out with the very greatest care. I only used bombing in the jungle or mountains in Malaya in order to flush out the Communists.[48]

In keeping with the British army culture of not universalizing country-specific solutions, "very little by way of doctrine was developed despite the operations in Borneo, Cyprus (1963), Radfan and Aden."[49] General Sir John Waters remarks, "Each theatre is so different that it requires its own policy and schools to shape the response to local needs. We've learned by hard experience what worked and what didn't."[50] The lessons that were learned during these operations were transmitted through the writings of those who fought in them, including Sir Robert Thompson, General Sir Frank Kitson, and Major General Richard Clutterbuck. Kitson notes: "Doctrine is prepared in order that the Army should have some basis for training and equipping itself. You certainly don't fight based on your doctrine! If you actually do fight based on your doctrine you're letting yourself in for disaster."[51] Even continuing operations in Northern Ireland were not reflected in official doctrine: "The only real indication that the experience gained in Northern Ireland had been reflected in Army units, was by the training of those units before they deployed to Northern Ireland for duty. The training was up to date, effective, and extremely flexible. Hostile tactics were studied, changes in training promulgated quickly, and troops informed immediately."[52]

The small size of the British army, its flexibility at the tactical level, and its traditional understanding of political-military operations and the principles of minimum force have combined to create an army well adapted to the demands of warfare in the wake of the cold war. Kitson remarks, "If the British army has any counterinsurgency principle, it is to regard use of force as only one plank in a combined political/economic/propaganda effort."[53] Echoing this principle, the British army's current author of doctrine writes, "The Army had taken note of the similarities, particularly at the tactical level, between counter insurgency, MACA [Military Assistance to the Civil Authority], and peace support operations on behalf of the UN in areas of strife or disturbance."[54] The British army published its consensus on the best way to deal with the demands it is most likely to face in its 1995 Army Field Manual, *Operations Other Than War: Counter Insurgency Operations.*

Nonetheless, the official doctrine remains secondary to the substantial experience of many British officers in counterinsurgency, as David Lloyd Owen explains: "I started my career in colonial policing in Palestine in 1938. So much of the Army of my generation and above have spent so much of their career doing colonial policing that we'd better bloody well be good at it."[55]

U.S. ARMY COUNTERINSURGENCY LEARNING AFTER VIETNAM

In marked contrast the British army in the evolutionary development of counterinsurgency learning since the Malayan Emergency, the U.S. Army has failed to form a consensus on the lessons of Vietnam and has not accepted the idea that revolutionary war requires a qualitatively different response from the conventional warfare it knows so well how to fight. Richard Downie, whose dissertation provided much of the theoretical framework for this study, examined the army's counterinsurgency doctrine in the post–Vietnam War era to seek evidence of organizational learning. Downie discovered "no significant conceptual change to the Army's counterinsurgency doctrine in the post–Vietnam War era." Although "the Army was well aware of deficiencies in its counterinsurgency doctrine," it "did not change its doctrine to correct or resolve those deficiencies." He concluded, "The Army did not learn from its Vietnam War and other LIC experiences."[56]

The commandant of the Army War College commissioned a review of army strategy in Vietnam in 1974. He explained the rationale for the study with these words:

I would emphasize my belief that it is most useful if one gets a force ready for an uncertain future rather than a certain future. There is great danger in being too certain about what the future will bring, and there's much greater assurance in preparing for a future which you frankly admit you cannot precisely define. So I think the lessons of Vietnam ought to help us move, not toward a rigid, final, unassailable doctrine, and certainly not a narrow doctrine, and not to assume that there's a point-to-point relationship between the lessons of Vietnam and what we would do "the next time," but toward an open, professionally stimulated and informed leadership corps, believing that anyone would be delinquent not to learn from all the blood of Vietnam and all the treasure spent there, and all the mistakes made, and all the good things that were done as well.[57]

It is easy to see why Major General Dewitt Smith's study became known as the "Vietnam lessons learned study."[58] The study quickly overwhelmed the War College and was turned over to the BDM Corporation, which published its findings in June 1980.[59] Downie summarizes the BDM findings: "Massive military power was not the best or the only weapon in LIC [low-intensity conflict] situations like Vietnam. In such cases, political aspects were more important than winning conventional military battles. . . . In short, the report validated the concept that military operations should support civil affairs objectives."[60]

Under the direction of Gen. William E. DePuy, who had served as Westmoreland's operations officer and commanded the First Infantry Division in Vietnam, the post-Vietnam army intentionally turned away from the painful memories of its Vietnam experience to focus on the kind of wars it knew how to fight and win: conventional warfare in Europe against the conventional armies of the Soviet Union.[61] The 1976 edition of FM 100–5 *Operations*, prepared under DePuy's direction, did not mention counterinsurgency.[62] Training was also shifted from unconventional warfare back to the army's conventional-warfare comfort zone; the Command and General Staff College cut the forty-hour Low Intensity Conflict curriculum to just nine hours in 1979.[63]

Disappointed with the conclusions of the BDM study, the War College commandant, General Smith, turned to Colonel Harry Summers of the Army War College, who used Clausewitz's *On War* as the framework for his modestly titled *On Strategy: A Critical Analysis of the Vietnam War*. Published in 1982, with a foreword written by Major General Jack Merritt, then the commandant of the Army War College, *On Strategy* quickly became the U.S. Army's approved version of why it lost the Vietnam War. Merritt notes the "overwhelmingly favorable comments that the War College has received since the book was originally published in paperback in the spring of 1981 . . . not only from the current leadership of the army . . . but also from many retired general officers who were intimately involved in the strategies and plans of the war at the highest level."[64]

The thesis of *On Strategy* that the army so approvingly digested was that "lack of appreciation of military theory and military strategy . . . led to . . . the exhaustion of the Army against a secondary guerrilla force."[65] Summers argues that the basic mistake . . . was that we saw their guerrilla operations as a strategy in itself. Because we saw it as a strategy, we attempted to understand it in terms of "people's war" theories of Mao Tse-Tung, and devised elaborate theories of counterinsurgency. We attempted to counter it by using such models as the British model in Malaysia . . . Instead of orienting on North Vietnam—the source of the war—we turned our attention to the symptom—the guerrilla war in the South.[66]

Rather than focusing so much of its effort on counterinsurgency, argues Summers, the army should have created a blocking position near the DMZ across Laos to Thailand to prevent infiltration[67]—ironically, the focus of the El Paso plan proposed by General Westmoreland in 1966.[68] The problem, contends Summers, was not that the army was too conventional in its approach to fighting the war in Vietnam, but that it was not conventional enough. This was just the message the army wanted to hear as it refocused its attention on European-style conventional warfighting in the 1970s and 1980s.

Comfortable as the Summers argument was for the army, some officers refused to accept the argument that the war in Vietnam was lost because the army was not allowed to use its firepower as widely and liberally as it would have liked. Andrew Krepinevich's *The Army and Vietnam*, published in 1984, is the most important. Krepinevich was pilloried by retired General Bruce Palmer for calling into question the widely accepted "lessons" the army had "learned" in the wake of Vietnam,[69] but even Palmer admits, "The Summers thesis, while popular in many circles, unfortunately tends to let the military off the hook, absolving them of all responsibility for our national failure and placing the blame elsewhere."[70]

Rather than squarely face up to the fact that army counterinsurgency doctrine had failed in Vietnam, the army decided that the United States should no longer involve itself in counterinsurgency operations. The "Weinberger doctrine" of 1983 made such involvement less likely by creating a series of tests that in practice precluded American participation in any wars that did not allow full exploitation of American advantages in technology and firepower. The army returned to its organizational roots, creating a force that triumphed in the extremely conventional Gulf War of 1990–1991.[71] The day after that victory, President George Bush crowed, "By God, we've licked the Vietnam syndrome once and for all."

In fact, the Gulf War simply confirmed the army's Jominian concept of fighting purely military battles with high-technology weaponry and overwhelming firepower.[72] By refusing to acknowledge that most wars, unlike the Gulf, are and will be fought on battlefields populated by people who may support one side or the other (or one of many), the army continued to prepare itself to fight wars as it wanted to fight them. Heavy reliance on firepower and technology and a poor appreciation for the political terrain in Somalia led to an ignominious retreat for U.S. forces engaged in a humanitarian operation in 1993,[73] and excellent military performance in the Implementation Force in the former Yugoslavia has been made largely irrelevant by a lack of concomitant political progress. By failing to learn the lessons of Vietnam, the U.S. Army continued to prepare itself to fight the wrong war.

NOTES

1. David A. Charters, "From Palestine to Northern Ireland: British Adaptation to Low-Intensity Operations," in David A. Charters and Maurice Tugwell, eds., *Armies in Low-Intensity Conflict: A Comparative Analysis* (Oxford: Brassey's, 1989), 182.

2. IWM DSR 009989/08 "Malayan Emergency 1948–1960," interview of Brig. J.M. Calvert, 21.

3. Ibid., 46.

4. Ibid., 27–28.

5. Thomas Mockaitis, *British Counterinsurgency 1919–1960* (New York: St. Martin's Press, 1990), 175. The author has been repeatedly struck by this trait of British army officers in the mess and elsewhere; British army captains habitually address their commanding officers as "Colonel Jim"—an offense punishable under the Uniform Code of Military Justice in the U.S. Army!

6. The fact that each regiment *has* its own mess uniform, distinct from those of all other regiments, is itself indicative of a spirit of independent thought separate from the center.

7. Ralf Dahrendorf, *The Modern Social Conflict: An Essay on the Politics of Liberty* (London: Weidenfeld and Nicholson, 1988), 53.

8. IWM DSR 10192/6 "The Malayan Emergency 1950–1955," interview of Sir Robert Thompson KGB, CMG, DSO, MC (1988) by CXW, 17–20.

9. The author is grateful to Lieutenant Colonel Simon Mayall of the Queen's Dragoon Guards for this point.

10. David Lloyd Owen interview, 11 November 1996.

11. John Cloake, *Templer: Tiger of Malaya: The Life of Field Marshall Sir Gerald Templer* (London: Harrap, 1985), 203.

12. Ibid., 61–2.

13. Ibid., 135.

14. Ibid., 209.

15. Morris Janowitz, *The Professional Soldier: A Social and Political Portrait* (New York: The Free Press, 1971), 234–235.

16. David Lloyd Owen interview, 11 November 1996.

17. William Westmoreland, *SOOHP, II*, 295, MHI.

18. First sentence of the section "Security Forces and Emergency Operations" in *Resistance Factors and Special Forces Areas: Malaya and Singapore* (Washington, DC: Georgetown University Research Project, under contract to ACSI, Headquarters, DA, 15 April 1959), 160.

19. Robert W. Komer, *Bureaucracy Does Its Thing* (Santa Monica, CA: RAND, 1973), 107. Komer's chapter VII, "Attempts at Adaptive Response," is a very valuable examination of how the United States adapted—or failed to adapt—and why.

20. See Robert S. Thompson, *No Exit from Vietnam* (London: Chatto and Windus, 1969), who argues that "the helicopter . . . exaggerated the two great weaknesses of the American character—impatience and aggressiveness. . . . It is probable that without the helicopter 'search and destroy' would not have been possible, and, in this sense, the helicopter was one of the major contributions to the failure in strategy" (136).

21. Lieutenant General John H. Hay, Jr., *Vietnam Studies: Tactical and Material Innovations* (Washington, DC: Department of the Army, 1974), 179, my emphasis. This statement, made by a very senior general officer in an official army publication, provides compelling support for the argument that the army as late as 1974 had not acknowledged Mao's revolution in military affairs. Revolutionary warfare, with limited logistical and technological demands but heavy political importance, was so far outside the experience of U.S. Army officers that they could not recognize its significance even at the conclusion of twenty-five years spent fruitlessly fighting it.

22. William Westmoreland, *A Soldier Reports* (New York: Da Capo, 1989), 283.

23. Ibid., 280.

24. Ibid., 281.

25. Ibid.

26. Andrew J. Krepinevich, *The Army and Vietnam* (Baltimore: Johns Hopkins University Press, 1986), 201.

27. Ibid., 210–211.

28. Royal United Services Institute, *Lessons of the Vietnam War*, 3, in ibid., 197.

29. Harold K. Johnson Oral History, Volume III, Section XV, 20, MHI.

30. General Creighton Abrams, quoted in Lewis Sorley, *Thunderbolt: General Creighton Abrams and the Army of His Times* (New York: Simon & Schuster, 1992), 355.

31. This may be an accurate judgment in McGarr's case. Krepinevich quotes a senior army officer, who said that the army "couldn't get McGarr out fast enough. He was a very poor MAAG chief, a stuffed shirt," Krepinevich, *The Army and Vietnam*, 57.

32. Westmoreland, *A Soldier Reports*, 275.

33. Lieutenant Colonel Lawrence P. Crocker, *The Army Officer's Guide*, 43rd ed. (Harrisburg, PA: Stackpole Books, 1985), 15.

34. Westmoreland, *SOOHP*, Volume 2, 73. MHI.

35. Quoted in Harry Summers, *On Strategy II: A Critical Analysis of the Gulf War* (New York: Dell, 1992), 128.

36. Crocker, *The Army Officer's Guide*, 8, my emphasis.

37. Janowitz, *The Professional Soldier*, 239.

38. Crocker, *The Army Officer's Guide*, 256.

39. Jay M. Parker, "Change and the Operational Commander," *Joint Force Quarterly* (Winter 1995/96), 95.

40. Chief of Staff of the Army Harold Johnson and Chairman of the JCS Maxwell Taylor prevented Vann's address to the Joint Chiefs and share some of the responsibility; they are examples of the same organizational culture. These officers

also did not fully implement President Kennedy's desires to reshape the army to make it a more effective counterinsurgency weapon.

41. Johnson Oral History, Section XIII, 31–32, MHI.

42. Ronald H. Spector, "U.S. Army Strategy in the Vietnam War" (review of Andrew Krepinevich's *The Army and Vietnam*), *International Security* 11/4 (Spring 1987), 134. Spector continues: "What was it about the U.S. Army in the 1960s that allowed such men to be appointed to posts for which they were so manifestly unsuited? What was it, in fact, that made it so difficult for the Army to adapt to conditions in Vietnam and so easy for it to embrace false or misleading measures of progress—whether Harkins' 'improvements' in ARVN performance or the body count of General Westmoreland?" The organizational culture of the United States Army is one explanation.

43. Westmoreland estimates that he spent on average "four out of seven days visiting the troops," Westmoreland, *A Soldier Reports*, 269. Then-captain Robert O'Neill recalls Westmoreland's "regularly visiting Australian and US Forces at the conclusion of major operations, especially those which had seen significant clashes between the opposing forces. These, more than any other aspects of the war, aroused Westmoreland's interest and won his commitment, support and time. There was no doubt that this was where Westmoreland's heart was inclined." O'Neill interview, 17 January 1997. O'Neill includes a photograph of Westmoreland's welcoming C Company, Fifth Royal Australian Regiment, to Vietnam on 2 May 1966 in *Vietnam Task: The 5th Battalion, Royal Australian Regiment, 1966/7* (Marrickville: Cassell Australia, 1968), facing page 33.

44. Thompson, *No Exit from Vietnam*, 130.

45. Westmoreland, *A Soldier Reports*, 240. Note that Westmoreland seeks an approved manual to guide his actions; Templer ordered that one be *written*, to be based on what the British army had learned about the situation in Malaya.

46. Lorenzo M. Crowell, "Thinking About the Vietnam War," *Journal of Military History* 60 (April 1996), 340.

47. Robert S. McNamara with Brian VanDeMark, *In Retrospect: The Tragedy and Lessons of Vietnam* (New York: Random House, 1995), 48. McNamara admits to some of the same errors, and to many others, in this apologia.

48. Granville Watts, 'Why the Americans Are Not Winning," *The Straits Times* (27 March 1968), in *Templer Papers*, Box 30.

49. Army Code No. 71596 AFM /Volume V, *Operations Other Than War*, Section B, "Counter Insurgency Operations," viii. The tale of British army performance and adaptation in these conflicts is told in Michael Dewar's *Brush Fire Wars: Minor Campaigns of the British Army Since 1945* (London: Robert Hale, 1990).

50. General Sir John Waters interview, 13 December 1995. Waters is echoed by Brigadier Gavin Bulloch, who states that British understanding of counterinsurgency is the "product of long, hard experience. . . . You Americans haven't been at this game very long." Bulloch interview, 19 December 1995.

51. Kitson interview, Devon, 12 December 1995.

52. Ibid. See also Brigadier (Retired) Gavin Bulloch, "Military Doctrine and Counterinsurgency: A British Perspective," *Parameters* XXVI, No. 2 (Summer 1996), 4–16. Bulloch described learning as passing through "verbal osmosis" from one campaign or regiment to another, always under the constraint of the British rule of law. Bulloch interview, 19 December 1995.

53. Kitson interview, Devon, 12 December 1995.

54. Army Code No. 71596 AFM/Volume V, *Operations Other Than War*, Section B, "Counter Insurgency Operations," ix.

55. David Lloyd Owen interview, 11 November 1996.

56. Downie, *Learning from Conflict*, 109.

57. BDM Corporation, *A Study of the Strategic Lessons Learned in Vietnam: Omnibus Executive Summary* Volume I (Washington, DC: BDM Corporation, 1980), vi.

58. Harry P. Ball, *Of Responsible Command: A History of the U.S. Army War College* (Carlisle Barracks, PA: U.S. Army War College, 1983), 478.

59. BDM Corporation, *A Study of the Strategic Lessons Learned in Vietnam: Omnibus Excutive Summary* (Washington, DC: BDM Corporation, 1980).

60. Downie, *Learning from Conflict*, 72.

61. Major Paul H. Herbert, *Deciding What Has to Be Done: General William E. DePuy and the 1976 Edition of FM 100–5, Operations* (Fort Leavenworth, KS: Leavenworth Papers Number 16, 1988).

62. Donald B. Vought, "Preparing for the Wrong War," *Military Review* 57 (May 1977), 29.

63. John Waghelstein, *Preparing for the Wrong War: The United States Army and Low Intensity Conflict 1755–1890* (Unpublished Doctoral Dissertation, Temple University, August 1990), 11.

64. Harry G. Summers, Jr., *On Strategy: A Critical Analysis of the Vietnam War* (Novato, CA: Presidio, 1982), xiii.

65. Merritt, in ibid., xiii.

66. Ibid., 86–88.

67. Ibid., 119.

68. Krepinevich, *The Army and Vietnam*, 262.

69. Bruce Palmer, Jr., review of *The Army and Vietnam*, *Parameters* XVI, 3 (Autumn 1988), 83–85. This review is very revealing, if somewhat schizophrenic: Palmer calls *The Army and Vietnam* "a long, rambling, one-sided discourse that lacks the balance, cohesion, and objectivity of a truly professional and scholarly book" (83). Palmer then enumerates Krepinevich's "numerous excellent points and sound judgments regarding the American performance in Vietnam that are worth remembering and heeding" (83). Palmer echoes many of Krepinevich's arguments in his own book, *The 25 Year War* (New York: Da Capo, 1984).

70. General Bruce Palmer Jr., "Introduction" to Lloyd J. Matthews and Dale E. Brown, eds., *Assessing the Vietnam War: A Collection from the Journal of the U.S. Army War College* (Washington, DC: Pergamon-Brassey's, 1987), xii. This compilation of articles from *Parameters*, the journal of the Army War College, is an outstanding reflection of the state of the debate within the army over the "lessons of Vietnam" in the late 1980s.

71. The author served as a tank platoon leader in the First Cavalry Division in this conflict, an experience that taught him a great deal about the organizational culture of the United States Army. If soldiers, machines, and firepower can win a war, the United States Army will win it. This is a good thing, as long as the enemy chooses to fight the United States symmetrically.

72. Retired General Barry McCaffrey has commented, "I fear the Majors of Desert Storm," for this very reason: it cemented for yet another generation of of-

ficers the concept of conventional attrition-based warfare as the "American Way of War." Whereas the Persian Gulf War of 1990–91 was "the right war, at the right time, at the right place, against the right enemy" so far as the U.S. Army was concerned, the rebuilding of the American army after Vietnam into a force that could again fight and win remains a remarkable achievement. See James Kitfield, *Prodigal Soldiers: How the Generation of Officers Born of Vietnam Revolutionized the American Style of War* (New York: Simon & Schuster, 1995).

73. For a convincing argument that the army's "Lessons Learning" system remains constrained by its organizational culture, see Sean D. Naylor, "Somalia Revisited: Is the Army Using Any of the Lessons It Learned?" *Army Times* (7 October 1996), 9–12.

9

Organizational Culture and Learning Institutions: Learning to Eat Soup with a Knife

The organizational culture of the British army allowed it to learn how to conduct a counterinsurgency campaign during the Malayan Emergency, whereas the organizational culture of the U.S. Army prevented a similar organizational learning process during and after the Vietnam War. This chapter attempts to place these conclusions in a wider context. It evaluates current ideas on military innovation, argues that organizational learning theory is a useful tool with which to analyze organizational change, and discusses the impact of varying organizational cultures on the learning abilities of different organizations. The chapter concludes with some ideas about how to make military forces adaptable in the light of emerging changes in warfare and about how to overcome institutional culture when necessary in building learning institutions.

IDEAS AND INTERNATIONAL RELATIONS

"Black box" theories of international relations suggest that states act only in order to increase their power in the international system; any state placed in the same situation would react in exactly the same way. The truth is more complicated. There are a number of factors other than power that

An earlier version of this chapter was published as "Learning to Eat Soup with a Knife: British and American Army Counterinsurgency Learning During the Malayan Emergency and the Vietnam War," *World Affairs* 161, 4 (Spring 1999), 193–199. Reprinted by kind permission of HELDREF Publishers.

affect the ability of states to achieve their goals and preserve their positions in the state system.[1] One of these factors is the organizational culture of a state's armed forces. The organizational culture of military forces is a decisive determinant in their effectiveness and hence helps to determine the course of international politics. The ability of military organizations to adapt to change—whether that change occurs in military technology, in the structure of the international system, or in the nature of war itself—is an important component of a state's ability to guarantee its own security and that of its allies.

In short, military organizations that are "learning institutions" add to the influence of their states in the international system. This was the case for the United Kingdom in the wake of the Malayan Emergency. Military organizations that are unable to learn can substantially damage the ability of their states to influence the international system; the United States suffered appreciably during and after the Vietnam War because its military was unable to learn how to counter insurgency. Understanding the organizational culture of military institutions, and the effects of that culture on their ability to learn, increases our ability to understand how states act and react in the international system.

EVALUATING THE LITERATURE ON MILITARY INNOVATION

Current literature on military innovation focuses on the question of whether armed services can innovate independently[2] or whether civilian leadership must force innovation on an unwilling military.[3] Some authors have found that civilian reformers and members of the military combine to create changes in doctrine, an integrative model of military innovation.[4]

Most research to date has focused on military innovation in peacetime rather than during conflict. However, the process of innovation is very different in wartime. Steven Rosen notes that military forces "exist in order to fight a foreign enemy, and do not execute this function every day. Most of the time, the countries they serve are at peace. . . . Instead of being routinely 'in business' and learning from ongoing experience, they must anticipate wars that may or may not occur."[5] One of the few studies of military innovation under the pressure of combat is Timothy T. Lupfer's *The Dynamics of Doctrine: The Changes in German Tactical Doctrine During the First World War.*[6] Although it examines only tactical level innovation, the study is significant for its description of the process through which the German army adapted to the demands of trench warfare.

Another examination of the relationship between civilian and military leadership and military innovation in wartime is Deborah Avant's *Political Institutions and Military Change: Lessons from Peripheral Wars.*[7] Avant compares British army innovation during the Boer War and the Malayan Emergency with American army innovation in Vietnam. Rather than focusing on the differences between the two armies as the critical variable explaining the different patterns of innovation, Avant believes that the different political systems of the United States and Britain led the two nations' politicians to create different militaries:

Civilian leaders in Britain, who had institutional incentives to act as a unit, had an easier time agreeing on both policy goals and oversight options to ensure that the Army followed these goals. Under these conditions, the British Army reacted more flexibility to changes in civilian leaders' goals. Conversely, civilian leaders in the United States, who had institutional incentives to act separately, found it harder to agree on policy goals and often chose more complex oversight mechanisms, which did not always induce the U.S. Army to respond easily to change.[8]

According to this view, British army officers responded directly to their political masters in the Cabinet, creating a more flexible military. In the American system the military had the ability to "trade off" demands made by the Congress against the president or vice versa. There are wider implications: "Differences in institutional structures that affect ensuing differences in the growth of parties, the issue-focus of voters, the interpretation of the international system, and the terms of delegation will lead to differences in the preferences of military organizations and civilian leaders. These variations explain the deviations in policy."[9]

This study reaches different conclusions, arguing along with Barry Watts and Williamson Murray that "the potential for civilian or outside leadership to *impose* a new vision of future war on a reluctant military service whose heart remains committed to existing ways of fighting is, at best, limited."[10] The critical independent variable is not the nature of national government, which in most cases has little impact on which policies the military chooses to adopt. It is the organizational culture of the military institution that determines whether innovation succeeds or fails.

EVALUATING THE EFFECTIVENESS OF LEARNING THEORY AS A TOOL FOR ANALYZING MILITARY INNOVATION

This study has attempted to explain why one military force successfully adapted to change whereas another failed to do so by tracing the processes through which the British army in the Malayan Emergency and the American army in the Vietnam War learned counterinsurgency. Using a theory of organizational learning first developed from observations of business management, the study focused on the process through which change developed or failed to develop. It found that the organizational culture—the "persistent, patterned way of thinking about the central tasks of and human relationships within an organization"[11]—played a key role in allowing an organization to create a consensus either in favor of or in opposition to proposals for change. Changes that conflict with the dominant group's ideas on preferred roles and missions—the essence of the organization—will not be adopted. Leaders of the organization, conditioned by the culture they have absorbed through years of service in that organization, will prevent changes in the core mission and roles. The key variable explaining when militaries will adapt to changes in warfare is the creation of a consensus among the leaders of the organization that such innovation is in the long-term interests of the organization itself.[12]

Unfortunately, organizational learning theory is not a succinct explanation for why some military forces innovate and others do not. Since it uses the technique of process tracing, learning theory demands in-depth study of individual cases of innovation or failure to innovate. Its emphasis on organizational culture and protection of the "essence of the organization" by elite decision makers within the organization similarly demands a high degree of familiarity with the organization under examination, as neither the identities of the dominant members of an organization nor their views on its core roles and missions are always immediately apparent.

But there is no other way to predict the likelihood of innovation nor to explain it once it occurs. If "a remembered past has always more or less constricted both action in the present and thinking about the future,"[13] then understanding that past, and understanding how it is remembered by those who direct an organization's present and future, is essential to understanding how that organization will adapt to changes in its environment.[14] To understand how and why an organization will change, it is essential to examine its past successes and failures—and those of the individuals who control the institution.[15]

THE IMPACT OF ORGANIZATIONAL CULTURE ON ORGANIZATIONAL LEARNING

The organizational culture of the British army, developed over many years of service in colonial wars—and, just as important, in prevention of colonial wars through sound administration in conjunction with British police forces and colonial administrators—reflected varied experiences outside conventional conflicts on the continent of Europe. The leadership of the British army shared a common belief that the essence of the organization included colonial policing and administration. When conventional tactics and strategy failed in Malaya, the British army had few problems creating an internal consensus that change was needed and that political rather than purely military solutions were well within the purview of the British army. An innovative and varied past created a culture amenable to the changes in organizational process required to defeat a complex opponent in a new kind of war.

The organizational culture of the American army permitted no doubt in the army's leadership about the essence of the organization: its core competency was defeating conventional enemy armies in frontal combat. The organization never developed a consensus that change to its procedures and to its definition of its responsibilities was required by the nature of the revolutionary war it confronted in Vietnam. An unshakable belief in the essence of the organization precluded organizational learning and has continued to prevent the formation of a consensus on the "lessons of Vietnam" and on changes required to make the army more capable there and in future conflicts. Words recently applied to the Soviet system also describe the U.S. Army of the time: "The person at the head of the hierarchical system was given great power—but he was given that power only so long as he did not use it in a way which threatened the continuation of the system."[16]

Gen. Harold K. Johnson's description of an officer's tenure in command can also be applied to explain why his ability to apply innovative solutions diminishes after years inside an organization: "The longer that a man is there, the greater is his loss of capability to innovate. When he comes in, he can be completely innovative. Ask all kinds of questions because he's attacking the status quo, but every time that he throws out something and adopts something of his own, then he has to defend it. Over a period of time, his defending time begins to exceed his innovative time."[17]

Organizations acquire personalities over time. They develop abilities in certain areas to accomplish the tasks of the organization but are constrained by their experience to innovate only within the self-defined parameters of what they see as their purpose. Even under the pressures for change presented by ongoing military conflict, a strong organizational culture can prohibit learning the lessons of the present and can even prevent the organization's acknowledging that its current policies are anything other than completely successful. In the words of a prominent student of organizational learning:

Most people so restrict their frame of reference, or context, for the problem they are facing that little change can occur. They get into such a routine with their work that they view virtually all problems in a similar way—back to all problems looking like nails when all you have is a hammer. Consequently, when asked to change matters, they tend to operate in a confined "single loop" of learning on which they can only do "more of" or "less of" the same thing because of the given context.[18]

BUILDING ARMIES THAT LEARN

Carl H. Builder noted, "How the services perceive the next major war they must fight is an important determinant of the types of forces they try to acquire, the doctrine they develop, and the training they follow for the use of those forces in combat."[19] Services' self-concepts determine not only how they will prepare for the next war, but also how flexible they will be in responding to unexpected situations when that war occurs. Chief of the General Staff General Sir Charles Guthrie recently paraphrased Michael Howard to the effect that "in structuring and preparing an Army for war you can be clear that you will not get it precisely right, but the important thing to ensure is that it is not too far wrong, so that you can put it right quickly."[20] The culture of the British army encourages such an attitude and such responses to changed situations. The culture of the American army does not, unless the changed situation falls within the parameters of the kind of war it has defined as its primary mission.[21]

Among the changes required are drastic modifications of military organizations to make their leadership more responsive to change in their environment. One Vietnam veteran, John Grinalds, recalls, "Entrenched operational procedures made it very hard to implement change."[22] Eliot Cohen points out that the management structure of the U.S. military has not evolved since World War II and still resembles that of the General Motors Corporation of 1950. Meanwhile, the world has moved on. "The modern corporation has stripped out layers of middle management, reduced or even eliminated many of the functional and social distinctions between management and labor that dominated industrial organizations. . . . The radical revision of these structures will be the last manifestation of a revolution in military affairs, and the most difficult to implement."[23]

Eric Heginbotham argues that American proficiency in the employment of combined arms improved more rapidly in the European theater of operations during World War II than did British combined arms proficiency— that the American army "learned" more effectively than did the British in the field of conventional armored warfare. Heginbotham highlights differences in the organizational infrastructures of the two armies to explain differences in learning performance:

The British Army had relatively few channels through which a dialogue among top officers could be sustained. The communication that did occur was hampered by a lack of common army-wide doctrine and the lack of tactical protocols for the orchestration of combined-arms units. Reliance on a combination of single-arm regimental standards and on *ad hoc* guidelines issued by theatre commander permitted continued innovation but little accumulation of knowledge. In contrast, American forces benefited from a dense network of channels that allowed for effective communication within the force.[24]

Given the organizational cultures of the two armies, these results are hardly surprising. The American army was focused from its inception on the idea of fighting decisive conventional conflicts despite the fact that most of the wars it actually fought were limited wars for political objectives. It evolved a standard organization and doctrine devoted to ensuring uniformity in the employment of American material and firepower superiority on the battlefield and encouraged innovation in line with these proclivities.

The British army, which had evolved to meet the needs of Imperial warfare and for which "conventional continental wars were an aberration" was unable suddenly to change its spots to meet the demands of a very different kind of warfare under the conditions of World War II in Europe. Williamson Murray, while praising the British conduct of grand strategy and mobilization, notes shortcomings in British operational and tactical performance during World War II: "On the one hand, there was no common doctrinal center in the army, as was the case with the Germans. Consequently, there was no consistent battle doctrine. On the other, there was no means of ensuring that the many decentralized training programs reflected similar approaches."[25] The very attributes that allowed the British army to respond to the demands of counterinsurgency in Malaya—decentralization, minimal use of firepower, independent and innovative theater commanders—made it a less effective learning organization on the conventional battlegrounds of World War II.

The demands of conventional and unconventional warfare differ so greatly that an organization optimized to succeed in one will have great difficulty in fighting the other. It will likely also be unsuccessful in efforts to adapt itself to meet changing requirements in the course of the type of conflict for which it was not originally designed and trained.[26] In fact, the very organizational culture that makes an institution effective in one area may blind it to the possibility that its strengths in that field are crippling deficiencies in a different situation—the more debilitating for being so deeply rooted in the culture that they are never even recognized, much less questioned.

The implications are dramatic. If it is in fact impossible for the same organization to perform effectively two very disparate tasks because the organizational culture that makes it effective in achieving one is counterproductive in accomplishing the other, then organizations should focus on achieving just one critical mission.[27] Those organizations that attempt to perform a mission for which they are unprepared and unsuitable by organization, training, doctrine, leadership style, organizational infrastructure, and equipment—all of which both contribute to and flow from organizational culture—will face grave difficulties in adapting to the new challenges they face. The U.S. Army in Vietnam is a classic example, but the relative weaknesses of the British and French armies in a high-technology combined arms conventional conflict in the Persian Gulf War of 1990–1991 should also be noted.[28] The difficulties of the United States Army in a peacekeeping role in Bosnia are another example of an organization's attempting to do something for which it is not designed, organized, or trained, at great cost to the health of the institution as a whole.[29]

DIRECTIONS FOR FUTURE RESEARCH

This study presents no overarching explanation for why some military forces are better at adapting to the demands of change in warfare than are others but does provide a framework for tracing the process of military innovation and highlights one variable within the organizational culture that appears to explain variations in learning outcomes. The evidence suggests that other cases of military innovation or failures to innovate could profit from study along the same lines, focusing on the organizational culture while tracing the organizational learning process. The efforts of the French army to defeat insurgency in Indochina and Algeria are two such cases[30]; there are many others, responses to conventional tactical and operational changes as well as to those in revolutionary warfare. The technique could also be applied to other questions of why states behave as they do, helping to explain both why states alter their policies in response to changes in the international system and, often even more interesting, why they do not.[31] International organizations such as the United Nations could also profitably be studied to determine the influence of organizational cultures on changes to procedures such as the creation and employment of peacekeeping forces.

BUILDING LEARNING INSTITUTIONS: MAKING MILITARY FORCES ADAPTABLE IN LIGHT OF CHANGES IN WARFARE

"Building learning organizations entails profound cultural shifts."[32]
—Peter M. Senge

Richard Downie concludes his examination of the United States Army's modifications to its low-intensity conflict doctrine after the Vietnam War with six recommendations for facilitating doctrinal change:

1. Institutionalize doctrinal development as a continually evolving set of theoretical guidelines.
2. Establish a systemic assessment process to ensure the validity of current doctrinal operation assumptions.
3. Develop an efficient process to gain organizational consensus on emerging doctrines.
4. Establish a systemic process through which to rapidly transmit and disseminate doctrine to units in the field.
5. Welcome the civilian leadership's inquiries concerning military capability and appropriateness of doctrine as useful challenges for the military institution.

6. Doctrine as a focus of inquiry concerning military effectiveness for potential threats and challenges.[33]

These recommendations emerge logically from an examination of the organizational learning cycle and would undoubtedly improve the adaptability of the U.S. Army if they were adopted. Their adoption and implementation, however, require an organizational consensus that the army currently suffers from an inability to learn and a further consensus that these steps would help to remedy that shortcoming. Unfortunately, this study has shown that even during a war in which organizational failures were obvious to much of the army, no consensus emerged among the army leadership that change was required. Downie's own study indicates that the army failed to learn from its Vietnam experience as a result of a failure to achieve organizational consensus on required changes to the definition of the army's roles and missions in low-intensity conflict. Only organizational self-awareness can change organizational culture.[34]

Until the army is willing to recognize its past failings, it will not adopt significant changes to increase its adaptability. In the words of U.S. Army Lieutenant General Theodore G. Stroup, Jr., "Our Army culture, however, can also be a liability when it is inappropriate and does not contribute to the Army's overall goals."[35] Colonel (Retired) Powell Hutton concurs: "The Army learns very slowly, because you have to change the culture. The culture changes slowly because innovators are forced out. If we're going to do one thing to make the organization healthy, we have to promote people who aren't like us."[36]

Lieutenant General John Cushman agrees:

Among other duties, the duty of generals is to observe, to think, and to *listen*, even to majors and colonels. Break down the compartments—wherever they exist—of service parochialism, of "turf," of hierarchical layering. Let insight evolve from an atmosphere of open, shared thought . . . from a willing openness to a variety of stimuli, from intellectual curiosity, from observation and reflection, from continuous evaluation and discussions, from review of assumptions, from listening to the views of outsiders, from study of history, and from the indispensable ingredient of humility.[37]

Evaluating Downie's and Cushman's recommendations in light of the British army's experience in Malaya reveals that most of the suggestions are and have long been integral parts of the British army's standard procedure. The British army's organizational culture, developed over many years of colonial policing, not just encouraged but actively expected innovation. For years, the resulting informally developed "doctrine" was disseminated by word of mouth and through the unofficial writing of participants in the campaigns; the fact that it is now officially prescribed from the new Doctrine and Training Directorate in Wiltshire may be the first step toward discouraging innovation in the British army. Organizational culture is hard to change, however; General Sir Frank Kitson's belief that "no one would read it if they did write it down" may yet preserve the institutional flexibility that played such an important role in defeating the Communist insurgency in Malaya. As the assistant under secretary (programmes) recently said to the Defence Committee in the House of Commons, "We have structured our forces precisely to deal with the unexpected."[38]

Is it possible for the U.S. Army to develop such a culture? Williamson Murray suggests that some improvements can be made, given efforts to "push cultural changes to encourage rather than discourage the process of innovation." Chief among these is a new "approach to military education that encourages changes in cultural values and fosters intellectual curiosity" in order to "foster a military culture where those promoted to the highest ranks possess the imagination and intellectual framework to support innovation."[39]

In the rapidly changing world of the post–Cold War era, such flexibility is a critical factor in the ability of military forces to meet the security needs their governments will demand of them. The Persian Gulf War of 1990–1991 may well have been an aberration, the last of the conventional industrial age conflicts; it was certainly a lesson to the states and nonstate actors of the developing world not to confront the West in conventional combat.[40] There are many other ways to use force to achieve political goals: terrorism, subversion, insurgency. Some years ago Eliot Cohen warned that America's increasing lead in weaponry created by digitized information, the so-called revolution in military affairs, would not guarantee her security. His words resound in the wake of 11 September 2001: "Just as nuclear weapons did not render conventional power obsolete, this revolution will not render guerrilla tactics, terrorism, or weapons of mass destruction obsolete. Indeed, the reverse may be true: where unconventional bypasses to conventional military power exist, any country confronting the United States will seek them out."[41]

The vast majority of armed conflict today occurs inside states rather than between them; as Steven Metz has noted, "For many countries in the world simmering internal war is a permanent condition."[42] The American army, so successful in waging and winning wars against other states, must adapt to increase its ability to moderate wars within states. The end of the cold war has returned to the front pages the small wars of the nineteenth century that were so critical an element in shaping the culture of the British army, including those in places like Afghanistan. U.S. Army Colonel Dan Bolger suggests that the trend toward these small wars is likely to continue: "To meet future challenges, America's Army must turn from the warm and well-deserved glow of its Persian Gulf victory and embrace, once more, the real business of regulars, the stinking gray shadow world of 'savage wars of peace,' as Rudyard Kipling called them."[43]

In these dirty little wars, political and military tasks intertwine and the objective is more often "nation building" than the destruction of an enemy army. The ability to learn quickly during such operations in order to create an organizational consensus on new ways of waging war—or of waging peace—may be of more importance for modern military institutions than ever before.[44] Armies will have to make the ability to learn to deal with messy, uncomfortable situations an integral part of their organizational culture. In T.E. Lawrence's metaphor, they must learn how to eat soup with a knife. The process will not be comfortable, but it could not be more important.

NOTES

1. Charles Powell, James Dyson, and Helen Purkitt, "Opening the 'Black Box': Cognitive Processing and Optimal Choice in Foreign Policy Decision Making," in Charles Herman, Charles Kegley, and James Rosenau, eds., *New Directions in the Study of Foreign Policy* (Boston: Allen & Unwin, 1987), 203–220.

2. The best known is Stephen P. Rosen, *Winning the Next War: Innovation and the Modern Military* (Ithaca, NY: Cornell University Press, 1991).

3. Barry R. Posen, *The Sources of Military Doctrine: France, Britain, and Germany Between the World Wars* (Ithaca, NY: Cornell University Press, 1984).

4. Kimberly Martin Zisk, *Engaging the Enemy: Organization Theory and Soviet Military Innovation, 1955–1991*; Ricky Lynn Waddell, *The Army and Peacetime Low Intensity Conflict, 1961–1993: The Process of Peripheral and Fundamental Military Change* (Unpublished Ph.D. Thesis, Columbia University, 1993).

5. Rosen, *Winning the Next War*, 8. Rosen discusses wartime innovation on pp. 22 to 24.

6. Timothy T. Lupfer, *The Dynamics of Doctrine: The Changes in German Tactical Doctrine During the First World War* (Fort Leavenworth, KS: Combat Studies Institute, 1981).

7. Deborah Avant, *Political Institutions and Military Change: Lessons from Peripheral Wars* (Ithaca, NY: Cornell, 1994).

8. Ibid., 130–131.

9. Ibid., 139.

10. Barry Watts and Williamson Murray, "Innovation in Peacetime," in Williamson Murray and Allan R. Millett, eds., *Military Innovation in the Interwar Period* (Cambridge: Cambridge University Press, 1996), 410.

11. James Q. Wilson, *Bureaucracy* (New York: Basic Books, 1989), 91.

12. "I'm not going to destroy the traditions and doctrine of the United States Army just to win this lousy war": an anonymous army officer quoted in Brian M. Jenkins, *The Unchangeable War* (Santa Monica, CA: RAND, 1972), 3, in Gunter Lewy, *America in Vietnam* (Oxford: Oxford University Press, 198), 138.

13. John Shy, "The American Military Experience: History and Learning," *Journal of Interdisciplinary History* 1, 2 (Winter 1971), 210.

14. Jay M. Parker, "Change and the Operational Commander," *Joint Force Quarterly* (Winter 1995/96), 92.

15. These results parallel those of Richard E. Neustadt and Earnest R. May in *Thinking in Time: The Uses of History for Decisionmakers* (New York: The Free Press, 1986), especially chapter 9, "Placing Strangers," and chapter 12, "Placing Organizations." For more insight into how early experiences condition cognition in decision makers, see Yuen Foong Khong, *Analogies at War: Korea, Munich, Dien Bien Phu, and the Vietnam Decisions of 1965* (Princeton, NJ: Princeton University Press, 1992).

16. Professor Archie Brown on Mikhail Gorbachev in Oxford, 28 October 1996.

17. Johnson Oral History, Volume II, Section IX, 28–29, MHI.

18. Bob Garratt, *The Learning Organization* (London: Harper Collins, 1994), 42–43.

19. Carl H. Builder, *The Masks of War: American Military Styles in Strategy and Analysis* (Baltimore: Johns Hopkins University Press, 1989), 128.

20. General Sir Charles Guthrie, "The British Army at the Turn of the Century," *RUSI Journal* 141/3 (June 1996), 6. The original citation is Michael Howard, "Military Science in the Age of Peace," *RUSI Journal* (March 1974), 3–4.

21. Sean D. Naylor, "War Games," *Army Times* (5 November 2001), 12–13.

22. Major General John Grinalds interview, Washington, D.C., 12 September 1996.

23. Eliot A. Cohen, "A Revolution in Warfare," *Foreign Affairs* 75, 2 (March/April 1996), 48. For a compelling explanation of how the U.S. Army should eliminate layers of bureaucracy, see Douglas A. MacGregor, *Breaking the Phalanx: A New Design for Landpower for the 21st Century* (Westport, CT: Praeger/CSIS, 1997).

24. Eric Heginbotham, *The British and American Armies in World War II: Explaining Variations in Organizational Learning Patterns* (Boston: MIT Defense and Arms Control Studies Program Working Paper, 1996), 1–2.

25. Williamson Murray, "British Military Effectiveness in the Second World War," in Allan R. Millett and Williamson Murray, eds., *Military Effectiveness.* Volume III, *The Second World War* (London: Unwin Hyman, 1988), 112.

26. See John A. Nagl and Elizabeth O. Young, "*Si Vis Pacem, Pare Pacem*: Improving U.S. Army Training for Complex Humanitarian Emergencies," *Military Review* LXXX, 2 (March/April 2000), 31–37.

27. The "conventionalization" of U.S. Army Special Forces throughout their history by the much more pervasive organizational culture of the conventional army shows this process at work; see Thomas Adams, *Military Doctrine and the Organization Culture of the United States Army* (Ph.D. Thesis, Syracuse University, 1990).

28. Among the generally self-congratulatory literature on the war, see Rick Atkinson, *Crusade* (New York: Random House, 1992), for references to the training, planning, and especially logistical problems of these two armies in the war. Reports that a banner proclaiming, "We only do deserts" appeared on the Pentagon the day of the cease-fire recognize the fact that the Gulf War was exactly the war the United States would have chosen to fight if it could have scripted the scenario: midintensity combined arms warfare on a battlefield generally free of civilians.

29. William Langewiesche, "Peace Is Hell," *The Atlantic Monthly* 288, 3 (October 2001), 51–80.

30. Christopher C. Harmon notes that the French "forgot all too well" their counterinsurgency successes of the nineteenth century in Indochina but does not trace the learning process nor discuss the organizational culture of the French army, in "Illustrations of 'Learning' in Counterinsurgency," *Comparative Strategy* 11 (1992), 30–33.

31. George W. Breslauer and Philip E. Tetlock, eds., *Learning in U.S. and Soviet Foreign Policy* (Boulder, CO: Westview, 1991). This book adopts such a perspective without focusing on organizational culture as a key factor in influencing learning.

32. Peter M. Senge, *The Fifth Discipline: The Art and Practice of the Learning Organization* (New York: Doubleday, 1990), xv.

33. Richard Downie, *Learning from Conflict: The U.S. Military in Vietnam, El Salvador, and the Drug War* (Westport, CT: Praeger, 1998), 261–265.

34. Carl H. Builder, *The Masks of War: American Military Styles in Strategy and Analysis* (Baltimore: Johns Hopkins University Press, 1989), 205.

35. Lieutenant General Theodore G. Stroup, Jr., "Leadership and Organizational Culture: Actions Speak Louder than Words," *Military Review* LXXVI, 1 (January/February 1996), 46.

36. Powell Hutton interview, Washington, D.C., 18 September 1996.

37. Lieutenant General John H. Cushman, USA, "Challenge and Response at the Operational and Tactical Levels, 1914–1945," in Millett and Murray, eds., *Military Effectiveness*, Volume III, 334–336.

38. Session 1991–2, Third Report, question 1190, quoted in Eric Grove, *The Army and British Security After the Cold War: Defence Planning for a New Era* (London: Strategic and Combat Studies Institute/HMSO, 1996), 10.

39. Murray, "Past and Future," in Murray and Millett, eds., *Military Innovation in the Interwar Period*, 326–327.

40. John A. Nagl, "Hitting Us Where We Don't Expect It: Asymmetric Threats to U.S. National Security," *National Security Studies Quarterly* 7, 4 (Autumn 2001), 113–121. See also Nagl, "Post–Cold War Priorities," *Military Review* LXXXI, 4 (July/August 2001), 104–106.

41. Eliot Cohen, "A Revolution in Warfare," *Foreign Affairs* 75 (March/April 1996), 51.

42. Steven Metz, "Insurgency After the Cold War," *Small Wars and Insurgencies* 5/1 (Spring 1994), 63.

43. Daniel P. Bolger, "The Ghosts of Omdurman," *Parameters* (Autumn 1991), 31–32.

44. See Gen. Wesley K. Clark, *Waging Modern War: Bosnia, Kosovo, and the Future of Conflict* (New York: Public Affairs, 2001), for insightful comments on how war has changed in the post–cold war world, and the current author's review essay, "Wes Clark's War," *The American Oxonian* LXXXVIII: 4 (Autumn 2001), 303–311, for less insightful reflections on the same topic.

Selected Bibliography

I. ARCHIVAL MATERIALS

U.S. Army Center for Military History (CMH), Washington, D.C.

Robert Komer Interview, 7 May 1970
Lieutenant General Julian Ewell Interview
The Westmoreland History Notes
Westmoreland COMUSMACV Signature Files
Abrams D/COMUSMACV and COMUSMACV Message Files

U.S. Army Military History Institute (MHI), U.S. Army War College, Carlisle Barracks, PA

Operational Readiness/Lessons Learned Reports (OR/LL)
>   1st Cavalry Division
>   3/4 Cavalry, 9th Infantry Division
>   25th Infantry Division

Colonel Jack G. Cornett Papers
General William DePuy Interview, SOOHP
Lieutenant General Julian J. Ewell Interview, SOOHP
General Paul D. Harkins Interview, SOOHP
General Harold K. Johnson Interview, SOOHP
General William Rosson Interview, SOOHP

Lieutenant Colonel John Paul Vann Papers
General William C. Westmoreland Interview, SOOHP
General Samuel T. Williams Papers

Lyndon B. Johnson Presidential Library

Robert Komer Interviews

Imperial War Museum, London Department of Sound Records

IWM DSR 008255/06, Richard Broome OBE, MC (24 July 1984)
IWM DSR 008943/7, Derek Frederick Blake (11 August 1985)
IWM DSR 009127/04, George Albert William Booker (5 November 1985)
IWM DSR 009989/08, Brigadier J.M. Calvert MA, DSO (1 October 1987)
IWM DSR 103392/9, Sir Richard Catling (1988)
IWM DSR 10175/4, Richard Joseph Wauchope Craig OBE, MC (1988)
IWM DSR 10727/4, Anthony Sean Harvey (1989)
IWM DSR 009187/6, Lt. Col. Robert Ian Hywel-Jones MC (14 January 1986)
IWM DSR 10672/4, Eric John Linsell (1989)
IWM DSR 009589/06, John Marsh (13 January 1987)
IWM DSR 10127/21, Sir John Nott KCB, PC (1988)
IWM DSR 10121/3, Wing Commander Charles O'Reilly OBE (1988)
IWM DSR 10200/4, John Sankey (1988)
IWM DSR 9797/07, William James Spearman (6 November 1987)
IWM DSR 10192/6, Sir Robert Thompson KBE, CMG, DSO, MC. (1988)

National Army Museum, Chelsea, London

Field Marshal Sir Gerald Templer Papers
General Sir Robert Lockhart Papers

Public Records Office, Kew, London

Records of the British Advisory Mission—Saigon
Records of the Far East Land Force Training Centre

Tactical Doctrine Retrieval Centre (TDRC), British Army Doctrine and Training Command, Pewsey, Wiltshire

TDRC 953. Lieutenant General Sir Harold Briggs, Director of Operations. *Report on the Emergency in Malaya from April, 1950 to November, 1951.* Kuala Lumpur: Federation of Malaya Government Press/H.T. Ross, 1951.

TDRC 5293. Lieutenant General Sir Frank Kitson, Kermit Roosevelt Lecture 1981. "Practical Aspects of Counterinsurgency."

TDRC 7220. Major General Sir Frank Kitson, Kermit Roosevelt Lecture 1976. "The Nature of Insurgency."

TDRC 10054. General Sir John Waters, Kermit Roosevelt Lecture 1990. "Challenges and Problems Facing the Army Conducting Counter Terrorist Operations."

TDRC 10171. Ian Beckett, *The Malayan Emergency 1948–1960*. Sandhurst: Department of War Studies, (No date).

TDRC 11291. *Staff College Notes on Counterinsurgency*. Camberley: British Army Staff College, 1994.

II. INTERVIEWS

Lieutenant Colonel (Retd) John Hunt, USA, Fort Leavenworth, 6 July 1995

Dr. John Fishel, Fort Leavenworth, 7 July 1995

Lieutenant Colonel Tom Adams, USA, Fort Leavenworth, 7 July 1995

Lieutenant Colonel Murray Swan, CAF, Fort Leavenworth, 7 July 1995

Colonel James R. Methered, USA, Doctrine and Training Command, Trenchard Lines, 30 October 1995

Lieutenant Colonel (Retd) Tim Harris, British Army, TDRC, Trenchard Lines, 30 October 1995

Brigadier (Retd) Gavin Bullock, British Army, Doctrine and Training Command, 30 October 1995

Lieutenant Colonel Larry Saul, USA, British Army Staff College, Camberley, 14 November 1995

Major Tim Kingsberry, British Army, British Army Staff College, Camberley, 14 November 1995

General (Retd) Sir Frank Kitson, British Army, Devon, 12 December 1995

General (Retd) Sir John Waters, British Army, Devon, 13 December 1995

Dr. Timothy J. Lomperis, Oxford, 17 January 1996

Major (Retd) Bill Tee, British Army, Oxford 19 January 1996

Colonial Policeman R.J.W. Craig OBE, MC, London 26 March 1996

Officers of the 4th Gurkha Regiment, Windsor, 14 June 1996

Colonel Danny Davis, USA, School of Advanced Military Studies, Fort Leavenworth, 21 August 1996

Dr. Ernest Evans, School of Advanced Military Studies, Fort Leavenworth, 21 August 1996

Major General (Retd) John Grinalds, USMC (Telephone) 22 August and 12 September 1996

General (Retd) William C. Westmoreland, USA, Kansas City, 24 August 1996

Major H.R. McMaster, USA, CGSC, Fort Leavenworth, 27 August 1996

Robert S. McNamara, 4 September 1996 (Telephone, Background Only)

Colonel Daniel Kaufman, USA, U.S. Military Academy, 4 September 1996

Colonel (Retd) Don Snider, USA, U.S. Military Academy, 6 September 1996

Major Michael Meese, USA, U.S. Military Academy, 6 September 1996

Lieutenant Colonel (Retd) Tim Lupfer, USA, NYC, 7 September 1996

Captain (Retd) John Tillson IV, USA, Washington, D.C., 9 September 1996
Major General (Retd) John Tillson III, USA, (Telephone), 9 September 1996
Dr Robert K. Wright, 25th ID Combat Historian, U.S. Army Center for Military History (CMH), 11 September 1996
Dr. Richard A. Hunt, CMH, 11 September 1996
Professor Williamson Murray, USMC Horner Professor of Military Theory, Quantico, 16 September 1996
Lieutenant General Paul K. Van Riper, USMC, Commander, U.S. Marine Corps University, 16 September 1996
Lieutenant Colonel (Retd) Andrew Krepinevich, USA, Washington, D.C., 17 September 1996
Lieutenant Colonel Richard Downie, USA, Strategic Plans & Policy, Joint Staff, the Pentagon, 19 September 1996
Lieutenant Colonel Thomas Adams, U.S. Army Peacekeeping Institute, Carlisle Barracks, 25 September 1996
Lieutenant Colonel Gregory A. Stone, U.S. Army War College, 25 September 1996
First Lieutenant (Retd) Robert Franks, 1/1–8 CAV/1 CD, 1966; Liaison to ROK Tiger Division, 1967; U.S. Army Military History Institute, 27 September 1996
General (Retd) Andrew J. Goodpaster, USA, (Telephone), 1 October 1996
Major Rod Sherman, USA, Operational Plans and Interoperability Directorate, Joint Staff, the Pentagon, 2 October 1996
Lieutenant Colonel Philip S. Coker, USA, Capabilities, Concepts, and Analysis, Joint Staff, 2 October 1996
Major General (Retd) David Lloyd Owen, British Army, Norwich, 11–12 November 1996
Major General (Retd) Richard Clutterbuck, British Army, Somerset, 10–11 December 1996
Derek Headly, Malayan Civil Service, Somerset, 11 December 1996
Major General (Retd) A.J. Trythall, British Army, Cheltenham, 21 December 1996
Brigadier (Retd) Michael Addison, British Army, Oxford, 29 January 1997

III. PUBLISHED SOURCES

Adams, Thomas K. "LIC (Low-Intensity Clausewitz.)" *Small Wars and Insurgencies* 1/3 (December 1990), 266–275.
———. *Military Doctrine and the Organization Culture of the United States Army.* Ph.D. Thesis, Syracuse University 1990.
Allen, Charles, ed. *Tales from the South China Seas: Images of the British in South-East Asia in the Twentieth Century.* London: Futura, 1984.
Allison, Graham T. *Essence of Decision: Explaining the Cuban Missile Crisis.* Boston: Little, Brown, 1971.
Ambrose, Stephen. *Rise to Globalism: American Foreign Policy Since 1938.* New York: Penguin, 1993.
Asprey, Robert B. *War in the Shadows: The Guerrilla in History.* New York: William Morrow, 1994.
Atkinson, Rick. *Crusade: The Untold Story of the Persian Gulf War.* New York: Houghton Mifflin, 1993.

———. *The Long Grey Line: West Point's Class of 1966*. London: Collins, 1990.

Avant, Deborah D. *Political Institutions and Military Change: Lessons from Peripheral Wars*. London: Cornell University Press, 1994.

Bacevich, A. J. et. al. *American Military Policy in Small Wars: The Case of El Salvador*. Washington, DC: Pergamon-Brassey's, 1988.

Barber, Noel. *The War of the Running Dogs: Malaya, 1948–1960*. London: Fontana, 1973.

Barnett, Correlli. *Britain and Her Army 1509–1970: A Military, Political, and Social Survey*. London: Penguin, 1970.

BDM Corporation. *The Strategic Lessons Learned in Vietnam* (Washington, DC: BDM Corporation, 1980).

Beckett, Ian F.W. *The Roots of Counterinsurgency: Armies and Guerrilla Warfare 1900–1945*. London: Blanford, 1988.

———. "The Study of Counter-Insurgency: A British Perspective." *Small Wars and Insurgencies* 1/1 (April 1990), 47–53.

Beckett, Ian F.W. and John Pimlott, eds. *Armed Forces and Modern Counter-Insurgency*. New York: St. Martin's Press, 1985.

Beyerchen, Alan. "Clausewitz, Nonlinearity, and the Unpredictability of War." *International Security* 17/3 (Winter 1992/93), 50–90.

Blaufarb, Douglas S. *The Counterinsurgency Era: U.S. Doctrine and Performance 1950 to the Present*. New York: The Free Press, 1977.

Blaxland, Gregory. *The Regiments Depart: A History of the British Army, 1945–1970*. London: Kimber, 1971.

Bolger, Daniel P. *Dragons at War: 2–34 Infantry in the Mohave*. Novato, CA: Presidio, 1986.

Breslauer, George W. and Philip E. Tetlock, eds. *Learning in U.S. and Soviet Foreign Policy*. Boulder, CO: Westview, 1991.

Brown, Dee. *Bury My Heart at Wounded Knee: An Indian History of the American West*. London: Pan Books, 1972.

Brownlee, Romie L. and William J. Mullen, III, *Changing an Army: An Oral History of General William E. DePuy, USA Retired*. Washington, DC: U.S. Government Printing Office, 1988.

Builder, Carl H. *The Army in the Strategic Planning Process: Who Shall Bell the Cat?* Santa Monica, CA: RAND, 1987.

Bulloch, Gavin B. "The Development of Doctrine for Counter Insurgency Operations." *British Army Review* 111 (December 1995), 21–24.

Cable, Larry. *Conflict of Myths: The Development of American Counterinsurgency Doctrine and the Vietnam War*. New York: New York University Press, 1986.

———. *Unholy Grail: The U.S. and the Wars in Vietnam*. London: Routledge, 1991.

Calwell, Charles E. *Small Wars: A Tactical Textbook for Imperial Soldiers*. London: Greenhill Books, 1990.

Cannon, Michael W. "The Development of the American Theory of Limited War, 1945–1963." *Armed Forces and Society* 19/1 (Fall 1992), 71–104.

Carruthers, Susan L. *Winning Hearts and Minds: British Goverments, the Media and Colonial Counter-Insurgency 1944–1960*. London: Leicester University Press, 1995.

Carver, Michael. *Tightrope Walking: British Defence Policy Since 1945*. London: Hutchinson, 1992.

Chaliand, G'erard. *Guerrilla Strategies: An Historical Anthology from the Long March to Afghanistan*. Berkeley: University of California Press, 1982.

Chapman, F. Spencer. *The Jungle Is Neutral*. London: Chatto and Windus, 1960.

Charters, David A. and Maurice Tugwell, eds. *Armies in Low-Intensity Conflict: A Comparative Analysis*. London: Brassey's, 1989.

Cincinnatus. *Self Destruction: The Disintegration and Decay of the United States Army During the Vietnam Era*. New York: W. W. Norton, 1981.

Clark, Wesley K. *Waging Modern War: Bosnia, Kosovo, and the Future of Conflict*. New York: Public Affairs, 2001.

Clarke, Jeffrey J. *Advice and Support: The Early Years, 1941–1960*. Washington, DC: Center of Military History, 1988.

Clausewitz, Carl von. *On War*. Translated and edited by Michael Howard and Peter Paret. Princeton, NJ: Princeton University Press, 1984.

Cloake, John. *Templer: Tiger of Malaya: The Life of Field Marshal Sir Gerald Templer*. London: Harrap, 1985.

Clutterbuck, Richard L. *Guerrillas and Terrorists*. London: Faber & Faber, 1977.

———. *The Long, Long War: The Emergency in Malaya 1948–1960*. London: Cassell, 1966.

———. *Riot and Revolution in Singapore and Malaya, 1945–1963*. London: Faber & Faber, 1973.

———. "Sir Robert Thompson: A Life of Counter-Insurgency." *Army Quarterly and Defence Journal* 120/2 (April 1990), 140–145.

Cohen, Eliot A. "Constraints on America's Conduct of Small Wars." *International Security* 9/2 (Fall 1984), 151–181.

Cohen, Eliot A. and John Gooch. *Military Misfortunes: The Anatomy of Failure in War*. New York: Vintage, 1991.

Colby, William. *Lost Victory*. New York: Contemporary Books, 1989.

Collins, John M. *America's Small Wars: Lessons for the Future*. Washington, DC: Brassey's, 1991.

Corr, Edwin G. and Stephen Sloan, eds. *Low-Intensity Conflict: Old Threats in a New World*. Oxford: Westview Press, 1992.

Creveld, Martin van. *The Training of Officers: From Military Professionalism to Irrelevance*. London: Collier Macmillan, 1990.

Crockatt, Richard. *The Fifty Year's War: The United States and the Soviet Union in World Politics, 1941–1991*. New York: Routledge, 1995.

Crocker, Lawrence P. *The Army Officer's Guide*, 43rd ed. Harrisburg, PA: Stackpole Books, 1985.

Cross, James E. *Conflict in the Shadows: The Nature and Politics of Guerilla War*. New York: Doubleday, 1963.

Department of the Army. Deputy Chief of Staff for Operations and Plans, Office of the Director of Strategic Plans and Policy, Special Warfare Division. *Counterinsurgency Operations: A Handbook for the Supression of Communist Guerrilla/Terrorist Operations*, Washington, DC: GPO, 1962.

———. Field Manual 7–98, *Operations in a Low-Intensity Conflict*. Washington, DC: U.S. Government Printing Office, 19 October 1992.

———. Field Manual 31–16, *Counterguerrilla Operations.* Washington, DC: U.S. Government Printing Office, 1963, 1967.

———. Field Manual 31–20, *Operations Against Guerrilla Forces.* Washington, DC: U.S. Government Printing Office, 1951.

———. Field Manual 31–22, *U.S. Army Counterinsurgency Forces.* Washington, DC: U.S. Government Printing Office, 1963.

———. Field Manual 31–23, *Stability Operations: U.S. Army Doctrine.* Washington, DC: U.S. Government Printing Office, 1967.

———. Field Manual 90–8, *Counterguerrilla Operations.* Washington, DC: U.S. Government Printing Office, 29 August 1986.

———. Field Manual 90–8, *Counterguerrilla Operations.* Washington, DC: U.S. Government Printing Office, 5 December 1990.

———. Field Manual 100–5, *Field Service Regulations: Operations.* Washington, D.C.: U.S. Government Printing Office, 1962.

———. Field Manual 100–5, *Operations.* Washington, DC: U.S. Government Printing Office, 1976.

———. Field Manual 100–5, *Operations.* Washington, DC: U.S. Government Printing Office, 20 August 1982.

———. Field Manual 100–5, *Operations.* Washington, DC: U.S. Government Printing Office, 5 May 1986.

———. Field Manual 100–5, *Operations.* Washington, DC: U.S. Government Printing Office, 14 June 1993.

———. Field Manual 100–20, *Low Intensity Conflict.* Washington, DC: U.S. Government Printing Office, 16 January 1981.

———. Field Manual 100–20, *Low Intensity Conflict.* Washington, DC: U.S. Government Printing Office, March 1990.

———. Field Manual 100–20, *Operations Other Than War.* (Draft) Washington, DC: U.S. Government Printing Office, 15 May 1995.

———. Field Manual 100–23, *Peace Operations.* Washington, D.C.: U.S. Government Printing Office, 30 December 1994.

Derry, Archie. *Emergency in Malaya: The Psychological Dimension.* Latimer, England: National Defence College, 1982.

Dewar, Michael. *Brush Fire Wars: Minor Campaigns of the British Army Since 1945.* London: Robert Hale, 1984.

Director General of Development and Doctrine. *Conference on the Origins of Contemporary Military Doctrine.* Larkhill: Royal School of Artillery, 28 March 1996.

Dixon, Howard Lee. *A Framework for Competitive Strategies Development in Low Intensity Conflict.* Langley, VA: Army-Air Force Center for Low Intensity Conflict Reports, 1988.

———. *Low Intensity Conflict: Overview, Definitions, and Policy Concerns.* Langley, VA: Army-Air Force Center for Low Intensity Conflict Reports, 1987.

Dixon, Howard Lee and Charles M. Ayers, *Operational Art in Low Intensity Conflict.* Langley, VA: Army-Air Force Center for Low Intensity Conflict Reports, 1987.

Dixon, Norman F. *On the Psychology of Military Incompetence.* London: Futura, 1979.

Doubler, Michael D. *Closing with the Enemy*. Lawrence, KS: University of Kansas Press, 1994.

Doughty, Robert A. *The Evolution of U.S. Army Tactical Doctrine, 1946–76*. Fort Leavenworth, KS: Combat Studies Institute, 1979.

Downie, Richard D. *Learning from Conflict: The U.S. Military in Vietnam, El Salvador, and the Drug War*. Westport, CT: Praeger, 1998.

———. *Military Doctrine and the Learning Institution: Case Studies in LIC*. Ph.D. Dissertation, University of Southern California, May 1995.

Dunbabin, J.P.D. *International Relations Since 1945: A History in Two Volumes*. London: Longman, 1994.

Elliott-Bateman, Michael. *Defeat in the East: The Mark of Mao Tse-tung on War*. London: Oxford University Press, 1967.

Ellis, John. *From the Barrel of a Gun: A History of Guerrilla, Revolutionary and Counter-Insurgency Warfare, from the Romans to the Present*. London: Greenhill Books, 1995. Revised and enlarged from *A Short History of Guerrilla Warfare*. London: Ian Allan, 1975.

Evans, Ernest. *Wars Without Splendor: The U.S. Military and Low-Level Conflict*. New York: Greenwood Press, 1987.

FitzGerald, Frances. *Fire in the Lake: The Vietnamese and the Americans in Vietnam*. New York: Vintage Books, 1972.

Frost, Peter J. *Doing Exemplary Research*. London: Sage Publications, 1992.

Frost, Peter J., et al., eds. *Organizational Culture*. Beverly Hills, CA: Sage Publications, 1985.

Furr, Willian F. *Low Intensity Conflict: Imperatives for Success*. Langley, VA: Army-Air Force Center for Low Intensity Conflict, 1987.

Gacek, Christopher M. *The Logic of Force: The Dilemma of Limited War in American Foreign Policy*. New York: Columbia University Press, 1994.

Gaddis, John Lews. "International Relations Theory and the End of the Cold War." *International Security* 17/3 (Winter 1992/93), 5–58.

Gallagher, James J. *Low-Intensity Conflict: A Guide for Tactics, Techniques, and Procedures*. Harrisburg, PA: Stackpole Books, 1992.

Galloway, K. Bruce and Robert Bowie Johnson, Jr. *West Point: America's Power Fraternity*. New York: Simon & Schuster, 1973.

Gates, John M. "People's War in Vietnam." *Journal of Military History* 54/3 (July 1990), 325–344.

Gelb, Leslie H. with Richard K. Betts. *The Irony of Vietnam: The System Worked*. Washington, DC: Brookings, 1979.

George, Alexander. "Case Studies and Theory Development: The Method of Structured, Focused Comparison." In Paul Gordon Larren, ed., *Diplomacy: New Approacues in History, Theory, and Policy*. New York: Macmillan, 1979, 43–68.

Grant, Arthur V. "Strategic Decisions: The Mire of Low-intensity Conflict." *Comparative Strategy* 10/2 (April-June 1991), 165–175.

Gray, Colin S. "National Style in Strategy: The American Example." *International Security* 6/2 (Fall 1981), 21–48.

Gregorian, Raffi. "Jungle Bashing in Malaya: Toward a Formal Tactical Doctrine." *Small Wars and Insurgencies* 5/3 (Winter 1994), 338–359.

Gwynn, Charles. *Imperial Policing*. London: Macmillan, 1939.

Hackett, John. *The Profession of Arms*. New York: Bantam, 1971.

Hackworth, David H. and Julie Sherman. *About Face*. New York: Simon & Schuster, 1989.

Halberstam, David. *The Best and the Brightest*. New York: Fawcett Crest, 1972.

———. *The Making of a Quagmire*. New York: Ballantine, 1965.

———. *War in a Time of Peace: Bush, Clinton, and the Generals*. New York: Scribner, 2001.

Hall, Christopher Jansen. *Defeating People's War: A Mental Blueprint*. Honors Thesis, Manchester University 1987.

Halperin, Morton H. *Bureaucratic Politics and Foreign Policy*. Washington, DC: Brookings, 1974.

Hammond, Grant T. "Low Intensity Conflict: War by Another Name." *Small Wars and Insurgencies* 1/3 (December 1990), 226–238.

Harmon, Christopher C. "Illustrations of Learning in Counterinsurgency." *Comparative Strategy* 11/1 (January–March 1992), 29–48.

Harris, J.P. *Men, Ideas, and Tanks: British Military Thought and Armoured Forces, 1903–1939*. New York: St. Martin's Press, 1995.

Hay, John H. *Tactical and Material Innovations*. Washington, DC: Department of the Army, 1974.

Hendrickson, Paul. *The Living and the Dead: Robert McNamara and Five Lives of a Lost War*. New York: Alfred A. Knopf, 1996.

Herbert, Paul H. *Deciding What Has to Be Done: General William E. DePuy and the 1976 Edition of FM 100-5, Operations*. Leavenworth Paper Number 16. Fort Leavenworth, KS: U.S. Army Command and General Staff College, 1988.

Hilsman, Roger. *To Move a Nation: The Politics of Foreign Policy in the Administration of John F. Kennedy*. Garden City, NY: Doubleday, 1967.

Hoffman, Bruce and Jennifer M. Taw. *Defense Policy and Low-Intensity Conflict: The Development of Britain's "Small Wars" Doctrine During the 1950's*. Santa Monica; CA: RAND 1991.

Hoffman, Stanley, et al. "Vietnam Reappraised." *International Security* 6/1 (Summer 1981), 3–26.

Hosmer, Stephen T. *The Army's Role in Counterinsurgency and Insurgency*. Santa Monica, CA: RAND, 1990.

Howard, Michael. *The Causes of Wars*. Cambridge, MA: Harvard University Press, 1983.

———. ed. *The Theory and Practice of War*. London: Indiana University Press, 1965.

———. *War in European History*. Oxford: Oxford University Press, 1979.

Hunt, Michael J. *Lyndon Johnson's War: America's Cold War Crusade in Vietnam, 1945–1968*. New York: Hill & Wang, 1996.

Hunter, Horace L. "Military Operations in Support of Counterinsurgency: A Primer for US Officers." *Marine Corps Gazette* 74/7 (July 1990), 40–45.

Huntington, Samuel P. *The Soldier and the State*. Cambridge, MA: Harvard University Press, 1957.

Jackson, Robert. *The Malayan Emergency: The Commonwealth's Wars 1948–1966*. London: Routledge, 1991.

Janowitz, Morris. *The Professional Soldier: A Social and Political Portrait*. New York: The Free Press, 1971.

Jervis, Robert. *Perception and Misperception in International Politics*. Princeton, NJ: Princeton University Press, 1976.

Jessup, John, E. and Robert W Coakley, eds. *A Guide to the Study and Use of Military History*. Washington, DC: Center of Military History, 1982.

Joes, Anthony James. *Guerrilla Warfare: A Historical, Biographical, and Bibliographical Sourcebook*. London: Greenwood Press, 1996.

Johnston, Alastair Iain. "Thinking About Strategic Culture." *International Security* 19/4 (Spring 1995), 32–64.

Jones, Archer. *The Art of War in the Western World*. Oxford: Oxford University Press, 1987.

Jones, Howard. *"A New Kind of War": American Strategy and the Truman Doctrine in Vietnam*. New York: Oxford University Press, 1989.

Kaiser, David E. "Vietnam: Was the System the Solution? A Review Essay." *International Security* 4/4 (Spring 1980), 199–218.

Karnow, Stanley. *Vietnam: A History*. New York: Viking, 1983.

Katz, Mark N., Ed. *Revolution: International Dimensions*. Washington, DC: CG Press, 2001.

Katzenbach, Edward L. "The Horse Cavalry in the Twentieth Century: A Study in Policy Response." *Public Policy* (1958), 120–149.

Khong, Yuen Foong. *Analogies at War: Korea, Munich, Dien Bien Phu, and the Vietnam Decisions of 1965*. Princeton, NJ: Princeton University Press, 1992.

Kier, Elizabeth. "Culture and Military Doctrine: France Between the Wars." *International Security* 19/4 (Spring 1995), 65–93.

King, Gary, et al. *Designing Social Inquiry: Scientific Inference in Qualitative Research*. Princeton, NJ: Princeton University Press, 1994.

Kingsberry, T.L. *Factors Contributing to the Differing American and British Approaches to Counterinsurgency Post-1945."* Camberley: British Army Staff College, 1995.

Kinnard, Douglas. *The Certain Trumpet: Maxwell Taylor and the American Experience in Vietnam*. London: Brassey's, 1991.

———. *The War Managers*. Hanover, NH: University Press of New England, 1977.

Kissinger, Henry A. "The Viet Nam Negotiations." *Foreign Affairs* 47/2 (January 1969), 211–234.

Kitfield, James. *Prodigal Soldiers: How the Generation of Officers Born of Vietnam Revolutionized the American Style of War*. New York: Simon & Schuster, 1995.

Kitson, Frank. *Bunch of Five*. London: Faber & Faber, 1977.

———. *Low Intensity Operations: Subversion, Insurgency, and Peacekeeping*. London: Faber & Faber, 1971.

———. *Warfare as A Whole*. London: Faber & Faber, 1987.

Kolenda, Christopher D. "Reconnaissance in the Offence: 'Command Push' vs 'Recon Pull'." *Armor* CV, 4 (July–August 1996), 45–49.

Komer, Robert W. *Bureaucracy at War*. Oxford: Westview, 1986.

———. *Bureaucracy Does Its Thing*. Santa Monica, CA: RAND, 1973.

———. *The Malayan Emergency in Retrospect: Organization of a Successful Counterinsurgency Effort*. Santa Monica, CA: RAND, 1972.

Krepinevich, Andrew. *The Army and Vietnam*. Baltimore: Johns Hopkins, 1986.

LaFeber, Walter. *Inevitable Revolutions: The United States in Central America*. New York: W. W. Norton, 1993.

Lang, Kurt. "Military Organizations." In James G. March, ed., *Handbook of Organizations*. Chicago: Rand McNally, 1965, 838–878.

Langewiesche, William. "Peace Is Hell." *Atlantic Monthly* 288, 3 (October 2001), 51–80.

Lansdale, Edward G. *In the Midst of Wars: An American's Mission to Southeast Asia*. New York: Harper & Row, 1972.

———. "Vietnam: Do We Understand Revolution?" *Foreign Affairs* 43/1 (October 1964), 75–86.

Laqueur, Walter. *The Guerrilla Reader: A Historical Anthology*. Philadelphia: Temple University Press, 1977.

Lawrence, T.E. *Seven Pillars of Wisdom: A Triumph*. London: Penguin, 1971.

Legro, Jeffry W. "Military Culture and Inadvertent Escalation in World War II." *International Security* 18/4 (Spring 1994), 108–142.

Lemelin, David J. "Force XXI: Getting It Right." *Military Review* LXXVI, 6 (November–December 1996), 81–84.

Levitt, Barbara and James G. March, "Organizational Learning." In Michael D. Cohen and Lee S. Sproul, eds., *Organizational Learning* (London: Sage, 1996), 516–540.

Levy, Jack S. "Learning and Foreign Policy: Sweeping a Conceptual Minefield." *International Organization* 48/2 (Spring 1994), 279–312.

Lewy, Guenter. *America in Vietnam*. Oxford: Oxford University Press, 1978.

Liddell Hart, B. H. *The British Way in Warfare: Adaptability and Mobility*. Middlesex: Penguin, 1942.

Linn, Brian McAllister. *The U.S. Army and Counterinsurgency in the Philippine War, 1899–1902*. Chapel Hill: University of North Carolina Press, 1989.

Lomperis, Timothy J. *From People's War to People's Rule: Insurgency, Intervention, and the Lessons of Vietnam*. London: University of North Carolina Press, 1996.

Lord, Carnes. "American Strategic Culture in Small Wars." *Small Wars and Insurgencies* 3/3 (Winter 1992), 205–216.

Lupfer, Timothy T. *The Dynamics of Doctrine: The Changes in German Tactical Doctrine During the First World War*. Fort Leavenworth, KS: Combat Studies Institute, 1981.

Luttwak, Edward N. *The Pentagon and the Art of War*. New York: Simon & Schuster, 1984.

Macgregor, Douglas A. *Breaking the Phalanx: A New Design for Landpower in the 21st Century*. London: Praeger, 1997.

Macmillan, Alan. "Strategic Culture and National Ways in Warfare: The British Case." *RUSI Journal*, 140/5 (October 1995), 33–38.

Manwaring, Max G., ed. *Uncomfortable Wars: Toward a New Paradigm of Low Intensity Conflict*. Oxford: Westview Press, 1991.

Manwaring, Max G. and John T. Fishel. "Insurgency and Counterinsurgency: Toward a New Analytical Approach." *Small Wars and Insurgencies* 3/3 (Winter 1992), 272–310.

Mao Tse-Tung. *Selected Military Writings*. Peking: Foreign Languages Press, 1966.

Mao Tse-Tung and Che Guevara. *Guerilla Warfare.* London: Cassell, 1965.

Marr, Captain S.R.D. Insurgency in the Post-Cold War Era. Camberley: British Army Staff College, 1995.

Mattingly, Richard Thomas and Wallace Earl Walker. "The Military Professional as Successful Politician." *Parameters* XVI, 1 (March 1988), 37–51.

May, Ernest R. *Lessons of the Past: The Use and Misuse of History in American Foreign Policy.* New York: Oxford University Press, 1973.

McMaster, H.R. *Dereliction of Duty: Johnson, McNamara, the Joint Chiefs of Staff, and the Lies that Led to Vietnam.* New York: Harper Collins, 1997.

McNamara, Robert S. *In Retrospect: The Tragedy and the Lessons of Vietnam.* New York: Times Books, 1995.

McNaugher, Thomas L. "Marksmanship, McNamara and the M16 Rifle: Innovation in Military Organizations." *Public Policy* 28/1 (Winter 1980), 1–37.

Meese, Michael J. "Institutionalizing Maneuver Warfare: The Process of Organizational Change," in Richard D. Hooker, Jr., ed., *Maneuver Warfare: An Anthology.* Boulder, CO: Westview, 1993, 193–219.

Metz, Stephen "AirLand Battle and Counterinsurgency." *Military Review* 70:1 (January 1990), 32–41.

———. "A Flame Kept Burning: Counterinsurgency Support After the Cold War." *Parameters*, XXV, 3 (Autumn 1995), 31–41.

Mileham, Patrick. *Ethos: British Army Officership, 1962–1992.* Camberley: Strategic and Combat Studies Institute, 1996.

Military Assistance Command—Vietnam (MACV). *Command Histories.* Saigon: 6PO, 1964–1970.

Miller, Harry. *Prince and Premier: A Biography of Tumku Abdul Rahman Putra Al-Haj, First Prime Minister of the Federation of Malaya.* London: George C. Harrap, 1959.

Millett, Allan R. and Wiliamson Murray, eds. *Military Effectiveness.* 3 Volumes. London: Allen & Unwin, 1988.

Millett, Allan R., Williamson Murray, and Kenneth H. Watman. "The Effectiveness of Military Organizations." *International Security* 11/1 (Summer 1988), 37–71.

Ministry of Defence. Army Code No. 70516 (Part 2), *Land Operations. Volume III-Counter Revolutionary Operations, Part 2—Internal Security.* London: Her Majesty's Stationery Office, 26 November 1969.

———. *Part 3—Counter Insurgency.* London: Her Majesty's Stationery Office, 5 January 1970.

———. Army Code No. 70516. *Land Operations.* Volume III *Counter-Revolutionary Operations.* Part 1. *General Principles.* London: Her Majesty's Stationery Office, August 1977.

———. Army Code No. 71451, *Design for Military Operations: The British Military Doctrine.* London: Her Majesty's Stationery Office, 1989.

———. Army Code No. 71596. *Army Field Manual* Volume V. *Operations Other than War.* Section B. *Counter Insurgency Operations.* Part 1: *The Concept and Practice of Insurgency.* London: Her Majesty's Stationery Office, 1995.

———. Army Code No. 71596 (Part 2), *Army Field Manual.* Volume V, *Operations Other than War.* Section B. *Counter Insurgency Operations.* Part 2:

The Conduct of Counter Insurgency Operations. London: Her Majesty's Stationery Office, 1995.

———. *The Conduct of Anti-Terrorist Operations in Malaya*. Kuala Lumpur: Director of Operations, 1958.

Mockaitis, Thomas R. *British Counterinsurgency, 1919–1960*. New York: St. Martin's Press, 1990.

———. *British Counterinsurgency in the Post-Imperial Era*. Manchester: Manchester University Press, 1995.

———. "Low-Intensity Conflict: The British Experience." *Conflict Quarterly* XIII/1 (Winter 1993), 7–16.

———. "A New Era of Counterinsurgency." *RUSI Journal* 136/1 (Spring 1991), 73–78.

———. "The Origins of British Counter-Insurgency." *Small Wars and Insurgencies* 1/3 (December 1990), 209–225.

Moore, Harold G. and Joseph Galloway. *We Were Soldiers Once . . . and Young*. New York: Random House, 1992.

Motley, James B. "U.S. Unconventional Conflict Policy and Strategy." *Military Review* LXX/1 (January 1990), 2–16.

Murray, Williamson, MacGregor Knox, and Alvin Bernstein, eds. *The Making of Modern Strategy: Rulers, States, and War*. Cambridge: Cambridge University Press, 1994.

Murray, Williamson and Allan R. Millett, eds. *Military Innovation in the Interwar Period*. Cambridge: Cambridge University Press, 1996.

Nagl, John A. "Defending Against New Dangers: Arms Control of Weapons of Mass Destruction in a Globalized World." *World Affairs* 162, 4 (Spring 2000), 158–173.

———. "Hitting Us Where We Don't Expect It: Asymmetric Threats to U.S. National Security." *National Security Studies Quarterly* 7, 4 (Autumn 2001), 113–121.

———. "Learning to Eat Soup with a Knife: British and American Army Counterinsurgency Learning During the Malayan Emergency and the Vietnam War." *World Affairs* 161, 4 (Spring 1999), 191–199.

———. "Post Cold-War Priorities." *Military Review* LXXXI, 4 (July–August 2001), 104–107.

———. "Wes Clark's War." *The American Oxonian* LXXXVIII, 4 (Autumn 2001), 303–311.

Nagl, John A. and Tim Huening. "Nearly War: Training a Divisional Cavalry Squadron for Operations Other Than War." *Armor* CV, 1 (January–February 1996), 23–24.

Nagl, John A. and Elizabeth O. Young. "*Si Vis Pacem, Pare Pacem*: Improving U.S. Army Training for Complex Humanitarian Emergencies." *Military Review* LXXX, 2 (March–April 2000), 31–37.

Neustadt, Richard E. and Ernest R. May. *Thinking in Time: The Uses of History for Decision Makers*. New York: The Free Press, 1986.

O'Ballance, Edgar. *Malaya: The Communist Insurgent War, 1948–60*. London: Faber and Faber, 1966.

Oldfield, John B. *The Green Howards in Malaya, 1949–1952*. London: Gale and Polden, 1953.

O'Neill, Bard E., et al., eds. *Insurgency in the Modern World*. Boulder, CO: West-view Press, 1980.

O'Neill, Robert J. *Vietnam Task: The 5th Battalion, Royal Australian Regiment*. Marrickville, Australia: Cassell Australia, 1995.

Osanka, Franklin Mark, ed. *Modern Guerrilla Warfare: Fighting Communist Guer-rilla Movements, 1941–1961*. New York: The Free Press of Glencoe, 1962.

Osborn, George K., ed. *Democracy, Strategy, and Vietnam*. Lexington, MA: Lex-ington Books, 1987.

Paget, Julian. *Counter Insurgency Campaigning*. London: Faber, 1967.

Palmer, Bruce. *The 25 Year War: America's Military Role in Vietnam*. New York: Da Capo, 1984.

———. *"The Army and Vietnam"* (Review of Krepinevich's *The Army and Viet-nam*. *Parameters* XVI, 3 (Autumn 1988), 83–85.

Paret, Peter. *French Revolutionary Warfare from Indochina to Algeria: The Anal-ysis of a Political and Military Doctrine*. London: Pall Mall Press, 1964.

———, ed. *Makers of Modern Strategy from Machiavelli to the Nuclear Age*. Princeton, NJ: Princeton University Press, 1986.

Paret, Peter and John W. Shy. *Guerillas in the 1960's*. New York: Frederick A. Praeger, 1962.

The Pentagon Papers: The Defense Department History of United States Decision-making on Vietnam, Senator Gravel Edition. 4 Volumes. Boston: Beacon Press, 1971.

Peters, Ralph. "After the Revolution." *Parameters* XXIV, 2 (Summer 1995), 7–14.

Pike, Douglas. *PAVN: People's Army of Vietnam*. New York: Da Capo Press, 1986.

Pocock, Tom. *Fighting General: The Public and Private Campaigns of Genreal Sir Walter Walker*. London: Collins, 1973.

Popplewell, Richard. "Lacking Intelligence: Some Reflections on Recent Approaches to British Counter-insurgency, 1900–1960." *Intelligence and National Se-curity* 10/2 (April 1995), 336–352.

Posen, Barry R. *The Sources of Military Doctrine: France, Britain, and Germany Between the World Wars*. London: Cornell University Press, 1984.

Prochau, William. *Once Upon a Distant War: Young War Correspondents and the Early Vietnam Battles*. New York: Random House, 1995.

Race, Jeffrey. *War Comes to Long An: Revolutionary Conflict in a Vietnamese Province*. Berkeley: University of California Press, 1972.

Record, Jeffrey. "Vietnam in Retrospect: Could We Have Won?" *Parameters* XXVI (Winter 1996–96), 51–65.

Rosen, Stephen P. "Military Effectiveness: Why Society Matters." *International Se-curity* 19/4 (Spring 1995), 5–31.

———. "New Ways of War: Understanding Military Innovation." *International Security* 13/1 (Summer 1988), 134–168.

———. "Vietnam and the American Theory of Limited War." *International Secu-rity* 7/2 (Fall 1982), 83–113.

———. *Winning the Next War: Innovation and the Modern Military*. London: Cornell University Press, 1991.

Rosencrance, Richard. "Explaining Military Doctrine" (Book Review of Posen's *Sources of Military Doctrine*). *International Security* 11/3 (Winter 1986–87), 167–174.

Rostow, W.W. "The Case for the Vietnam War." *Parameters* XXVI, 4 (Winter 1996–97), 39–50.

Rotter, Andrew J. *The Path to Vietnam: Origins of the American Commitment to Southeast Asia*. London: Cornell University Press, 1987.

Sampson, Martin W. III. "Cultural Influences on Foreign Policy." In Charles F. Hermann, Charles W. Kegley, and James N. Rosenau, *New Directions in the Study of Foreign Policy*. Boston: Allen & Unwin, 1987, 348–408.

Sarkesian, Sam C. *Unconventional Conflicts in a New Security Era: Lessons from Malaya and Vietnam*. London: Greenwood, 1993.

Scales, Robert H., Jr. *Firepower in Limited War*. Washington, DC: National Defence University Press, 1990.

Schwarz, Benjamin C. *American Counterinsurgency Doctrine and El Salvador: The Frustrations of Reform and the Illusions of Nation Building*. Santa Monica, CA: RAND, 1991.

Shafer, D. Michael. *Deadly Paradigms: The Failure of U.S. Counterinsurgency Policy*. Princeton, NJ: Princeton University Press, 1988.

Shafritz, Jay M. and J. Steven Ott. *Classics of Organization Theory*. Chicago: The Dorsey Press, 1987.

Sheehan, Kevin P. *Preparing for an Imaginary War? Examining Peacetime Functions and Changes of Army Doctrine*. Ph. D. Thesis, Harvard University, 1988.

Sheehan, Neil. *A Bright Shining Lie: John Paul Vann and America in Vietnam*. New York: Vintage Books, 1988.

Sheehan, Neil, et al., eds. *The Pentagon Papers (The New York Times Edition)*. New York: Bantam, 1971.

Short, Anthony. *The Communist Insurrection in Malaya, 1948–1960*. Plymouth: Frederick Muller, 1975.

———. *The Origins of the Vietnam War*. London: Longman, 1989.

Shy, John. "The American Military Experience: History and Learning." *Journal of Interdisciplinary History* 1, 2 (Winter 1971), 205–229.

Simpson, H. J. *British Rule, and Rebellion*. London: William Blackwood, 1937.

Slim, Field-Marshal Viscount. *Defeat into Victory*. London: Papermac, 1986.

Sloan, Stephen. "US Legacy for LIC: An Enduring Legacy or a Passing Fad?" *Military Review* LXX/1 (January 1990), 42–29.

Smith, E. D. *Malaya and Borneo*. London: Ian Allan, 1985.

Smith, James M., Ed. *Searching for National Security in an NBC World*. Colorado Springs, CO: USAF Institute for National Security Studies, 2000.

Snider, Don M., John A. Nagl, and Tony Pfaff. *Army Professionalism, the Military Ethic, and Officership in the 21st Century*. Carlisle, PA: U.S. Army War College Strategic Studies Institute Monograph, 1999.

Sorley, Lewis. *Thunderbolt: General Creighton Abrams and the Army of His Times*. New York: Simon & Schuster, 1992.

Spector, Ronald H. *Advice and Support: The Early Years, 1941–1960*. Washington, DC: Center of Military History, 1985.

———. "U.S. Army Strategy in the Vietnam War" (Book Review of Krepinevich's *The Army and Vietnam*.) *International Security* 11/4 (Spring 1987), 130–134.

Starry, Donn A. *Armored Combat in Vietnam*. Poole: Blandford Press, 1981.

Stockwell, A.J., ed. *British Documents on the End of Empire: Malaya*. 3 Volumes. London: HMSO, 1995.

Stroup, Theodore G. "Leadership and Organizational Culture: Actions Speak Louder than Words." *Military Review* LXXVI, No.1 (January–February 1996), 44–49.

Stubbs, Richard. *Hearts and Minds in Guerrilla Warfare: The Malayan Emergency, 1948–1960*. Oxford: Oxford University Press, 1989.

Summers, Harry R. *On Strategy: A Critical Analysis of the Vietnam War*. Novato, CA: Presidio, 1981.

———. *On Strategy II: A Critical Analysis of the Gulf War*. New York: Dell, 1992.

Sun Tzu. *The Art of War*. Translated by Samuel B. Griffith. Oxford: Oxford University Press, 1971.

Swinton, E.D. *The Defence of Duffer's Drift*. Wayne, NJ: Avery, 1986.

Tee, William S. "Ingredients of Victory in Counter Revolutionary Warfare." *Army Journal* 234 (November 1968), 3–13.

Thompson, Robert. *Defeating Communist Insurgency: Experiences from Malaya and Vietnam*. New York: Frederick A. Praeger, 1966.

———. *Make for the Hills: Memories of Far Eastern Wars*. London: Cooper, 1989.

———. *No Exit from Vietnam*. London: Chatto and Windus, 1969.

———. *Peace is Not at Hand*. London: Chatto and Windus, 1974.

Thompson, W. Scott, and Donaldson D. Frizzell, eds. *The Lessons of Vietnam*. London: Macdonald and Jane, 1977.

Timbers, Robert. *The Nightingale's Song*. New York: Touchstone, 1995.

Tocqueville, Alexis de. *Democracy in America*. New York: Mentor, 1984.

Toczek, David. *They Did Everything but Learn from It: The Battle of Ap Bac, Vietnam*. Westport, CT: Greenwood Press, 2001.

Townshend, Charles. *Britain's Civil Wars: Counterinsurgency in the Twentieth Century*. Boston: Faber & Faber, 1986.

Trinquier, Roger. *Modern Warfare: A French View of Counterinsurgency*. New York: Praeger, 1964.

United States Marine Corps. *Small Wars Manual, 1940*. Washington, DC: U.S. Government Printing Office, 1940.

U.S. Army, Vietnam. *Armored Combat in Vietnam (ARCOV)*. Saigon: 6PO, 1966.

———. *Mechanized and Armor Combat Operations in Vietnam (MACOV)*, Washington DC: 6PO, 1967.

U.S. Congress. *Background Information Relating to Southeast Asia and Vietnam*. Washington, D.C.: U.S. Government Printing Office, 1969.

U.S. Congress/Ann Hollick. *Vietnam Commitments 1961*. Washington, DC: U.S. Government Printing Office, 1972.

van Creveld, Martin. *On Future War*. London: Brasseys', 1991.

Van Evera, Steven, "The Cult of the Offensive and the Origins of the First World War." *International Security* 9/1 (Summer 1984), 58–107.

Vetock, Dennis J. *Lessons Learned: A History of U.S. Army Lesson Learning*. Carlisle Barracks, PA: U.S. Army Military History Institute, 1988.

Waddell, Ricky Lynn. *The Army and Peacetime Low Intensity Conflict, 1961–1993: The Process of Peripheral and Fundamental Military Change*. Ph. D. Thesis, Columbia University, 1993.

Waghelstein, John D. "Ruminations of a Pachyderm or What I Learned in the

Counterinsurgency Business." *Small Wars and Insurgencies* 5/3 (Winter 1994), 360–378.

Walt, Lewis. *Strange War, Strange Strategy: A General's Report on Vietnam.* New York: Funk & Wagnalls, 1970.

Waltz, Kenneth N. *Man, the State, and War.* New York: Columbia University Press, 1959.

Weigley, Russell F. *The American Way of War.* Bloomington: Indiana University Press, 1973.

———. *Eisenhower's Lieutenants: The Campaign of France and Germany, 1944–1945.* Bloomington: Indiana University Press, 1981.

Welch, David A. "The Organizational Process and Bureaucratic Politics Paradigms: Retrospect and Prospect." *International Security* 17/2 (Fall 1992), 112–194.

Westmoreland, William C. *A Soldier Reports.* New York: Da Capo, 1989.

Wirtz, James J. "Counterinsurgency Paradigms." *International Security* 14/1 (Summer 1989), 184–194.

Woodham-Smith, Cecil. *The Reason Why.* London: Constable, 1955.

Woodman, Stewart. "Defining Limited Conflict: A Case of Mistaken Identity." *Small Wars and Insurgencies* 2/3 (December 1991), 24–43.

Zaffiri, Samuel. *Westmoreland.* New York: William Morrow, 1994.

Zisk, Kimberly Martin. *Engaging the Enemy: Organization Theory and Soviet Military Innovation, 1955–1991.* Princeton, NJ: Princeton University Press, 1993.

Index

About the Author

Lieutenant Colonel John A. Nagl is a Military Assistant to the Deputy Secretary of Defense. A West Point graduate and Rhodes Scholar, he earned an MPhil and DPhil in International Relations from Oxford University before teaching national security studies at West Point. Nagl led a tank platoon in the First Cavalry Division in Operation Desert Storm and, from September 2003 through September 2004, served as the Operations Officer of Task Force 1-34 Armor in Khalidiyah, Iraq.